MW00618351

Howdy Doody

Collector's Reference and Trivia Guide

Jack Koch

COLLECTOR BOOKS

A Division of Schroeder Publishing Co., Inc.

The current values in this book should be used only as a guide. They are not intended to set prices, which vary from one section of the country to another. Auction prices as well as dealer prices vary greatly and are affected by condition as well as demand. Neither the Author nor the Publisher assumes responsibility for any losses that might be incurred as a result of consulting this guide.

Searching For A Publisher?

We are always looking for knowledgeable people considered to be experts within their fields. If you feel that there is a real need for a book on your collectible subject and have a large comprehensive collection, contact us.

On the cover, from left to right:
Back row: Welch's Jelly Jar Glass (2nd series), $8.00; Welch's Cookbook, $38.00; Peter Puppet Playthings Princess hand puppet, $18.00; Peter Puppet Playthings Howdy marionette, $50.00.
Front row: Small head hand puppet, $25.00; Peter Puppet Playthings salt and pepper shakers, $75.00; Smith-Taylor ceramic plate, $45.00; Welch's Jelly Jar Glass (series 2), $10.00; Luce Cookie-Go-Round Tin, $90.00

Cover Design: Beth Summers
Book Design: Benjamin R. Faust

Additional copies of this book may be ordered from:

COLLECTOR BOOKS
P.O. Box 3009
Paducah, KY 42002-3009

@ $16.95. Add $2.00 for postage and handling.

Copyright: Jack Koch, 1996

This book or any part thereof may not be reproduced without the written consent of the Author and Publisher.

Printed by IMAGE GRAPHICS, INC., Paducah, Kentucky

To my wife, Nancy, who started my quest for Doodyana. Without her Howdy Doody features and smile, Doodyville would have been another distant memory.

Foreword by Buffalo Bob Smith

For all you trivia fans and Howdy Doody Alumni — this book is priceless. It recalls many interesting, unusual, and pleasant memories for Howdy and me and I know it will do the same for you. It's really "Howdy Doody Time" all over again.

©BOB SMITH, FROM THE SCOTT BRINKER COLLECTION

Howdy receiving mail from the Letter-Getter.

Contents

Acknowledgments 6

Copyrights 6

Introduction 7

Cast of Characters 10

People, Places & Things 12

Time Line 86

Collectibles Price Guide 112

Howdy Doody Firsts 157

About the Author 158

Acknowledgments

I am indebted to the following for their help: Robert E. "Buffalo Bob" Smith, Edward Kean, and Howard Davis for taking their valuable time reviewing material. Scott Brinker for this hospitality and his loan of photos and scripts, Milt Neil, and Robert Rippen for their time and information. Ralph MacPhail Jr. and Bob Reed for graciously sharing their collections. Henry J. Bassman and Mike Jacobs for photography help. Mark E. Chase of *Collector Glass News,* and Stanley Pollinger and Andrea Bruno of Hollander for insights on product marketing. Fran Cubello of NBC Clip Licensing for her time and knowledge.

Portions have been reprinted with permission from TV Guide® Magazine. Copyright© 1951 – 1964 where appropriate, by News America Publications, Inc. and *Howdy Doody Times,* a publication of the Doodyville Historical Society.

©BOB SMITH, FROM THE SCOTT BRINKER COLLECTION

Clarabell (Bob Keeshan) helps Howdy talk to Mother Goose on the Honka Doodle.

Copyrights

We have acknowledged the copyright holder and licensee when known. Any ommissions or errors are unintentional.

CONDITION

A survey of item condition definitions showed the usual collectible inconsistency. Some definitions of "VG" or "C8" were identical to other dealers "EX" or even "NM." Terms such as "Rare," "Scarce," or "Very Rare" were occasionally added to a description, but that identical item might be advertised elsewhere in the same publication without the designation. Many ads stated a condition without defining the grade they advertised. Items arriving from a mail order ad or auction sometimes failed to live up to the advertised grade description. (Return policies were usually liberal.) Most dealers noted minor problems.

All the products listed here are without a major defect. Items may have minor wear (i.e., scuffs, light fading, etc.); with or without the original box, card, or instruction brochure (if any). Damaged items, parts missing, or those "needing work" are not included here.

PRICING INFORMATION

The items listed in the Collectibles Price Guide were compiled from published retail price lists, flea markets, auctions, and antique shops over a two year period, and rounded to the nearest dollar. Large price range discrepancies have little to do with item condition. An item with box and instruction manual may be offered by one dealer for less than another dealer without those items. Prices only reflect that individual dealer's selling price. Some dealers are consistently at the high end or low end of the range. Occasionally, dealers will lower or raise the price of an unsold item as it ages in their inventories. Items with minor defects are not necessarily less expensive than those without problems.

Geographic location, established retail store, a competitive ad in a national publication, or a weekend flea market had little effect on the selling price of memorabilia. Auctions generally receive higher prices than a retailer, but some auctions will offer their unsold items at a good discount from their original suggested or minimum bid. Some dealers have large quantities of an item and will sell 10 or 100 pieces at a much larger discount than a single piece.

These prices are to be used as a reference guide only and are not intended as a retail price list. Since there is a wide disparity in grading and pricing, collectors should familiarize themselves with Howdy Doody items in their specific region(s) and should be cognizant of their dealers grading prior to making any purchase or valuation of personal items.

COLLECTING

There are two challenges to collecting Howdy Doody memorabilia. First is the completion of a collection. Doodyville collectibles were released primarily in the early 1950s with additional items produced in 1976 and 1988. With the exception of probable 50th Anniversary souvenirs, authorized Howdy Doody memorabilia has reached its limits. A complete collection is difficult, but possible.

Most Howdy Doody collectibles are reasonably priced. They do not have the demand of Star Trek, Sports, or Super Heroes collectibles because Howdy is absent from TV reruns. The younger generation really doesn't know all that much about him, thus the demand is modest. There are cross-over pieces, such as dolls, salt & pepper shakers, tin toys, and cookie jars, where the collector demand in those areas keep related prices up.

The second challenge is finding Doodyville related toys to collect. Hundreds of thousands of each item were manufactured, sold and given away; however, they are from the days parents threw them away as children outgrew them. Great numbers of items survived, some in large quantities and excellent condition. At a show, one finds searching for and locating these items pleasurably rewarding. This hunt is more enjoyable than finding the best price among the multitude of tables with identical articles (e.g. sport cards)!

BACKGROUND

In 1997, Howdy Doody will turn 50 years young. To those of us who watched him between 1947 and 1960, he brings back warm memories of happier and simpler times. Howdy kept us entertained; he helped teach us the values of right and wrong, kindness, charity, fellowship, friendship, good habits, treating animals well, forgiveness, obeying the laws, and more; Buffalo Bob encouraged us to participate in the religion of our choice.

Howdy is not the dynamic, violent, action-packed show kids view today. There was no killing or shoot-outs. Except for a brief period near the end of the show's 13 year run, Mr. Bluster's petty tricks and Clarabell's seltzer bottle squirts were the meanest the program became. Howdy was our friend, our buddy. His friends were our friends. Advertisers sold us wholesome products. If we ate too many Hostess Twinkies or Mars candy bars, then we could use Colgate tooth paste to fight Mr. Tooth Decay. Questionable products were not promoted.

We, the Howdy Doody Alumni, lost that touch of warmth as we saw a president assassinated, fought or opposed the war in Viet Nam, saw the fall of the Nixon and Agnew Administration, etc. The Howdy Doody generation (erronously referred to as the Baby Boomers) has become the leaders and workers of today's United States. Many of us still look for those simpler times, but only memory and memorabilia remain.

Howdy continues to draw the faithful to this day. "Buffalo Bob" Smith and Lew "Clarabell" Anderson make regular appearances throughout the country to sign autographs, appear in parades, and sometimes entertain the hundreds that flock to these events. The Doodyville Historical Society (founded in 1978) publishes a monthly newsletter for members (*The Howdy Doody Times*) and holds conventions. Membership information can be obtained by mailing a SASE to the author.

CAN YOU HELP?

We apologize in advance for errors and omissions. Any additional information or corrections can be sent to the author at: P.O. Box 428, Yardley, PA 19067, or e-mail at JACKK87289@AOL.com. Please include documentation, i.e. related photographs and photocopies, with your letter. All information will be considered for future editions, with appropriate credit given if used.

Buffalo Bob Smith live! Buffalo Bob is available for appearances in your area. Requests for information should be sent to the address above.

©BOB SMITH, FROM THE SCOTT BRINKER COLLECTION

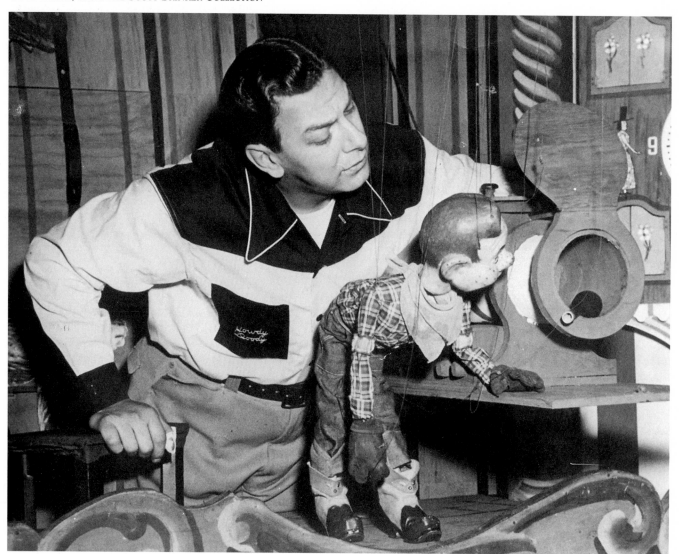

Buffalo Bob in an early costume and Howdy inspect a new Scott Brinker creation!

11-14-94

Seeing Jack Koch's incredible treatise, and I do mean **TREAT**ise, on HOWDY DOODY is a 4-D delight to me. After writing the scripts and music of Howdy's first 2,000-odd (Odd?) shows, I never dreamed that 40 years later such a fabulous, skilled Love Opus — Jack's remarkable 3rd Testament — would preserve the existence of the efforts of Buffalo Bob Smith, myself and countless others, for the Star Trek generations to see! Or am I wrong in being reminded of Clarabell every time I see Spock's ears?

Reader, do enjoy Jack's book half as much as I have and it'll still be the best read of your life. And you're sure to win back the price of admission and more, next time you get a Howdy Doody question in some Trivia Contest.

Edward Kean
Detroit, Michigan
Nov. 14, 1994

Letter from Edward Kean.

Cast of Characters

MARIONETTES

Bargaining Bill 1952	John J. Fedoozle . . . . .1948 – 1960
Bloop . . . . .1955 – 1960	Grandpa Doody . . . . .1953 – 1960
Don Jose Bluster .1948 – 1956	Hop, Skip & Jump .1953 – 1960
Hector H. Bluster .1948 – 1956	Mike Hatchet . . . . .1958 – 1960
Petey Bluster . . . . .1957 – 1960	Hyde and Zeek. .1954 – 1960
Phineas T. Bluster . . . . .1948 – 1960, 1976	Mr. Huff 1948
Buzz Beaver . . . . .1954 – 1960	Mambo . . . . .1954 – 1960
Chickapoodle 1953	Outter Orbit 1976
Dilly Dally . . . . .1948 – 1960, 1976	Paddle . . . . .1954 – 1960
Double Doody . . . . .1948 – 1960	Poll Parrott 1953
Heidi Doody . . . . .1955 – 1960	Sandra Witch . . . . .1958 – 1960
Howdy Doody I .1948	Capt. Windy Scuttlebutt . . . . .1953 – 1960
Howdy Doody II .1947 – 1960	Princess . . . . .1950 – 1951
Howdy Doody III 1976	Tizzy . . . . .1954 – 1960
Flub-A-Dub . . . . .1949 – 1960, 1976	Tom Turtle . . . . .1954 – 1960
Flub-A-Dub Jr 1952	Lillie Belle Widgeon 1953
Eustice 1948	

CHARACTERS

Abra K. Dabra . . . . .1955 – 1956	Oil Well Willie . . . . .1948 – ?
Bahpoo 1953	Oscar . . . . .1948 – 1952
Bargain Bill 1952	Papoose Hattaheela 1954
Big Ben 1952	Papoose Runningwater 1954
Bison Bill . . . . .1954 – 1955	Peppi Mint . . . . .1959 – 1960
Buffalo Bob . . . . .1947 – Present	Pesky 1957
Hefflesniffer Booglegut 1948	Pierre . . . . .1949 – 1952
Carnival Cal . . . . .1955 – 1956	Princess (Tyler) .1951 – 1953
Val Carney 1957	Princess (Marsh) .1957
Clarabell (Keeshan) . . . . .1948 – 1952	Princess (Genardi) . . . . .1954 – 1955
Clarabell (Lamb) .1952	Princess Bottelwasher 1954
Clarabell (Nicholson) . . . . .1952 – 1955	Professor Bellringer . . . . .1955 – 1956
Clarabell (Anderson) . . . . .1955 – Present	Poobah 1953
Chief Featherman . . . . .1948 – 1952	Rancher Robb 1956
Chief Thunderchicken . . . . .1953 – 1956	Rodeo Ray 1954
Chief Thunderthud . . . . .1953 – 60, 76	Salami Sam 1949
Cornelius Cobb .1952 – 1960	Sarabell 1954
Doctor Singasong . . . . .1949 – 1955	Signore DoReMiFaSoLaTiDo 1953
Fletcher, the Sketcher 1976	Sir Archibald . . . . .1949 – 1952
Gonkletwerps 1950	Story Princess . . . . .1955 – 1956
Happy Harmony .1976	Timothy Tremble .1955 – 1956
Lanky Lou . . . . .1949 – 1952	Ugly Sam . . . . .1949 – 1952
Larsony E. Grand 1960	Van Der Flugel Twins 1955
Professor Fitznoodle 1955	Windy, the dog . . . . .1952 – 1953
Monsieur Fountainebleau . . . . .1953 – 1960	Witch Hazel . . . . .1958 – 1960
Sandy McTavish .1954 – 1955	Zippy, the chimp .1952
Nicholson Muir .1976	
Nino . . . . .1947 – 1949	

ACTORS

Dayton Allen	1949 – 1952	Bill LeCornec	1948 – 1960
Lew Anderson	1953 – Present	Gina Genardi	1954 – 1955
Marti Barris	1959 – 1960	Gil Lamb	1952
Ted Brown	1954 – 1955	Milt Neil	1948 – 1960, 1976
Henry Calvin	1952	Robert Nicholson	1952 – 1960, 1976
Jackie Davis	1976	Marlyn Patch	1976
Arlene Dalton	1955 – 1956	Robert E. Smith	1947 – Present
Ray Forrest	1954	Allen Swift	1953 – 1956
Bob Keeshan	1947 – 1952	Judy Tyler	1951 – 1953

MARKETING

Bob Smith	1948 – 1950	NBC	1972, 1976
KAGRAN Corp	1951 – 1954	King Features/NBC	1987 – 1988, 1994 – Present
California National Products	1955 – 1960		

©BOB SMITH, FROM THE SCOTT BRINKER COLLECTION

Clarabell (Bob Keeshan) and Howdy at the Scopedoodle.

A HOWDY DOODY CHRISTMAS

A 1951 RCA Victor 45 rpm record, #5324, originally sold for $1.00; on the flip side of The Popcorn Song.

A TRIP TO FUN LAND

An 8mm Castle Film, #831.

A VISIT TO THE HOWDY DOODY SHOW.

A 35mm black & white still film produced by Tru-Vue.

A.O. TODD

See: TODD, A.O.

AAA SIGN CO.

Ohio company reproduced two Howdy Doody advertising tin signs. One sign for "Howdy Doody Twin Pops," the other for "Howdy Doody Fudge Bar"; with a wholesale price of $5.25 each (common at flea markets).

ABRA K. DABRA

See: DABRA, Abra K.

ADCO LIBERTY

New Jersey company that manufactured metal lunch boxes from 1954 to 1956.

ADVERTISING SERVICES DIVISION

Manufactured tags and labels for Howdy Doody products, such as Hollander Umbrellas.

AFRICAN CONFUSY-DOOZY JUICE

Juice that confused the user. From a July 1955 program.

AFRICAN FLUTTERBY

Insect in a program; July 1955.

AFRICAN-AWAKE-A-WEEK NUT

Plant that kept the user awake; July 1955.

AHMCO

Manufactured a Princess Summerfall Winterspring doll, 1954.

AIR-O-DOODLE

1. Part auto, part ship, part train, and part plane.
2. RCA 45 rpm and 78 rpm records in 1949 about the Air-O-Doodle.

ALASKAN ADVENTURE

Howdy Doody film shown on the show in July 1957. Howdy rescued a professor.

ALBERION, ED

One of the part time Clarabells for Poll Parrot road promotions.

ALLEN, DAYTON

See: BOLKE, Dayton Allen

ALLEN, ROBERT Y. (b.1909)

Original co-inventor and co-designer of the second Howdy Doody with Melvin Shaw.

ALLIE

Cat who helped Mr. Bluster at Boiling Lake in November 1955.

ALWAYS ALWAYS LAND

Introduced in December 1957; home of the Witches (April 1960) and the Invisible Man (June 1960); attacked by Captain Hook and the Pirates.

AMA

African witch doctor and friend of Simon Sly in a February 1956 series.

AMERICAN KUNKEL DISTRIBUTING CO.

Wentzville, Missouri, company that manufactured various Howdy Doody shoe polishes.

AMERICAN PAPER GOODS CO.

Manufactured the 8 oz. tubs for "Howdy Doody Ice Cream" from their manufacturing facilities in Chicago, Illinois, and Kensington, Connecticut.

AMOS

The South American republic that elected El Bandito; March 1959.

ANDERSON, JACK

Sound effects man for the show; early 1950s.

ANDERSON, LEW (1922 –)

Started portraying Clarabell on March 16, 1955. He was the voice of Tommy the Turtle and played Trapper Tyrone in 1955. Prior to the Howdy Doody Show, Lew was a member of the Honey Dreamers appearing on the Dave Garroway, Bob Smith, Kay Kayser, and Steve Allen shows. He is the director of the Lew Anderson All-American Band and appears as Clarabell in malls and parades.

ANDY HANDY

See: HANDY, Andy.

APPLAUSE INC.

Manufactured satin-faced and painted-feature Howdy Doody dolls and wrist watches in 1988.

ARCHIBALD, SIR

English explorer born in 1904; played by Dayton Allen. His costume was an explorer's outfit, pith helmet, and long beard. The judge who counted the Wonder Bread ballots in the 1952 "President of all the Kids in the USA" election.

ARGUS COMMUNICATIONS

Division of DLM Industries. Manufactured a series of Howdy Doody postcards and posters; 1988.

ARKADOODLE

Doodyville ship used for exploration; November 1955.

ARMY, U.S.

Purchased Doodyville from Mr. Bluster in December 1955. They wanted to use the town to test bombs.

ARNOLD TOYS

West German manufacturer of a tin Howdy Doody Trapeze toy. The toy measures 9" wide by 12" tall. It was imported by the Toy Novelty Associates; 1950s.

ART AWARD COMPANY, THE

North Bergen, New Jersey, company manufactured the "Howdy Doody Acrylic Paint By The Number Set"; 1976.

AT THE RODEO

Title of film for the Sun-Ray brand camera.

AUNT HAZEL

Mr. Bluster's aunt; visited Doodyville; spring of 1953.

BAGE, GARFIELD

Friend of Mr. Bluster in Bali-Hoo. He tried to help Mr. Bluster keep Buffalo Bob, Howdy, and Clarabell on the island in August 1959.

BAGWELL, ROSS

Started as a cue card boy on the Howdy Doody show and stayed until it ended in 1960. Owner and founder of Bagwell Productions in Knoxville, Tennessee, acquired by Scripps-Howard in 1994. He now operates CINETEL Productions in Knoxville.

BAPOOH

Played by Allen Swift, the Hindu twin of Poobah.

BALI-HOO

South Seas vacation island for Howdy, Buffalo Bob, and Clarabell; August 1959.

BALLAD OF JACK AND THE BEANSTALK, THE

Song sung by Buffalo Bob in honor of an upcoming NBC spectacular; November 1956.

BALLOON BERRIES

Brought to Doodyville by Liona in April 1957. The berries caused the eater to blow up like a balloon!

BALUNA

Place where Clarabell was taken to stand trial for breaking Gus Gasbag's balloons; April 1960.

BARGAIN BILL

Marionette made by Scott Brinker who traded a horse for Clarabell's six-leaf clover in December 1952. He was revised as a living person in the late 1950s and played by Robert Nicholson. Bill's marionette head is owned by Scott Brinker.

BARRIS, FRANCES MAUREEN (April 6, 1938 –)

Played Peppi Mint, a vivacious teenager, starting in December 1959. After the Howdy Doody Show, she was a cast member on *Comedy Tonight* from July 5 to August 23, 1970, and a cast member on *The Late Summer, Early Fall Bert Convy Show* from August 25 to September 1976 on CBS. She was the daughter of Harry Barris, song writer, and sang with Bing Crosby as a member of the Rhythm Boys singing with Paul Whitman's Orchestra in the 1950s.

BARRIS, MARTI

See: BARRIS, Francis Maureen.

BARRON, JOHN

Wrote the Whitman Tel-A-Tale book *Howdy Doody's Clarabell Clown and the Merry-Go-Round*, in 1955.

BEAT BENNY

See: Benny, Beat

BEATY, MARY RODGERS

Wrote the words and music for the Golden Record *Charles Dickens' A Christmas Carol*.

BE A VENTRILOQUIST

A 33⅓ rpm record, #HD35, from Goldberger Doll Manufacturing, Inc. The record was released with a series of Goldberger ventriloquist dolls.

BEAVER, BUZZ

Character that arrived in Doodyville in January 1953, made by Margo Rose. Generally aligned himself with Mr. Bluster to play tricks on the other cast members. He now resides with Margo Rose.

BECK'S

Produced a Christmas catalog with a Howdy Doody photo cover; 1951.

BEE BREAKS CLARABELLE'S BALLOON, THE

Blue Bonnet® Margarine's first Howdy Doody Coloring Comics; printed August 1953. (Note: Clarabell spelling!)

BEEFO

Strong Man at the circus; a coloring book character; 1955.

BELAIR, HARVEY

The #1 cameraman on the Howdy Doody Show.

BELINDA FROG

Whitman Fun Book character.

BELLRINGER, PROFESSOR

Played by Allen Swift; January 1955.

BEN HUR INDUSTRIES, INC.

Manufactured a bath sponge; 1950s.

BEN, BIG

Played by Henry Calvin; took over the Doodyville circus grounds to build a gravel dump; June 1952.

BENGOR PRODUCTS

A New York, New York, company that manufactured the Howdy Doody Clock-A-Doodle in the early 1950s.

BENNY, BEAT

Substitute for Buffalo Bob during his vacation.

BERNHARD ULMANN CO.

Manufactured the Howdy Doody 7" x 8" terry cloth washcloth hand puppets; 1950s.

BERNSTEIN, CARL

News reporter and co-author of *All the President's Men*, winner of a Howdy Doody look alike contest.

BEST SEAL CORP.

Manufactured an inflatable Howdy cushion; 1980s, product #1341.

BESTWAY PRODUCTS INC.

Pressed Howdy Doody records for Simon & Schuster.

BIBBLE BOARD

Device used to ask questions to the Question Quasher Squasher.

BICYCLE INSTITUTE OF AMERICA

Made an 18" bicycle with 10" wheels for Howdy Doody to promote bike safety on the program.

BIG BEN

See: BEN, Big.

BIG CHIEF

Little Golden Record; the flip side of *Cowabunga*; 1955.

BIG GOLDEN BOOK

Book product line published by Simon & Schuster. Their Howdy title was:
#475 *Howdy Doody in the Wild West* (1952).

BISON BILL

Played by Ted Brown. Replaced Buffalo Bob while he was recuperating from his heart attack from September 27, 1954, to July 29, 1955, and while Buffalo Bob was on vacation in March 1956. Bison Bill made his entrance to the show seated on a horse.

BJORNSON, B.J.

The #2 camera man on the Howdy Doody show; 1949. He retired after a long career with NBC.

BLACK BILL

Pirate and villain of a Howdy Doody comic and color cartoon serial *Ghost Ship*; September 1955.

BLACK KNIGHT, THE

Gumby film shown in February 1957.

BLACK QUEEN

Name of a pirate ship in a Dell Howdy Doody Comic; 1950.

BLACKBURN, NORMAN

A vice president of NBC in 1949. He hired the Disney animation artists that created the Velma Dawson Howdy Doody on May 22, 1948. He participated in the decision of which rendering would be the second Howdy Doody.

BLACKJACK

Resident of Bubblegumia in a March 1953 Dell comic, where Dilly Dally is crowned king.

BLACKWOOD, PADY

Master puppeteer who manipulated Howdy Doody in the 1976 revival program and again in the 1987 40th Anniversary show.

BLAINE, JIMMY

Played Jersey Jim on the show while Buffalo Bob was on vacation in February 1949, and again in 1955 during Buffalo Bob's heart attack absence, and later in August 1959. Blaine was a repeat guest on *Stop the Music* (May 1949 – 1952), was emcee on *Hold That Camera* (August – September 1950), hosted *Jimmy Blaine's Junior Edition* (January – August 1951), hosted *The Billy Daniel's Show* (October – December 1952), and hosted *Music At Meadowbrook* (May 1953 – April 1956).

BLAND CHARNOS CO.

Manufactured the "Howdy Doody Wonderland" costumes; early 1950s.

BLOOP

Flying bird-like creature wearing a bow tie, hat, and shoes with a propeller on its tail that appeared whenever anyone said a word with an "oop" in it. In September 1955, he was frightened by the Tootle-Stick.

BLUE BONNET®

Brand name of oleomargarine. A sponsor and premium maker. Premiums included:
•Playroom Portraits
•Coloring Comics (1953)
•Howdy Doody Stars and Stage Props (1954).

BLUE BONNET SUE

Female face; logo of Blue Bonnet® Margarine; she appeared in most of their Howdy tie-in advertising.

BLUE BONNET SUE AND HOWDY DOODY MYSTERY PICTURE COLORING CONTEST

1953 contest. Entries were to be on official forms with children connecting dots to form a Flub-A-Dub (the mystery) in a Howdy Doody picnic picture, and coloring in the picture; parents had to complete the statement, "I like Blue Bonnet Margarine because..." in 25 words or less. Prizes were 150 Raleigh bikes, 200 Ingerham Howdy Doody Wristwatches, 400 Howdy Doody Acro-Doodles, and 1,000 Howdy Doody Crazy Balls. The contest ended on November 28, 1953, and was judged by the Ruben H. Donnelley Corp.

BLUE MAGIC

Product of the Luce Manufacturing Co. The Blue Magic crystals were housed in a Dri-Nob on a tin can. As the knob turned pink, the crystals absorbed moisture and allowed the can's contents to remain crisp and tasty at all times, 1950s.

BLUSTER BOUNCE

Dance created by Mr. Bluster; January 1955.

BLUSTER BROTHERS CIRCUS

What Phineas and Don Jose Bluster wanted to name the circus after they cheated Howdy out of it in November 1949.

BLUSTER BULLET

Doodyville newspaper published by Mr. Bluster in August 1955. Filled with lies. Doodyville Bugle inaugurated to compete with it.

BLUSTER CLAUS

See: CLAUS, Bluster.

BLUSTER'S BALONEY BONANZA

Doodyville radio program; August 1955.

BLUSTER, ANNABELL

Sister of Phineas T. Bluster in the book *Howdy Doody and Mr. Bluster*; 1954.

BLUSTER, BUSTER B.

Introduced in an August 1955 show.

BLUSTER, DON JOSE (1880 –)

One of the Bluster triplets that was born in South America. He was conceived by Edward Kean, designed by Milt Neil, and built by Scott Brinker. Voice of Dayton Allen. Don Jose usually was tricked into being used by his brother, Phineas, against Howdy.

BLUSTER, HECTOR HAMHOCK (1880 –)

One of the Bluster triplets that was born in England; he was suspected of being a likely Mr. X in the summer of 1952. He was conceived by Edward Kean, designed by Milt Neil, and built by Scott Brinker.

BLUSTER NATIONAL BANK

A bank owned by Phineas T. Bluster that held the mortgage on Doodyville; he tried to foreclose in November 1955.

BLUSTER, PETEY

Marionette and the nephew of Mr. Bluster; conceived by Willie Gilbert and Jack Weinstein, built by Margo Rose. He was a pawn in many of Uncle Phineas's plots (e.g. the frown contest, April 1957).

BLUSTER, PHINEAS T. (1880 –)

One of the Bluster triplets. Named after P.T. Barnum. Fourth puppet conceived by Edward Kean (1948), named by Roger Muir, designed by Milt Neil, built by Scott Brinker, and voice of Dayton Allen until 1952, and then Allen Swift. One of the few villains — but a mild one — in the show. A Howdy Doody nemesis, mayor of Doodyville, and a mean-spirited, egomaniac usually scheming to spoil everyone's fun and control the Doodyville Circus, he ran against Howdy for President of the Kids in 1948. Phineas was one of three marionettes brought back for the New Howdy Doody Show. He now resides with Margo Rose.
CANADA: Claude Roe was his voice in the Howdy Doody show from November 1954.

BLUSTER, THADDEUS

Ancestor of Phineas T. Bluster. Chief Thunderthud found him in prison after the Chief used the Time-A-Tub time machine; April 1955.

BLUSTER, UNCLE LOUIS

Discovered a mystery chemical; August 1955.

BLUSTERVILLE

Community established in 1950, and reappeared to compete with Doodyville; April 1956.

BOGART, PAUL

An assistant director of the Howdy Doody show until 1952. After Howdy Doody he directed numerous shows including *All in the Family*. He won four Emmy Awards: 1965 in Outstanding Individual Achievement in Entertainment (Director) for The "700-Year-Old Gang" on *The Defenders*; in 1968 in Outstanding Directorial Achievement in Drama for "Dear Friends" on the CBS Playhouse; again in 1971 for "Shadow Game" on the CBS Playhouse; and 1978 for Outstanding Director in a Comedy Series for "Edith's 50th Birthday" in *All in the Family*. He directed: *Marlow* (1968), *Skin Game* (1971), *Cancel My Reservation* (1972), *Class of '44* (1973), *Oh God, You Devil* (1984), *The Canterville Ghost* (1986), *Power, Passion and Murder* (1987), and *Torch Song Trilogy* (1988).

BOILING LAKE

An underworld lake; November 1955.

BOLKE, DAYTON ALLEN (1914 –)

Stage name: Dayton Allen. Hired in 1949 to operate and speak for the new Phineas T. Bluster marionette. He went on to play the live characters Lankey Lou, Sir Archibald,

Salami Sam, Ugly Sam, Pierre the Chef, and also was the voice and manipulator of Hector Hamhock Bluster, Don Jose Bluster, Flub-A-Dub, Inspector John J. Fedoozle, Poll Parrot, and the evil Mr. Tooth Decay in the Colgate commercials. He returned to the show for the December 28, 1957, anniversary as Pierre. He was the voice of the sadistic ravens in the Terry Tunes for five years prior to the Howdy Doody show, the voice of Oky Doky the puppet on the *Adventures of Oky Doky* TV show from November 4, 1948, to May 26, 1949, on the Dumont Network. After Howdy Doody, he played Mr. Bungle on the *Winky Dink* show and then appeared regularly on the *Steve Allen Show* from September 1958 to December 27, 1961, on NBC and ABC, as the "Why Not?" man.

BOLOGINA

Location where Buffalo Bob saves the Inspector; December 1955.

BONE, HAMLET

Phantom of the Doodyville theater and foreign spy; January 1959.

BOOGLEGUT, HEFFLESNIFFER

Campaign manager for Mr. X in the 1948 Presidential Election. He became a close friend of Howdy after the election and frequently called him during the program, but never appeared on the show.

BOOGLEGUT, HEFFLESNIFFER SR.

Father of Hefflesniffer Booglegut.

BOOM, BIM BAM

A hard-of-hearing judge for the Noise Abatement Week contest; April 1959.

BOOMER ZOOMER

A flying machine that looked like an arrow with a chair and steering wheel on top. This gadget allowed Mr. Bluster to fly to the Lost and Lonesome Lagoon; December 1955.

BOONE, CAPT.

Character that advertises for a man of steel; May 1958.

BORIS

Henchman to Mr. Bluster in Littlelandia; December 1955.

BORSCHT, B.P.

Hollywood producer who wants to make a movie in Doodyville; December 1958.

BOSCO

1. Talking bear Howdy meets in *Howdy's Camping Adventure* in Dell comic; 1950.
2. A dancing bear and character in the *Howdy Doody Circus* from a Dell Comic; 1951.

BOTTLEWASHER, PRINCESS FRYINGPAN

Played by Lee Carney, she was counterpart to Princess Summerfall Winterspring.

BOYSEN, RICKIE

From Haddonfield, New Jersey, and one of four winners of the TV Digest Howdy Doody Coloring Contest; 1951.

BRAGGINS, CLIFF

Scriptwriter and songwriter for the Canadian version of Howdy Doody from November 1954. He wrote *Flub-A-Dub is Gone Away*; 1955.

BRINKER, EDYTHE

Late wife of Scott Brinker. Helped make props, produced, and held cue cards on the TV show.

BRINKER, SCOTT

Engaged in 1948 to replace Frank Paris to build marionettes. He built the Blusters, The Inspector (using the Velma Dawson Howdy Doody head), Princess Summerfall Winterspring, Dilly Dally, Bargaining Bill, Poll Parrot, and Double Doody as a back up. He designed the body for the Velma Dawson Howdy Doody head. He also made sets for the Johnny Jupiter. He produced most of the brilliantly creative props and sets through 1955. Scott Brinker still makes repairs on the Howdy marionette that travels the country with Buffalo Bob today.

BRISTOL, LEE

Stage manager for the Howdy Doody show and son of the founder of Bristol-Myers Inc.

BROWN, TED

Played Bison Bill from September 27, 1954, through March 25, 1955. Before Howdy Doody, he played King Cole on the *Birthday Party* TV show in 1949 carried by the Dumont Network; was the emcee for *The Greatest Man on Earth* quiz program from December 3, 1952, to January 15, 1953. Ted Brown continues to be a radio personality in the New York City area.

BROWNING, KIRK

Early stage manager of the Howdy Doody show. He directed the movie *You Can't Take it With You* (1984). He became famous for directing live Lincoln Center, New York, productions.

BRUNO

Henchman for Mrs. Izbing, attempting to kidnap Heidi and take her to Sweden; March 1956.

BUBBLEGUMIA

Location of an adventure story in an issue of Howdy Doody comics. Dilly Dally is crowned king because of his yellow hair; March 1953.

BUBBLESCHMIDT, PROFESSOR

One of many visiting academicians. Gave Flub-A-Dub an intelligence test; July 1955.

BUFFALO BOB

Was and is played by Robert E. Smith. The name, history, and story of this character were created by Edward Kean in late 1949. He was Howdy's voice, friend, and confidant. Buffalo Bob was the key member of show. He introduced the commercials and products; participated in every story plot, usually as a peace-maker and guardian of Doodyville. He was the Chief of the Sigafoose Indian tribe, inheriting his "Buffalo" title from his grandfather, "Buffalo Tom" in 1955. Buffalo Bob was often referred to as "the man every little boy idolized and every little girl wanted to marry." Buffalo Bob makes appearances with Howdy throughout the United States today.

BUFFALO BOB SMITH DAY

August 1, 1952, in Buffalo, New York.

BUFFALO BOB SMITH LIVE AT BILL GRAHAM'S FILLMORE EAST

A 33⅓ rpm album on the Project 3 label, PR5055SD, from Total Sound, Inc. A recording of Buffalo Bob's 1970 – 1971 University and College revival tour. Songs such as *It's Howdy Doody Time, The Clarabell Song, Brush Your Teeth With Colgate,* and many more were recorded.

BUFFALO BULLETS

One of the three fat Tons of Fun characters on the Old-Time Movies, named by Bob Smith.

BUFFALO CLINT

One of the three fat Tons of Fun characters on the Old-Time Movies, named by Bob Smith.

BUFFALO EMMA

The name used by Bob Smith's mother when she made a guest appearance on the show in 1949.

BUFFALO FRANK

Father of Marty Stone; made off-TV appearances for the show.

BUFFALO TOM

Buffalo Bob's grandfather and a member of the Sigafoose tribe.

BUFFALO VIC

1. Victor Smith, brother of Bob Smith.
2. One of the three fat Tons of Fun characters on the Old-Time Movies, named by Bob Smith.

BUNGATHUD, CHIEF

A founder of Doodyville; ancestor of Chief Thunderthud.

BUNNYLAND

Located at the bottom of a hole. Petey Bluster falls into the hole in April 1957.

BUNYIP

Animal that is part Kangaroo and part Teddy Bear. It is the highlight of a September 1958 program.

BURRY'S

Makers of Howdy Doody Cookies in 1952. Cookie boxes came with one of 14 denominations of Howdy Doody Play Money. Burry's also produced a set of Magic Trading Cards.

BURT

Also known as 'Pretty Boy' Burt. He was an escaped convict recaptured by Flub-A-Dub in Dell comic #19.

BUZZ BEAVER

See: BEAVER, Buzz

BYRNE, MURIEL

Buffalo Bob's secretary from 1947 – 1954; the sister of New Jersey's former governor, Brendan Byrne.

CABOOSE CABBAGE

A vegetable and the only cure for Diesel Measles. Found only in the cave of the Stick Men, September 1959.

CACTUS CARL

Character in a January 1956 series.

CADBURY'S HOWDY DOODY BAR

A 1951 – 1954 candy distributed in Canada; had eight butterscotch centered pieces sold for $.10 per bar.

CALIFORNIA NATIONAL PRODUCTIONS, INC.

Fully owned by NBC. Succeeded Kagran to license the Howdy Doody Show tie-ins. Sold rights from 1956 through 1960.

CALVIN, HENRY

Played Big Ben in 1952. From 1957 – 1959, he played Sgt. Garcia in the Walt Disney TV show Zorro and again in the 1960 movie *The Sign of Zorro*. In 1960, he played in the Disney movie *Toby Tyler*.

CAMPBELL, VIC

Writer for the early morning Bob Smith radio shows from 1946 to 1952. He helped develop the radio program *The Triple B Ranch* in 1947, where Howdy Doody was created.

CAPT. BOONE

See: BOONE, Capt.

CARDINAL CAMERA CORPORATION

Long Island City, New York, firm that manufactured the Howdy Doody white sailor cap. Originally sold for $.69.

CARNEY, LEE

Puppeteer hired in December 1952 to replace Rhoda Mann. The wife of Mike King, another show puppeteer. She also played Aunt Hazel in the spring of 1953, plus the roles of Sarabell and Princess Fryingpan Bottlewater.

CARNEY, VAL

Played by Robert Nicholson in 1958, hired Clarabell for

his carnival and made him walk the high wire.

CARNIVAL CAL

Played by Allen Swift. Character hired to run the April 1955 Doodyville fair; returned to Doodyville in November 1955.

CAROUSEL

Makers of a 1988 Howdy Doody slipper.

CASTLE FILMS

Brand name for United World Films. They manufactured 8 mm films such as:
#831 *A Trip to Funland* and *Howdy Doody's Christmas* (1951).

CATHEY FURNITURE MFG. CO.

Lewisburg, Tennesee, manufacturers of the Howdy Doody Platform Rocker. Originally priced at $12.95.

CAVE OF THE WIND

A cave in Underworld, November 1955.

CBC

Canadian Broadcasting Corp., the company that produced the Howdy Doody show in Toronto, Canada.

CHAMPREL COMPANY

A New York company that manufactured an early 1950s Howdy Doody Bubble Bath.

CHANGING ISLAND

Located in the Gulf of Mexico. Mr. Bluster was shipwrecked there in January 1953. He was rescued there by Buffalo Bob, and Nick Nicholson was introduced as the third Clarabell there.

CHARLES DICKENS' *A CHRISTMAS CAROL*

A Golden Record #R261 with the story and song by Bob Smith, originally sold for $.29. Howdy played Bob Crachet, Dilly Dally played Tiny Tim, Captain Scuttlebutt played Scrooge, orchestra directed by Mitch Miller, and the story was written by Mary Rogers Beaty.

CHELSEY NOVELTY COMPANY

Manufactured a 3½" Howdy Doody Talking Pin.

CHESTER QUACKENHAM

See: QUACKENHAM, Chester Q.

CHICAPOODLE

A puppet that was a cross between a chicken and a poodle. Mr. Bluster captured it and returned it to its owner, Lulu Belle Widgeon, for the reward in 1952.

CHIEF FEATHERMAN

See: FEATHERMAN, Chief.

CHIEF BUNGATHUD

See: BUNGATHUD, Chief.

CHIEF THUNDERCHICKEN

See: THUNDERCHICKEN, Chief.

CHIEF THUNDERTHUD

See: THUNDERTHUD, Chief.

CHILDREN'S SONGS, INC.

Published the *Music is Fun with Howdy Doody* songbook in 1949.

CHODER, JILL

She played Cynthia Goodheart in a 1971 show. After Howdy Doody, she played the part of Sandy Galloway on the NBC drama *Number 96* from December 10, 1980, to January 2, 1981.

CHURCH-CRAFT PRODUCTS, INC.

A St. Louis, Missouri, manufacturer of Stori-Views and Stori-Viewers in the early 1950s.

CINDERELLA

A play produced in Doodyville in August 1957.

CLARABELL

See: HORNBLOW, Clarabell.

CLARABELL

Song written by Edward Kean.

CLARABELL BANANA BAR

"Ice Milk Chocolate Flavored Coating" bar made by the Rivers Manufacturing Company. It was eligible for prize redemption from the Doughnut Corporations' Prize Doodle List in 1954 – 1955.

CLARABELL DANGLE-DANDY

An 8" x 10" back panel from a Kellogg's cereal box. Clarabell's face could be cut out and assembled with string for a mobile.

CLARABELL HURDY GURDY

1950s toy manufactured by FBA Industries.

CLARABELL TEE-SHIRT

A premium from the Howdy Doody's Big Prize Doodle list. It could be obtained for 20 specially marked ice cream bags and $.75 shipping or 375 bags and no money. The shirt was available in small, medium, or large sizes and Clarabell's nose had a built-in beeper on the shirt.

CLARABELLE [sic] CLOWN

A series of three dolls made by Madame Alexander. (Note: Clarabell spelling.)

CLARABUS

A golf cart like vehicle that Clarabell rode in 1955, and used as a taxi by Clarabell in May 1956.

CLAUS, BLUSTER

What Mr. Bluster wants to become after he deposes Santa Claus in December 1955.

CLIFT, BROOKS

A stage manager for the Howdy Doody show, and brother of Montgomery Cliff, the actor.

CLOKEY, ART

He created Gumby and Pokey characters. In 1956, he directed 10 Gumby movies.

CLONE, CY

An unscrupulous salesman that sells overpriced goods to the residents of Doodyville in August 1959.

CLOWN TOWN

Birthplace of Clarabell Hornblow.

CLOWNSTRETCHER

Invented by Edward Kean to help the viewing public make the transition from a chubby Bob Keeshan Clarabell to a lanky Gil Lamb Clarabell in 1952.

COBB'S HAIR FAIR

An invention created by Mr. Cobb in September 1958.

COBB, JASPER CORNELIUS

(November 5, 1952) Played by Nick Nicholson, later by Allen Swift, and then again by Nicholson. This shopkeeper had a strong dislike for clowns, placing him at odds with Clarabell. In the 1976 revival series, he became a prop man.

COCORICO

Publishers of "Un Petit Livre D'or" books in Paris, France. Publishers of the French version of the Little Golden Books.

COG, CAPTAIN

Leader of the Xenon spacemen that capture Dilly and Howdy.

COLECO

Brand from the Connecticut Leather Company. They produced the Chief & Princess hobby kits.

COLGATE PALMOLIVE PEET COMPANY

Began advertising on the show in April 1948.
Manufactured a 7" tall die cut Palmolive Soap sign and a miniature TV viewer. Sponsored the 1955 "Name the Tug Boat" contest.

COLLEGEVILLE PRODUCTS

Manufactured the Pl'a-Time Costumes in the early 1950s.

COLLYER, BARBARA

Produced the 1952 *Welch's Howdy Doody Cookbook* for the Welch's Grape Juice Co. She also invented the drink "Purple Cow," which was half milk and half grape juice; the drink had a very short life span.

COLORING CARDS

See: ROYAL Coloring Cards.

COLORING COMICS

See: HOWDY Doody Coloring Comics.

CONE, BOB

Writer for the Saturday NBC radio program *Howdy Doody*.

CONFUSION JUICE

Given to Buffalo Bob by Pesky in November 1957. This drink put the user in a state of confusion.

CONFUSY-DOOZY JUICE

See: African Confusy-Doozy Juice.

CONNECTICUT LEATHER COMPANY

A Hartford, Conneticut, company that manufactured a series of 1950s do-it-yourself craft kits including:
#298 The Official Chief & Princess Moccasin Kit
#H101 Howdy Doody & Clarabell Puppet Mitten Kit
#H102 Howdy Doody & Clarabell Slipper & Sock Kit
#H207 Howdy Stufftoy Kit
#H208 Flub-A-Dub Stuftoy Kit
#H209 Clarabell Hug-Me-Toy or Laundry Bag
Howdy Doody Needlepoint Kit.

CONRAD MANN

See: MANN, Conrad.

CONTINENTAL BAKING CO.

Parent company of Wonder® Bread and Hostess® Twinkies, sponsors of the Howdy Doody Show starting in April 1948. They spent $100,000 per year for the use of Howdy Doody characters on the end seals of Wonder Bread loaves in 1950.

COOTS, J. FRED (1898 – 1985)

Songwriter on the show from 1954 – 1956. He worked on the Heidi Doody story with Howard Davis. He was the composer of the well known song of *Santa Claus is Coming to Town*. J. Fred Muggs, the chimp on the *Today* show, was named after him.

COPELAN, RAYE

Designer of the 1950 Peter *Puppet Playhouse* Marionettes. Previously she created the 30" Oky Doky puppet that was introduced in a 1948 Children's Fashion Show; hosted a TV program on the Dumont Network through 1949.

COPPERSMITH, JERRY

Author of the Tell-A-Tale book *Howdy Doody and the Magic Lamp* in 1954.

COWABUNGA

1. A greeting and exclamation used by Chief Thunderthud. Created in the early 1950s by Edward Kean, it was written in scripts as "KAWA BONGA" (two words). This expression was adopted by The Simpsons and the Teenage Mutant Ninja Turtles in their cartoon shows. Snoopy of the Peanuts comic strip occasionally uses the term in the strip and in Hallmark greeting cards. The "Kawa-" prefix was frequently adapted for other uses, e.g. in the January 27, 1954, Thunderthud used "Kawa-Kaploata," "Kawa-Caboose," "Kawa-Locomotive," "Kawa-Deisel," "Kawa-Weasel," "Kawa-Papoose," "Kawa-Goose," and "Kawa-Mazoola" in the first few minutes of the program. The Oxford English Dictionary has accepted Cowabunga as a word.

2. A 78 rpm record published under the "Little Golden Records" label.

COWAGOOPA

Friendly greeting used by Princess Summerfall Winter-spring. Created by Edward Kean.

COZY CORNER

A Whitman Publishing Company line of books. They produced:
#2410 *Howdy Doody's Island Adventure.*

CRAWFORD, MEL

Illustrator of the Whitman's Tell-A-Tale books *Howdy Doody and the Magic Lamp* in 1954 and *Howdy Doody's Clarabell Clown and the Merry-Go-Round* in 1955.

CROWE, JACK

Illustrated the 1953 Whitman *Television's Famous Howdy Doody Fun Book.*

CROWN SILVER PLATE

Manufactured silver-plated utensils including:
Long-handled ice iea spoon.
#A-13 Educator Set — spoon and fork.

CUSACK, PATRICIA

From Philadelphia, Pennsylvania, and one of the four winners of the 1951 TV Digest Howdy Doody Coloring Contest.

CY CLONE

See: CLONE, Cy.

CYNTHIA GOODHEART

See: GOODHEART, Cynthia.

D & R INDUSTRIES

Toledo, Ohio, firm that manufactured the Howdy Doody Oil Painting Set for Beginners.

DABRA, ABRA K.

Played by Allen Swift. A magician created in 1953, and friend of Mr. Bluster in June 1955. His magic gets out of control and works backwards! Arrives in Doodyville in February 1956.

DALLY, DILLY

(October 1949) Introduced on the 400th performance of the show; cast after the Frank Paris' Eustice. He was the fifth new puppet on the program, created by Edward Kean, designed by Milt Neil, and built by Scott Brinker, manipulated and voiced by Bill LeCornec. He was cast as a circus roustabout born in 1938, who wore a sweater with a big "D" (for being the waterboy on the Doodyville High School Football team) on it. Dilly had the ability to wiggle his ears. Dilly was Howdy's friend, and frequently Phineas T. Bluster's dupe. Dilly was one of three marionettes brought back for the 1976 New Howdy Doody Show. He now resides with Margo Rose.
CANADA: Voice was performed by Jack Mather from November 1954.

DALTON, ARLENE (– 1986)

Played the Story Princess from September 12, 1955. She replaced Gina Genardi. Arlene was the voice of Heidi Doody.

DALTON, KITTY

She was in charge of the program's wardrobe in the early 1950s.

DALY, KATHLEE

Author of the 1956 Little Golden book *Howdy Doody's Animal Friends.*

DANDYVILLE

The hometown of Dandy Doodle and Elephant Bob in a June 1955 episode.

DANTY APRON MFG. CO

Manufactured the Howdy Doody and Princess Cobbler aprons in New York City.

DAUBER, LIZ

Illustrated the 1950 book *Howdy Doody's Circus* with Dan Gormley.

DAVIS, HOWARD (1917 –)

Was first hired as co-director to work with Bob Hultgren in 1952, as well as co-director of *The Gabby Hayes Show*. Part-time writer and script supervisor for the Howdy Doody Show in 1954, replacing Edward Kean; helped write the lyrics for the song *Will My Dog Be Proud of Me?* with Robert Nicholson. He wrote the "Jersey Jim" scripts in 1955, and helped with the Heidi Doody story line. He was succeeded by Willie Gilbert and Jack Weinstock in 1954. After Howdy Doody, he directed the *Today* show with Dave Garroway until 1959 and directed *Wide Wide World* until 1958.

DAVIS, JACKIE

A singer, organist, and conductor of the Doodyville Doodlers in the 1976 revival series.

DAVIS, OWEN JR.

Vice President of Casting for NBC in 1947. He wanted children's programming and brought the Frank Paris marionettes together with Bob Smith. Davis also produced the NBC *Repertory Theater* from April 17 – July 10, 1949.

DAWSON, THELMA

An early Disney animator that was hired to design the post "Elmer" Howdy Doody. Was paid $2,000 by NBC for the manufacture and rights of the second Howdy Doody. The best known version of Howdy was shipped from California to New York in two boxes, one for the head and one for the body.

DE LUNA, RAYO

Princess Summerfall Winterspring's counterpart on Spanish version of Howdy Doody.

de BAUN, STEVEN

A contract writer for the program with Howard Davis in early 1955. He wrote Shakespearean adaptations for early TV.

DEBOX, JACQUIN PROFESSOR

Passed through Doodyville in April 1958 with his invention, the "electickle."

DECAY, MR. TOOTH

A Colgate Toothpaste character who was always trying to attack Happy Tooth. He could be vanquished by brushing with Colgate. His voice was by Dayton Allen until 1952, and then Alan Swift.

DELL PUBLISHING CO.

Published 38 Howdy Doody Comics from January 1950 through July/September 1956. Issues one through five had photographic covers. In 1957 Dell published two additional Howdy Doody comics under the Four Color series.

DENNIS, CLARK

A tenor and regular on *The Bob Smith Show* radio and TV program on NBC Network.

DEPARTMENT OF PIONEERS

Government agency responsible for certifying Pioneers; from a July 1955 program.

DIESEL MEASLES

Disease infecting Flub-A-Dub in September 1959. Cured only with Caboose Cabbage.

DILLY DALLY

See: DALLY, Dilly.

DILLY DALLY WADDLE

A 1953 Whitman race where the runners bend over, grabbed their ankles and ran.

DILWORTH, BETTINA

Floor manager of the Howdy Doody show 1949.

DLM INC.

Parent company of Argus Communications, makers of 40th Howdy Doody Anniversary tie-ins.

DO'S AND DON'TS ON MANNERS

Stori-View set #602 consisting of 12 slide cards.

DO DO, KING

The Martian King in October 1955.

DO NOTHING MACHINE

An invention created by Flub-A-Dub in September 1958.

DOBBIN, DOUGHFACE

Character in August 1955 that wanted to take Hobby, the pony from Doodyville.

DOBRINSKA, TIMMY

Children's winner of the 1978 Milwaukee, Wisconsin, Howdy Doody Look-Alike Contest.

DOC DITTO

An old toy maker.

DOC LEMON

See: LEMON, DOC.

DOLAN, LINDA

West Virginia child who won the I'd Like Clarabell to Visit Me Because... contest in 1952. Clarabell visited in September.

DONALD ART COMPANY

A New York, New York, company that produced an 8" x 10" series of TV Time Pictures.

DONNELLEY, REUBEN H., CORPORATION

Judges in the 1953 Blue Bonnet Sue and Howdy Doody Mystery Coloring Contest and the 1955 Colgate-Palmolive Co. Name the Tug Boat Contest.

DOODLE

An anti-gravity ray invented by Dr. Doodle in January 1956.

DOODLE, DANDY

Howdy Doody's double that tries to get everyone to move from Doodyville to Dandyville in June 1955.

DOODLE, DR.

Comes to Doodyville in January 1956 with an anti-gravity ray.

DOODY DIME-A-DAY DEPUTY

The 1955 March of Dimes campaign launched on the program in June. This appeal collected in over 300,000 dimes.

DOODY, DOUBLE

Duplicate of Howdy Doody made by Scott Brinker in 1948. Was Howdy Doody's twin brother and Mr. X in the 1948 President of all the Kids election. He is now enshrined at the Smithsonian Institute in an exhibit with Charlie McCarthy, Mortimer Snerd, and Froggie the Gremlin.

DOODY, GRANDPA

One of Doodyville's oldest citizens, this puppet, made by Margo Rose in 1953 was a knock off from one of the Howdy Doody extras; wearing an Army uniform, he donned cane and beard. His voice was performed by Bob Smith. He now resides with Margo Rose.

DOODY, HEIDI

A puppet conceived by Howard Davis, built by Margo Rose and voice by Arlene Dalton. She was introduced as a stranger who saved Buffalo Bob's life in Africa. Howdy adopts her as his sister in August 1955 to keep her from being expelled from Doodyville. Heidi's song was written by J. Fred Coots. She now resides with Margo Rose.

DOODY, HOWDY

Howdy began his career as a voice on radio. His opening line included the greeting "Howdy Doody" and eventually took on the name. There were three distinct versions of this main character:
#1 The Frank Paris Howdy (January – May 1948). He was commonly called "Elmer" and was abruptly removed from the program by Paris over marketing rights disputes. He looked like a country bumpkin. He was manipulated by Frank Paris; voice by Bob Smith. Howdy #1 was destroyed by Paris in an agreement with NBC.
#2 The Velma Dawson/Scott Brinker Howdy (1948 – 1960). This is the most common face seen on the majority of the shows and promotional items. The Dawson version was top heavy. Scott Brinker modified him into the Inspector and created another head from the original mold. Other copies were made from the mold by Scott Brinker and used in the Canadian, Cubian, and Mexican programs. It is believed that the Mexican Howdy was boiled in a cauldron by striking Mexican television workers. Additional Howdy duplicates were made for the Double Doody and Photo Doody characters. He was controlled by Rhoda Mann (1948 – 1952) and Rufus Rose, Margo Rose, and Lee Carney (1953 – 1960); voice by Bob Smith and Allen Swift (1954 – 1955). Howdy #2 now lives and travels with Bob Smith.

©BOB SMITH, FROM THE SCOTT BRINKER COLLECTION

Edyth Brinker, Inspector John J. (Boing) Fedoozle, Howdy, and Scott Brinker. The Brinkers built many of the sets, props, and puppets. The inspector was originally made as Howdy but the head was too heavy. A new Howdy head was made and the inspector was created.

#3 The Revival Howdy (1976). Created for the syndicated shows, Howdy was modernized with long vinyl hair. Manipulated by Pady Blackwood; voice by Bob Smith.

DOODY, PHOTO

Built by Rufus Rose in January 1952, he was a duplicate of Howdy Doody with ball joints instead of strings. Photo was used for publicity photos and public appearances. He was called Howdy's cousin. In 1983, he was damaged by a vandal at Roger Muirs' office and restored by Pady Blackwood. He now resides with Roger Muir.

DOODYVILLE BIRD CLUB

A club that met in February 1958 to hear Professor Whipporill speak.

DOODYVILLE BUGLE

Newspaper started by Howdy in August 1955. Buffalo Bob was the editor.

DOODYVILLE HISTORICAL SOCIETY

Organization created in 1978 for the study and enjoyment of Howdy Doody related items and experiences.

DOODYVILLE LAWS

Highlighted by law #1: "Anyone absent from Doodyville for more than ten days would not be allowed back."

DOODYVILLE NATIONAL BANK

The bank pictured on the backs of Howdy Doody play money issued by Burry's Cookies and The Ogilvie Flour Mills Co. Ltd. Howdy Doody was the Treasurer and his face was engraved on the building.

DoRaMiFaSoLaTiDo, SIGNORE

Played by Bill LeCornec starting in 1953; he was an Italian lyrical singer.

DOUGHFACE DOBBIN

See: DOBBIN, Doughface.

DOUGHNUT CORP. OF AMERICA

Brooklyn, New York, manufacturer who created a premium exchange in 1954 – 1955 for wrappers from several different licensed ice cream makers. They tied-in a Howdy Doody Ice Cream Club with membership cards, etc. for the promotion. Prizes could be selected from their Prize Doodle List. Additional prizes were available on the backs of the wrappers. Prizes were again offered in the 1955

Howdy Doody Prize List Featuring Flags for Bags, and again in 1957 through their Jackpot of Fun Comic Book.

DR. DOODLE

See: DOODLE, Dr.

DR. SINGASONG

See: SINGASONG, Dr.

DRI-NOB

Patented device of the Luce Manufacturing. Co. Located on top of a Krispy Kan, its crystals absorbed moisture allowing the contents of the can to remain fresh. When the crystals turned from blue to pink, they could be refreshed by being heated in an oven for 15 – 30 minutes.

DRURY, JACK

Public relations man who helped develop the NBC show revival in 1976.

DUDI, JAUDI

Spanish version of Howdy Doody Show distributed in Mexico and pre-Castro Cuba that had a live police dog replace Clarabell.

DUNCAN HOUNDS

See: HOUNDS, Duncan.

DUNNE, DOMINICK

A stage manager for the Howdy Doody show in 1949. He became a best-selling novelist contributing show business pieces to *Vanity Fair* magazine.

ECUYER, LEE

Zippy the Chimp's trainer.

ED-U-CARDS MANUFACTURING CORP.

Manufactured the 1950s Howdy Doody Dominoes game from their New York factory, originally sold for $1.00.

EEGEE CO.

They manufactured three 1972 Howdy Doody dolls. There was a 12" (30.5cm), 19" (48.3cm), and 26"

(66.0cm) doll with vinyl head and cloth body. The smallest and largest ones have a moveable mouth. The smallest is marked "style #H D 12." All were manufactured in Hong Kong. Manufactured a Clarabell doll in 1973. In the 1970s, manufactured the Howdy Doody plastic heads used for the Goldenberger Doll Manufacturing Co.

EFFANBEE DOLL CORPORATION

Manufactured a 19" and 23" Howdy Doody hard plastic doll which sold for $5.98 and $9.95 in February 1948.

EL BANDITO

Visits Doodyville on March 26, 1960, to kill Buffalo Bob; he is captured by Howdy and Clarabell.

EL PUPETERO

Visits Doodyville on March 26, 1960, to aid El Bandidito in killing Buffalo Bob.

ELECTICKLE

A machine invented by Professor Jacquin DeBox that can tickle everyone invisibly.

ELECTROMINDOMIZER

A device used to read peoples' minds; made up of "a bunch of gears and wheels and screws and dials and . . ." It was composed of an antihistamine tube, a cathode glass tube, and a sink generator. The Electromindomizer was used on the program for two months.

ELEPHANT BOB

Buffalo Bob's rival in Dandyville.

ELMER

Original name of the Howdy Doody character, this was the first marionette for the part. Created by Bob Smith in the late 1940s. Had an Oafs voice, jug ears, a messy mop of blond hair, and a moronic grin. Elmer always addressed the kids with "Howdy Doody, Kids." Created for a $500 fee. His first appearance was January 1948. Buffalo Bob described the character as "Mortimer Snerd-ish country bumpkin-type." This first Howdy Doody was destroyed by Paris in the RCA building in December 1955.

EMENEE INDUSTRIES

A New York, New York, manufacturer of a 1950s Howdy Doody Ukulele; originally sold for $.98. The Ukulele could also be obtained via the Doughnut Corporation's Prize Doodle List for ice cream bags. They also produced a ukulele for the 1976 revival.

ENCHANTED TREASURE

A cartoon on a September 1956 show starring Dilly Dally and Captain Scuttlebutt.

EUSTACE

A Frank Paris puppet and the predecessor of Dilly Dally. Created in February 1948. He was pulled from the show by Paris over a merchandising dispute. Eustace was destroyed by Paris in the RCA building in December 1955.

EZ Do, Co.

Manufactured a 1950s set of wooden stools with characters' pictures painted on them.

FAIRYLAND THEATER

A live theater in the Howdy Doody Circus in a 1950 Whitman Coloring Book. Mother Goose stories were performed there.

FALCON, ERROL

The director during the revival series in 1976 – 1977.

FARMER WIBBET

Carrot farmer.

FAT VAT

A machine that Pesky the clown used to drastically reduce Buffalo Bob's weight in February 1958.

FAUST, JIMMY

Chosen as the "Midwest Howdy Doody Boy" in May 1950

FBA INDUSTRIES

Manufactured a 1950s 8" long Clarabell Hurdy Gurdy toy.

FEATHERMAN, CHIEF

Played by Bob Keeshan. Member of the Tinka Tonka tribe. Created By Edward Kean in 1948. Featherman disliked Clarabell and searched for him. Since Keeshan played both parts, the Chief never found Clarabell.

FEDOOZLE, JOHN J. (1922 –)

A.K.A. The Inspector. Born in 1922 according to the 1950 Poll Parrot news. Became America's No. 1 BOING Private Eye. Modified by Scott Brinker in 1948 from the original Velma Dawson Howdy Doody. Voice by Dayton Allen until 1952 and then Allen Swift. His specialty was searching for two kinds of people: those that are missing and those that have to be found! He was also a Lieutenant Colonel in the South American Foreign Legion, holding identity card #274183. He now resides with Margo Rose.

FELTON, HAPPY

Took charge of Doodyville for the first week after Buffalo Bob's heart attack in September 1954, replaced by Bison Bill. Previously he broadcast the *Happy Felton's Knot Hole Gang* show on NBC, Saturdays at 10 AM from November 20, 1954, through February 26, 1955. This 30 minute live children's program was a combination quiz show and European vaudeville film clip presentation.

FIB-A-DOODLE

Machine in a March 1956 adventure.

FICE, FRANK

Producer for the Canadian version of Howdy Doody Show starting in November 1954.

FITZNOODLE, PROF.

Arrives in Doodyville to make ink out of water or oil so that the Doodyville Bugle can be published in August 1955.

FIVE L'S

Stood for "The Lucky Left Leg of the Lima Llama."

FLAPDOODLE

A 1949 device that gave anyone anything they wanted, as long as the end result was good. Shaped like a one foot diameter pipe; it was invented by Howdy Doody and Dilly Dally.

FLEISCHMANN'S.

Produced Blue Bonnet® brand oleomargarine.

FLETCHER THE SKETCHER

An artist/sketcher played by Milt Neil in the 1976 revival series.

FLIGHT TO ADVENTURE

Short color films produced and presented by Lowell Thomas Jr. on the show beginning September 12, 1955.

FLIP-A-RING, INC.

A Waterbury, Connecticut, company that manufactured the Flub-A-Dub Flip-A-Ring toy.

FLIPFLOP, FRED

Visited Doodyville in March 1960.

FLUB-A-DUB (December 1947 –)

Found in South America in February 1949, by Buffalo Bob while on a vacation. Flub-A-Dub was created by Edward Kean, designed by Milt Neil, and built by Scott Brinker. His voice was described as "a mixture of a foghorn and a woodsaw" and movements were performed by Dayton Allen through 1952. At first, the controls were worked by wire cable, and then by string. He was eight animals in one: the head of a duck, the ears of a cocker spaniel, the neck of a giraffe with rings around it, a dachshund's body, a seal's flippers, a pig's tail, a cat's whiskers, and the memory of an elephant. At first he had a diet of flowers, but when parents complained that their children were emulating the Flub and eating flowers, the diet was changed to meatballs and spaghetti. Flub-A-Dub was one of three marionettes brought back for the 1976 New Howdy Doody Show.
His voice was Larry Mann in the Canadian version of the Howdy Doody show from November 1954.

FLUB-A-DUB FLIP-A-RING

Game manufactured by Flip-A-Ring, Inc. in the early 1950s, originally sold for $.39. A doughnut sized ring on a string had to be caught on the Flub-A-Dub's beak.

FLUB-A-DUB IS GONE AWAY

Song written by Cliff Braggins for the Canadian Howdy Doody show in 1955.

FLUB-A-DUB JR.

Son of Flub-A-Dub. He was a short lived character in the early 1950s and helped find the election ballots in November 1952. Flub-A-Dub Jr. was described as looking like a Flub-A-Dub, but smaller.

FLUGEL'S CASTLE

Home of the Van Der Flugel twins in the early 1950s. The castle was built by the Brinkers.

FLY-AWAY-MACHINE

A June 1955 invention of Chief Thunderthud to allow him to soar over Doodyville.

FLYING CAMERA, THE

A 1951 camera that had two short orange-colored wings. The camera flew around taking pictures.

FLYING CARPET, THE

A five part cartoon series from January through February 1956.

FONTAINEBLEAU, MONSIEUR

Played by Allen Swift starting in 1953; he was an artist.

FORREST, RAY

Played Rodeo Ray in 1954. He was an announcer and emcee on such shows as the *NBC News* (1944), Boxing (1948 – 1949), and *TV Screen Magazine* (1948 – 1949).

FORTISSMO, PROF.

World's greatest entertainer. Visited Doodyville in May 1956.

FOSTER CITY PRODUCTS, INC.

A Cleveland, Ohio, company that manufactured the 1950s Howdy Doody Adhesive Bandage Strips.

FOUR COLOR COMICS

A series of comic books produced by the Dell Publishing Company from September 1939 to June 1962. After the Howdy Doody Comics were discontinued, two more were produced under the Four Color label:
#761 Howdy wind surfing on ice (January 1957);
#811 Dilly viewing painted stars in telescope (June 1957).

FRAME TRAY INLAY

Name of the Whitman Publishing Co. product line. The Howdy Doody Picture Puzzles were puzzles contained in a frame. Among their puzzles were:
#2603 Clarabell through the Hoop (1953)
#2603 Ice Cream Shop (1953)
#2603 Is That You Clarabell? (1952)
#2603 Ringmaster Howdy (1953)
#2603 Dilly the Human Bullet
#2628 Clarabell Picture Puzzle (1954)
#2984 Howdy Goes West
#4428 Howdy and skunk (1953)
#4428 Howdy, Dilly & Mr. Bluster on plane (1953)
Howdy on a Bronco
Howdy Doody at the Circus.

FRAUD, FRED

A boxing promoter who helped raise money for football uniforms in October 1959.

FRIEND SONG, THE

Song written by Edward Kean.

FRIES ENTERTAINMENT INC.

Manufactured a 40th anniversary Howdy Doody buttons and posters.

FRIES PRODUCTION

An independent television syndication company. Together with Roger Muir, produced a two-hour 40th Howdy Doody Anniversary special in 1987.

FROSTY SPRAY SNOW

Cans of snow primarily sold at Christmas. In the late 1950s, the 12.5 oz. Howdy Doody promotional cans came with Howdy's picture on the front and 20 free decorating stencils (including Howdy and Clarabell).

FROWN CONTEST

Creation of Mr. Bluster to compete with the Smile Contest in November 1957. Since Petey does not smile, Mr. Bluster wants him to win something.

FREY, GEORGE

NBC Vice President of Sales in 1948 who perceived the Howdy Presidential Campaign as a marketing boon for television.

FRY-CADBURY LTD.

A Montreal, Canada, candy company that manufactured a butterscotch candy from 1951 – 1954.

FUN FEET

Brand name of the 1980s Howdy Doody Carousel slippers.

FUN HAUS

Illustrated the 1988 series of Howdy Doody posters and postcards.

FUN HOUSE

The gallery of eight boys and girls for the *Puppet Playhouse* programs starting in December 1947, the earliest version of the Peanut Gallery.

FUNLAND

An entertaining land used by the Pied Piper in June 1957.

GABBY HAYES

See: HAYES, George.

GALLU, SAMUEL

A 1950s script writer for the Howdy Doody show. Also performed as a tenor in New York Concert Hall. In 1959 he produced the 39 syndicated adventures of *The Blue Angels*.

GASBAG, GUS

Maker of animal balloons in April 1960. Clarabell broke them.

GAUDSCHMIDT BROTHERS

A vaudeville act with poodles; an act on the first *Puppet Playhouse*, December 27, 1947.

GENARDI, GINA (1938 –)

Replacement for Judy Tyler as Princess Summerfall Winterspring. Initially introduced as Papoose Gina Runningwater on January 26, 1954. She ended as the third Princess on September 9, 1955.

GENERAL MILLS

Manufacturers of Wheaties® brand cereals; a show sponsor.

GEORGE

A giraffe in the circus presented by Dell Comics. He wanted to use paste rather than pins in the Halloween Pin the Tail on the Giraffe game.

GEORGE FOSTER PEABODY AWARD

Awarded to Bob Smith for the Howdy Doody Show, voted the most outstanding children's show on TV and Radio in 1948.

GERARD, JOHN R.

A writer on the Canadian Howdy Doody show. Married to Maxine Miller (Princess Hilda).

GIDDY-GIDDY WATER FOUNTAIN

A Mr. Bluster find that made the drinkers talk backwards. The November 1949 plot backfired affecting Phineas and Don Jose Bluster.

GIGGLYA

Laughing fish in the circus; appeared in a 1950 Whitman coloring book.

GILBERT, WILLIE

Writer for the show with Jack Weinstock. They conceived marionettes and characters such as Tiz, Mike Hatchet, Tom Turtle, Paddle, Sandra and Hazel Witches, Peppi Mint, and Petey Bluster. He had previously written for the *Captain Video Show*. He wrote *The Laughing Song* with Weinstein and R. Nicholson in 1955; and helped write The New Howdy Doody Show in 1976 with Robert Nicholson. He co-authored the Broadway show *How to Succeed in Business without Really Trying* with Weinstock and Abe Burrows. They won a Pulitzer Prize in 1962 and the New York Drama Critic's Circle Award in 1961 – 1962.

GILES, KEN

Produced the 1950s Howdy Doody's Poll-Parrot Easy as ABC Coloring Book and the Poll-Parrot Tuk-A-Tab masks and Detective Disguises.

GINGER NUT

A color cartoon aired from September 12, 1955.

GINGER SNAPPER

See: SNAPPER, Ginger.

GNIK

A peddler on an August 1960 show who gives Peppi Mint a magic mirror.

GOLDBERGER DOLL MFG. CO.

Manufactured a 1970s series of ventriloquist dummies and dolls in Hong Kong distributed through their Brooklyn, New York, office. Dolls produced were 24" and 30". In conjunction with the dolls, they sponsored an LP record *Be a Ventriloquist*.

GONKLETWERP, GLEEFUL

A December 1950 character and one of the Three Flying Gonkletwerps.

GONKLETWERP, MISERABLE

A December 1950 character and one of the Three Flying Gonkletwerps.

GONKLETWERPS, THREE FLYING

Invisible characters created in December 1950. Parents complained that their children were afraid of characters they couldn't see. They were renamed the Three Friendly Invisible Gonkletwerps. This did not calm the kids, and the Gonkletwerps were retired from the program.

GOOD DEED PILLS

Invented by Buffalo Bob in January 1959. Taking them makes one do good things, but when diluted they cause the reverse effect.

GOODBYE SONG, THE

Written by Edward Kean in 1950 to close each week's program.

GOODHEART, CYNTHIA

Played by Jill Choder. A character in a 1971 show.

GOOLA-GOOLA BEAR

A prehistoric bear that Howdy brings back from the frozen north pole.

GORMLEY, DAN

Illustrated the 1950 book *Howdy Doody's Circus* with Liz Dauber.

GOULET, ROBERT

Occasionally played Timber Tom, the Buffalo Bob counterpart in the Canadian version of the show.

GRAND, LARSON E.

Played by Bill LeCornec. Steals the Baseball Diamond (a gemstone) in an April 1960 show. On a May show he convinced Buffalo Bob to start a circus with local talent.

GRAUER, BEN

Announcer for the NBC Toscannini conducted Symphony Orchestra. He once substituted for Buffalo Bob, and he swore Howdy into office as President of all the Kids of the United States in January 1949.

GREAT GRANDFATHER GRAVITY LOSER

Mr. Bluster's anti-gravity invention.

GRIBBROEK, ROBERT

Illustrated the 1955 Cozy Corner book *Howdy Doody's Island Adventure*.

GRINNY

A laughing fish in the circus; appeared in a 1950 Whitman coloring book.

GROTHKOPF, CHAD

Drew the 1950s Howdy Doody comic strip with Milt Neil; copy by Edward Kean. Introduced on November 7, 1949, when Howdy announced the new Sunday newspaper comic strip.

GROUCHY

An unpleasant clown who wanted to take Pesky's place in March 1958.

GULF ROAD SHOW

Also known as *The Gulf Road Show Starring Bob Smith*. NBC variety and talent show airing Thursday nights 9:00 to 9:30 PM from September 2, 1948, to June 30, 1949. Howdy Doody made two appearances on the program and sang *All I Want for Christmas is My Two Front Teeth* on December 22, 1948.

GUMBY

Plasticine clay figure created by Art Clokey and introduced on a June 1956 Howdy Doody program in "The Adventures of Gumby." Gumby was spun off as its own program in March of 1957. That show was hosted first by Bobby Nicholson and later by Pinkie Lee.

GUMBYLAND

Where Gumby lived. Buffalo Bob visited Gumbyland in January 1957.

GUND

Manufactured hand puppets with cloth bodies. They included Howdy Doody, Princess Summerfall Winterspring, Clarabell, Dilly Dally, Flub-A-Dub, and Phineas T. Bluster.

HADLEY COMPANY

Manufactured pre-1951 Figurine Painting Kits. Figures consisted of all the main characters measuring approximately 6½" high.

HAIDA, PRINCESS

Played by Caryl McBain. She was the Canadian version of Princess Summerfull Winterspring from November 15, 1954. She was a member of the Western Canadian Thunderbird tribe with inherited medicine man powers from her grandfather.

HALLMARK CARDS

Manufactured the 1991 Ambassador series of Howdy Doody greeting cards.

HALO SHAMPOO

A product of Colgate-Palmolive advertised on the program.

HANDY, ANDY

A tycoon to whom Buffalo Bob tries to sell a fountain and Mr. Bluster tries to sell him a do-it-yourself clothes cleaner in May 1957.

HAPPY FELTON

See: FELTON, Happy.

HAPPY HARMONY

See: Harmony, Happy.

HAPPY TALK

Bob Smith's Welsh corgi; appeared in March and June 1955 episodes.

HAPPY TOOTH

See: Tooth, Happy.

HARETT-GILMAR INC.

Far Rockaway, New York, manufacturer of Howdy Doody boxed games such as:
Howdy Doody Electronic Carnival Game (1950) and #621 Howdy Doody 3 Ring Circus (Wiry Dan Electronic label) (1951).

HARMONY, HAPPY

A Doodyville school teacher; played by Marilyn Patch in the 1976 revival series.

HARRY

A Dell comic circus hippopotamus that sat on Tom Thumb.

HARRY THE HIPPOPOTAMUS

A Whitman Fun Book character.

HARVEY HOTPLATE

See: HOTPLATE, HARVEY

HASKELL, KIT

Performer in the 1976 revival series.

HATCH-A-HUTCH

From a September 1955 program.

HATCHET, MIKE

A marionette conceived by Willie Gilbert and Jack Weinstein and built by Margo Rose; August 1958; detective called into Doodyville to locate a stolen football.

HATT, RONALD RAY

From Reading, Pennsylvania, and one of the four winners of the 1951 TV Digest Howdy Doody Coloring Contest.

HATTAHEELA, PAPOOSE

A candidate for Princess Summerfall Winterspring introduced on January 28, 1954.

HAYES, CHRISTOPHER COLUMBUS

Great-great-grandfather of Gabby Hayes, mentioned on a September 1955 program.

HAYES, GEORGE "GABBY"
(May 7, 1885 – February 9, 1969)

Was a substitute for Buffalo Bob and a frequent guest on the show. Most of his career he was a sidekick to cowboys like Hopalong Cassidy, Gene Autry, Roy Rogers, and John Wayne in 174 performances from 1923 – 1951. He had his own NBC children's program, *The Gabby Hayes Show* from October 1, 1950, to December 23, 1951 (directed by Doody's Howard Davis and Bob Hultgren), and on ABC from May 12 to July 14, 1956.

HAYES, OLIVER WENDEL

Poet uncle of Gabby Hayes mentioned in a September 1955 show.

HEFFLESNIFFER BOOGLEGUT

See: BOOGLEGUT, Hefflesniffer.

HEIDI DOODY

See: DOODY, Heidi.

HERO, THE

Name of a movie being made by Farley Flickey in Doodyville in July 1956.

HESS, JUDITH (October 9, 1934 – July 4, 1957)

Professional name: Judy Tyler. Portrayed the first real life Princess Summerfall Winterspring of the Tinka-Tonka Tribe from the last half of 1951 through October 1953. Jimmy Durante selected her from of a Copacabana chorus line for his show in 1951. She left the program in November 1953 to star in Richard Rogers Broadway musical *Pipe Dream*. She co-starred in *Jailhouse Rock* with Elvis Presley. She died tragically in an auto accident at age 23.

HICK CUP

Award given in March 1959 show for the person who best dresses like a clown.

HICKENLOOPER, MISS

Howdy's schoolteacher appearing at the end of 1954.

HIGHCHIEF, SKY

The puppeteer who manipulated the bandaged Howdy Doody after Frank Paris withdrew his puppet from the program.

HILDA, PRINCESS

Played by Maxine Miller. Replacement for Princess Sumerfall Winterspring.

HINES, FRANNY

An actor christened by Buffalo Bob in the Old-Time Movies. The name was also that of a friend of Buffalo Bob, who appeared on a few shows.

HOBBY

A pony brought to Doodyville by the princess in August 1955. Hobby contained a mysterious message.

HOLLANDER & SONS, INC., F.

Manufactured the 1951 Howdy Doody Umbrellas. Stanley Pollinger, president of Hollander stated that hundreds of thousands were manufactured, wholesaling at $1.40 and retailing for $2.00. They were commissioned by Martin Stone using designs by Milt Neil. A plastic Howdy head on the handle was supplied from a lamp manufacturer.

HONKADOODLE

A machine invented by Howdy Doody for Mother Goose. When the goose quacked into it, the Honkadoodle would type out the statement in English.

HONNEWINKLE, HULDA

The name of an actress christened by Buffalo Bob in the Old-Time Movies. The name was that of a friend of Buffalo Bob's mother.

HOOK, CAPTAIN

Attacked Always Always Land in an April 1960 show.

HOP

One of three kangaroo puppets made by Margo Rose in 1953.

HOPKINS, BOB

Stage director of the show in 1954.

HORN, MR.

Character in a November 1958 program.

HORNBLOW, CLARABELL

Created in February 1948 and played by Bob Keeshan, an NBC page. Original make up by award-winning Dick Smith. Clarabell was a mute clown using his horn-equipped box to communicate a "yes" or a "no." He was generally lovable but wild and unruly in his early years. Squirting Buffalo Bob and Chief Thunderthud with a seltzer bottle was his favorite pastime. He feared Chief Featherman and always fled when he thought that the Chief was near.
Clarabell was played by:
    Bob Keeshan 1948 – 1952
    Gil Lamb 1952
    Robert Nicholson 1952 – 1955
    Lew Anderson 1955 – Present
CANADA: Played by Alfie Scopp in Canadian version of the Howdy Doody show from November 1954.

HOSTESS CUPCAKE®

A product of Continental Baking Co.; advertised on the show.

HOSTESS TWINKIE®

A product of Continental Baking Co.; advertised on the show.

©Bob Smith, from the Scott Brinker Collection

Howdy, puppeteer Rhoda Mann, and Dilly Dally (with early hair style).

HOTPLATE, HARVEY

A generous stranger in a May 1955 episode; he sponsored a Doodyville invention contest. Impersonated by Mr. Cobb in March 1956.

HOUNDS, DUNCAN

Famous chef that visited Doodyville in September 1957 to give the Best Chef Award.

HOUSE OF CARDS

Location of the Wizard series; December 1955.

HOWDY BLUSTER SHOW, THE

This program was announced by Mr. Bluster after he dispatched Buffalo Bob in a spaceship in the spring of 1953.

HOWDY DOODLERS, THE

A June 1956 musical combo.

HOWDY DOODY

See DOODY, Howdy.

HOWDY DOODY & BUFFALO BOB SMITH AT THE PIANO

A wind-up two-piece mechanical toy manufactured by Unique Art in 1950, originally sold for about $3.00. One part was a stand-alone Howdy Doody. The other was Buffalo Bob, seated at a piano.

HOWDY DOODY & PALS

A plastic lunch box with a matching dome thermos manufactured in 1977 by the King Seeley Thermos Company.

HOWDY DOODY – RADIO PROGRAM

Sixty minute, five day a week NBC radio program starting in 1951 written by Bob Cone. An audio version of the TV program. Bob Smith, Bob Nicholson, Judy Tyler, Dayton Allen, and Bill LeCornec voiced their TV personalities. Edward Kean and Robert Nicholson wrote the music.

HOWDY DOODY 3-PIECE DISH SET

Manufactured by the Taylor-Smith Company, it consisted of a plate, cup, and bowl originally sold for $2.19.

HOWDY DOODY ACRYLIC PAINT BY THE NUMBER SET

Manufactured by the Art Award Company in 1976; each kit contained two 8" x 10" character panels, 12 acrylic paints, and a brush. The kits were:
#8101 Howdy and Phineas T. Bluster
#8102 Howdy and Clarabell
#8103 Howdy and Dilly Dally
#8104 Howdy and Flub-A-Dub.

HOWDY DOODY ADHESIVE BANDAGE STRIPS

Manufactured by Forest City Products, Inc. There were 36 (18 large and 18 small) bandages in each package originally selling for $.29. Each package had six pictures of the show characters to cutout and trade; a trading card in each package. These cards were the same photos as on the Mars candy Christmas cards and a series of note pads.

HOWDY DOODY AIR-O-DOODLE CIRCUS TRAIN

A 16" long wind-up toy from the 1950s.

HOWDY DOODY AND CLARABELL

Little Golden Book #121 published in 1951, written by Edward Kean and illustrated by Art Seiden.

HOWDY DOODY AND CLARABELL COLORING BOOK

A 1955 Whitman coloring book #1188 originally sold for $.25.

HOWDY DOODY AND CLARABELL PUPPET MITTEN KIT

1950s kit that allowed the user to make a set of children's mittens with the picture of Howdy on one hand and Clarabell on the other.

HOWDY DOODY AND CLARABELL SLIPPER SOCK KIT

Manufactured by Connecticut Leather Company in the 1950s. The kit allowed the user to make a set of children's slippers with the picture of Howdy on one hand and Clarabell on the other.

HOWDY DOODY AND CLARABELL THE CLOWN

A Tru-Vue photo card #T-4 made in 1954. In this adventure, Clarabell seeks a useful job.

HOWDY DOODY AND HIS MAGIC HAT

Little Golden Book #184 published in 1954. It was based on a UPA cartoon; illustrated by Art Seiden.

HOWDY DOODY AND HIS PALS

Stori-View set #601 consisting of 12 slide cards.

HOWDY DOODY AND MOTHER GOOSE

An RCA Victor record album.

HOWDY DOODY AND MR. BLUSTER

Little Golden Book #204 published in 1954, written by Edward Kean and illustrated by Elias Marge.

HOWDY DOODY AND PRINCESS COBBLER APRONS

Sanforized pink or blue denim broadcloth aprons from the Danty Apron Manufacturing Co. sold for $1.00.

HOWDY DOODY AND SANTA CLAUS

1. Little Golden Book #237 published in 1955, written by Edward Kean and illustrated Art Seiden.
2. A pre-1951 RCA Victor record album starring Howdy and Buffalo Bob.

HOWDY DOODY AND THE AIR-O-DOODLE

The name of the first Howdy Doody RCA Victor story record on the Little Nipper label released in December 1949. Howdy takes us for a trip around the world in the Air-O-Doodle. There were two versions of this album: a 45 rpm single #WY397 originally sold for $2.26, and two 78 rpm albums #Y397 originally sold for $2.31. The story and music were by Edward Kean and the orchestra was conducted by Henri Rene. The record sold as many as 30,000 per week.

HOWDY DOODY AND THE MAGIC LAMP

A Tell-A-Tale Book #944 published in 1954; written by Jerry Coppersmith and illustrated by Mel Crawford.

HOWDY DOODY AND THE MONKEY TALE

A Tell-A-Tale Book #902 published in 1953.

HOWDY DOODY AND THE MUSICAL FOREST

The name of an RCA Victor story record.

HOWDY DOODY AND THE PRINCESS

Little Golden Book #135 published in 1952, written by Edward Kean and illustrated by Art Seiden.

HOWDY DOODY AND YOU

Name of an RCA Victor Little Nipper label 45 rpm record number EYA 41. The orchestra was conducted by Robert Nicholson, with story and songs written by Edward Kean.

HOWDY DOODY ANIMAL FRIENDS

Little Golden Book #252 published in 1956, written by Edward Kean and illustrated by Art Seiden.

HOWDY DOODY AT THE CIRCUS

A Howdy Doody Television Film from the early 1950s.

HOWDY DOODY AT THE ZOO

Sun-Ray Camera's first package of pre-exposed negatives. Exposing these early 1950s negatives to light for 30 seconds produced a character photo.

HOWDY DOODY AU PAYS DES JEUX

The French version of *Howdy Doody in Funland* published in 1953 for Canada under the Un Petit Livre D'or label; book #71.

HOWDY DOODY BALLOON ZOO

Long balloons that came with instructions for twisting into animal shapes.

HOWDY DOODY BALLOONS

Assorted sized balloons with Howdy's picture on them. Sold in the 1950s from $.05 to $.50 each.

HOWDY DOODY BANANA FUDGE BAR

A milk sherbet bar made by the Rivers Manufacturing Company. It was eligible for gifts from the Doughnut Corporation's Prize Doodle List of 1954 – 1955.

HOWDY DOODY BANK

A ceramic 7" bank depicting Howdy riding a pig. This same design was used in the 1988 Leadworks desk lamp.

HOWDY DOODY BEACH BALL

A premium from the Howdy Doody Big Prize Doodle List. It could be had for 20 specially marked ice cream bags plus $.60 shipping, or 300 bags and no money.

HOWDY DOODY BIRTHDAY DECORATION SET

A 1950s six plastic candle holder set for birthday cakes; made by Tee-Vee Toys sold for $.19.

HOWDY DOODY BOBBING HEAD FIGURE

A seated Howdy nodding doll; manufactured by Leadworks.

HOWDY DOODY BOY OF 1950

Look-alike contest.

HOWDY DOODY BUBBLE BATH

A 6" cylindrical container with 50 bath gels, manufactured by the Champrel Company in the early 1950s.

HOWDY DOODY CARD GAME

Made by Russell Manufacturing Co. in 1955 originally sold for $.19.

HOWDY DOODY CHARACTER BUBBLE PIPES

Assorted colored plastic bubble pipes made in the 1950s by Lido Toy Company. The bases of the pipes had the faces of characters Howdy, Clarabell, Flub-A-Dub, and Mr. Bluster. The pipes were blue, red, yellow, and silver; sold individually boxed, in boxes of two with a soap dish on display cards.

HOWDY DOODY CHARACTER GLASS LAMP-SHADE

A 13" 1950s overhead glass lampshade depicting Howdy Doody circus events.

HOWDY DOODY CHARACTER PUPPET

Series of 1950s toys manufactured by Peter Puppet Playthings, Inc. in Scope Doodle boxes.

HOWDY DOODY CHOCOLATE COVERED ICE CREAM

Manufactured by Schlosser Brothers, Inc. This ice cream bar was eligible for prize redemption from the Prize Doodle List in 1954 – 1955.

HOWDY DOODY CHOCOLATE COVERED ICE MILK

Manufactured by Rivers Ice Cream Co. It was eligible towards a premium from the Doughnut Corporation's Prize Doodle List in 1954 – 1955.

HOWDY DOODY CHRISTMAS STOCKING

A 19" flannel stocking (1951 – 1954) with the message "Seasons Greetings from Howdy Doody and his friends" with a drawing on the front.

HOWDY DOODY CLIMBER

A Welch's 1950s premium. A Howdy attached to string; when pulled, Howdy climbs up the string.

HOWDY DOODY CLOCK-A-DOODLE

A cuckoo type clock manufactured by Bengor Products in the early 1950s. It has Flub-A-Dub at the top and Howdy on the pendulum. Some antique toy dealers regard this as the scarest Howdy Doody item.

HOWDY DOODY COLOR COMICS — SUNDAY NEWS

A button with Howdy's picture, given away from October 1949 promoted the new comic strip in the *New York Sunday News*. The strip ceased publication in 1953.

HOWDY DOODY COLORING BOOK

Books #2018 and #2953, produced by the Whitman Publishing Company in 1957 and originally sold for $.05.

HOWDY DOODY COLORING COMICS

A series of one page cartoons inserted in packages of Blue Bonnet® Margarine; beginning in August 1953.

HOWDY DOODY COMICS

A series of 38 comic books produced by the Dell Publishing Company from 1950 through 1956. Six million comics were sold each year. (See also Four Color Comics.) The covers were:
1. Howdy Doody (photo cover January 1950)
2. Howdy & toy circus wagon (photo cover)
3. Howdy & Clarabell (photo cover July – August 1950)
4. Howdy & Mr. Bluster on a duck (photo cover September – October 1950)
5. Howdy on horse (November – December 1950)
6. Howdy & Dilly in cannibal pot (January – February 1951)
7. Howdy & Hobby horse (March – April 1951)
8. Howdy as artist (May – June 1951)
9. Elephant giving Howdy a bath (July – August 1951)
#10. Howdy sleepwalking (September – October 1951)
#11. Dilly catching Howdy in butterfly net (November 1951)
#12. Howdy and the dog catcher (December 1951).
#13. Santa Howdy (January 1952)
#14. Howdy winter wind surfing (February 1952)
#15. Snowman Clarabell (March 1952)
#16. "Howdini" magic show (May – June 1952)
#17. Howdy stops TV bandit (July – August 1952)
#18. Howdy hooks Dilly (September – October 1952)
#19. Election Parade (November – December 1952)
#20. Howdy painting totem pole (January – February 1953)
#21. Howdy reading ghost stories (March – April 1953)
#22. Howdy catching butterflies (May – June 1953)
#23. Howdy in swimming tube (July – August 1953)
#24. Howdy and Dilly rowing (September – October 1953)

#25. Howdy and Dilly playing football (November – December 1953)

#26. Howdy celebrates New Year (January – February 1954)

#27. Howdy on Merry-Go-Round (March – April 1954)

#28. Station attendant Howdy (May – June 1954)

#29. Howdy pets skunk (July – August 1954)

#30. Howdy vacuums leaves (September – October 1954)

#31. Howdy cuts spaghetti for Dilly (November – December 1954)

#32. Howdy and Dilly making cookies (January – March 1955)

#33. Howdy eating ice cream sundae (April – June 1955)

#34. Howdy and gang on train ride (July – September 1955)

#35. Howdy skates in soap box (October – December 1955)

#36. Howdy ice skating (January – March 1956)

#37. Howdy fishing (April – June 1956)

#38. Howdy eats watermelon (July – September 1956)

HOWDY DOODY CRAZY BALL

A 10" diameter plastic ball with a peculiar bounce.

HOWDY DOODY DOMINOES

Game manufactured by the Ed-U-Cards Manufacturing Co. in the early 1950s.

HOWDY DOODY DOODLE SLATE

A premium from the Howdy Doody's Big Prize Doodle list. It could be obtained for 10 specially marked ice cream bags and $.20 shipping, or 100 bags and no money. This was a variation of the Etch-A-Sketch.

HOWDY DOODY DOODLERS

An eight member musician group who performed on the 1976 revival series.

HOWDY DOODY EGGS

A February 1950 license to White Gold Enterprises. Howdy Doody's picture was stamped on each egg. The cartons contained cut-out cartoons.

HOWDY DOODY ELECTRIC CARNIVAL GAME

An electric midway game produced by the Harett-Gilmar Inc. in 1951.

HOWDY DOODY ELECTRIC LAPEL PIN

A 1950s pin with pull string produced by the E.J. Kahn Co. Originally sold for $.69.

HOWDY DOODY EXPLAINS TV

Stori-View set #606 consisting of six slide cards.

HOWDY DOODY FIGURINE PAINTING KIT

Manufactured by the Hadley Company before 1951. The kit consisted of 6½" show characters made of white plaster and colored paints.

HOWDY DOODY FLICKER KEY CHAIN

See: POLL Parrot's Howdy Doody Key Chain.

HOWDY DOODY FLICKER RING

See: POLL Parrot's Howdy Doody Flicker Ring.

HOWDY DOODY FOR PRESIDENT

The campaign theme song for Howdy's 1948 presidential campaign.

HOWDY DOODY FROSTY SNOW SPRAY

A 12.5 oz can of giant snow flakes manufactured by the U.S. Packaging Corporation. These cans came with a 20 Free Stencils offer.

HOWDY DOODY FUDGE BAR MILK SHERBET

Manufactured by Rivers Ice Cream Co. It was eligible towards a premium from the Doughnut Corporations Prize Doodle List in 1954 – 1955.

HOWDY DOODY FUN BOOK

A Whitman Publishing Co. activity book #2169 published in 1951 and originally sold for $.25.

HOWDY DOODY GOES HUNTING FOR RABBITS

A Howdy Doody Television Film from the early 1950s.

HOWDY DOODY GOES TO ALASKA

A Howdy Doody Television Film from the early 1950s.

HOWDY DOODY GOES TO THE BEACH

A Howdy Doody Television Film from the early 1950s.

HOWDY DOODY GOES TO THE ZOO

A Howdy Doody Television Film from the early 1950s.

HOWDY DOODY HALLOWEEN PARTY

A story in the November 1951 Dell comic written by Edward Kean.

HOWDY DOODY ICE CREAM

Manufactured by the Rivers Ice Cream Co. This Water Ice and Ice Milk bar was eligible for prize redemption from the Doughnut Corporation's Prize Doodle List in 1954 – 1955.

HOWDY DOODY ICE CREAM CLUB

A club organized by the Doughnut Corporation of America. For $.10 members received a membership card, membership button, and an 8" x 10" color photo of Howdy.

HOWDY DOODY IN FUNLAND

Little Golden Book #172 published in 1953, written by Edward Kean and illustrated by Art Siden.

HOWDY DOODY IN THE WILD WEST

A Big Golden Book #475 written by Edward Kean in 1952.

HOWDY DOODY LUNCH BOX

A metallic lunch box manufactured by ADCO Liberty Company in 1955; designed by Milt Neil.

HOWDY DOODY MAGIC PUZZLE BALL

A Howdy Doody 1950s puzzle in a ball shape.

HOWDY DOODY MAGIC SHOW FEATURING POLL-PARROT

A 1950s Poll-Parrot premium jigsaw puzzle.

HOWDY DOODY MAGIC TRADING CARDS

A set of 42 trading cards manufactured in 1951 by Specialty Advertising Service of New York. The front showed a color Doodyville drawing of the characters; the reverse had a magic trick or puzzle with the card number. At least two sets of these cards were issued; one given away in pairs of cards with Burry's Howdy Doody Cookies on white stock, and the other as individual cut cards with Howdy Doody Ice Cream on buff stock, slightly wider. These same cards were used in strips of three, without the magic trick on the reverse, to decorate the Howdy Doody Wallets. Although the Magic Trading Cards were numbered, that number applied to the trick/puzzle side only; e.g. card #26 was the Magnetic Forehead trick, the flip side on the Burry's set was Howdy Feeds Jerry Giraffe and Dilly Dally the Snake Charmer on the Ice Cream set. The following list represents the Burry's set:

1. Howdy Doody
2. Clarabell
3. Dilly Dally
4. Mr. Phineas T. Bluster
5. Howdy and the Princess canoeing
6. Howdy Doody leads the parade
7. Howdy Doody and Buffalo Bob
8. Flub-A-Dub steals the show
9. Flub-A-Dub
#10. Princess Summerfall Winterspring
#11. Howdy Doody out west
#12. The Princess and her friends
#13. Big Chief Dilly Dally
#14. Clarabell does a self-portrait
#15. Howdy Doody's Air-O-Doodle
#16. Howdy Doody at the Circus
#17. Dilly Dally the Snake Charmer
#18. Howdy MacDoody
#19. Oil Well Willie
#20. Inspector
#21. Clarabell rides the Zingo-Cycle
#22. The Princess playing her drums
#23. Senor Howdy Doody
#24. Clarabell having a drink
#25. Dilly Dally goes hunting
#26 Howdy feeds Jerry Giraffe
#27. The Princess and her doll
#28. Clarabell's juggling act
#29. Flub-A-Dub knits a sweater
#30. Clarabell and Dilly enjoy a soda
#31. Chief Featherman
#32. Oscar
#33. Clarabell fixes the Scope-Doodle
#34. Howdy Doody and the Honk-A-Doodle
#35. Mr. Bluster meets Mr. Walrus
#36. Howdy and Dilly fishing
#37. Ugly Sam
#38. Pierre the Chief
#39. Flub-A-Dub takes a bath
#40. Howdy Doody's Magic Show
#41. Howdy Doody's Totem Pole
#42. Dilly and Clarabell play hide and seek

HOWDY DOODY MAKE IT YOURSELF BEE-NEE KIT

A 1950s craft kit that instructed the user how to make a beanie cap.

HOWDY DOODY MODELING COMPOUND

Marketed by the Kid-O Co. in 1957.

HOWDY DOODY NAVY, THE

Song written by Edward Kean.

HOWDY DOODY OFFICIAL OUTDOOR SPORTS BOX

1950s toolbox picturing a ranch manufactured by the Liberty Steel Chest Co. in the early 1950s.

HOWDY DOODY OFFICIAL PL'A-TIME COSTUME

Halloween costumes produced between 1951 and 1954. The costumes of Howdy, Clarabell, Dilly Dally, Flub-A-Dub, and Princess Summerfall Winterspring were packaged in boxes with a Howdy Doody cut-out face on the front. Boxes were rubber stamped on the side with the costume's character and size.

HOWDY DOODY OIL PAINTING SET

Painting set manufactured by D & R Industries in the 1950s.

HOWDY DOODY PAINT SET

A water color paint kit, #4312, manufactured by Milton Bradley in the early 1950s. It contained one brush, 14 paint tabs, water dish, and painting papers.

HOWDY DOODY PAPER MASK

A cut out mask from a 1954 Kelloggs® Rice Krispies cereal box.

HOWDY DOODY PHONODOODLE

A 1950s record player produced by Shura-Tone Productions, Inc. Five different models originally sold from $8.95 to $27.95.

HOWDY DOODY PICTURE PUZZLES

Whitman Publishing Co. frame puzzles produced in 1953 for their Frame Tray Inlay line.

HOWDY DOODY PLASTIC TOYS

A 1950s five-piece character set manufactured by Tee-Vee Toys.

HOWDY DOODY PLATFORM ROCKER

Children's rocking chair made by the Cathey Furniture Manufacturing. Co.; sold for $12.95.

HOWDY DOODY PLAY GYM SET

Tubular steel gym with a safety seat and wooden seat swing and steel ride-glide sold for $24.95. Accessories included slide-attachment, basketball board, and shower-head for $9.95.

HOWDY DOODY PLAY MONEY

Fourteen denominations supplied by Burry's cookies as a premium. In 1953, the Ogilvie Flour Mills Co., Limited gave away play money with their products. The Ogilve money was redeemable for a prize; one million Doodyville Bank dollars were exchangeable for a BSA bicycle. Money denominations were:
$100 Oscar
$500 Dr. Sing-A-Song
$1,000 Flub-A-Dub
$5,000 Phineas T. Bluster
$10,000 Princess Summerfall Winterspring
$25,000 Dilly Dally

HOWDY DOODY PRIZE LIST

The 1955 Doughnut Ice Cream Bag Prize List, similar to the Prize Doodle List.

HOWDY DOODY PUMP-MOBILE

A 1950s 8½" long, 7" high wind-up toy manufactured by Nylint.

HOWDY DOODY PUPPET WASH CLOTHS

A washing mitt depicting Howdy, Princess, Clarabell, or Mr. Bluster manufactured by the Bernard Ulman Corporation. Originally sold for $.49, or with a squeaking noise for $.59.

HOWDY DOODY PUT-IN-HEAD

An early 1950s clay molding kit similar to the Mr. Potato Head toy; Howdy, Dilly, Mr. Bluster, and Clarabell could be re-created on foods.

HOWDY DOODY QUIZ SHOW

An action guide wheel, 12" diameter produced by the Multiple Products Corporation in 1951. An opening at the top asks a question and a Magic Window flap at the bottom displays the answer.

HOWDY DOODY RANCH HOUSE TOOLBOX

A steel tool box, 14" x 6" x 6", with handle manufactured by the Liberty Steel Chest Corporation in the 1950s.

HOWDY DOODY READY TO MAKE TOY KITS

Craft kits manufactured by Connecticut Leather Company for making stuffed toys with pattern and yarn. They include:
#H207 Howdy Doody Toy
#H208 Flub-A-Dub Toy
#H209 Clarabell Hug-Me-Toy or Laundry Bag.

HOWDY DOODY RUBBER BALL

A 1950s 4½" diameter rubber ball with a picture of Howdy Doody on one side and Clarabell on the other.

HOWDY DOODY SAND FORMS

Molded plastic faces of Howdy, Clarabell, Flub-A-Dub, and Mr. Bluster with a plastic shovel manufactured by Ideal and originally sold for $.59 in 1952.

HOWDY DOODY SAND SET

Similar to the Howdy Doody Sand Forms but included a plastic bucket, 1954.

HOWDY DOODY SHOW PUNCHOUT BOOK

A Whitman Publishing Company activity book #2119 produced in 1952. Cardboard character puppets could be punched out and made to move, controlled with string.

HOWDY DOODY SHOW, THE

1. Name of the program from early 1949 through September 1960. Previously it was known as *Puppet Playhouse*.
2. Stori-View set #605 consisting of six slide cards.

HOWDY DOODY SNAP-A-WINK

See: POLL Parrot's Howdy Doody Snap-A-Wink.

HOWDY DOODY SPINNING BLOCK SET

A 1950s transparent block set with Doodyville character pictures inside. Sold for $1.98.

HOWDY DOODY STARS AND TV STAGE PROPS

A Blue Bonnet® Margarine premium. Consisted of 23 items, 12 show stars and 11 stage props. The 12 show stars were punchouts on the backs of the Blue Bonnet® packages; stars are:
Clarabell and Clarabus
Howdy Doody and five hats
Dilly Dally and Scope Doodle
Mr. Bluster and Talk-A-Scope
The Inspector and Telescope
Captain Windy and Ship's Wheel
Chief Thunderthud and Totem Pole
Oil Well Willie and Wampum Wagon
Hop, Skip, and Jump
Princess with a spotlight
Flub-A-Dub
Dr. Sing-a-Song with a Floodlight

HOWDY DOODY STICKER FUN

A Whitman Publishing Company activity book #2158 produced in 1953.

HOWDY DOODY STICKER FUN CIRCUS

A Whitman Publishing Company activity book #2155 produced in 1955.

HOWDY DOODY STICKER FUN CIRCUS

A Whitman Publishing Company book #2165 produced in 1955.

HOWDY DOODY SUITE

A musical composition written by Bob Nicholson, performed on the show in April 1955 with a 25-piece orchestra.

HOWDY DOODY WEEKEND COMICS

A newspaper cartoon strip illustrated by Milt Neil and Chad Grothkopf, and written by Edward Kean; began November 20, 1949.

HOWDY DOODY SUNGLASSES

Manufactured by the Rockglas Corp. Originally sold for $.39.

HOWDY DOODY TALKING PIN

Premium from the Howdy Doody Ice Cream Club that spoke "Howdy Doody." Send one ice cream wrapper and a quarter to the fulfillment center and Premium Associates returned the talking pin, an Ice Cream Club membership card, and a premium booklet. It could be had for 10 specially marked ice cream bags and $.15 shipping, or 75 bags without money. The pin said "Howdy Doody."

HOWDY DOODY TELEVISION FILM

A comic-type strip produced vertically on a roller to be displayed on a plastic TV. Manufactured by the Lido Toy Company in the early 1950s.

HOWDY DOODY TELL-TALE BOOKS

A Whitman Publishing Co. label; they produced assorted 1950s books.

HOWDY DOODY TIMES, THE

Official publication of the Doodyville Historical Society.

HOWDY DOODY T.V. MERRIMAT

An 8½" x 14" placemat showing the USA with an action character in each of the states except Hawaii and Alaska. The map was made by Specialty Advertising Services in 1952.

HOWDY DOODY TV STUDIO

A 1950s boxed game.

HOWDY DOODY TV TIME

A set of eight 8" x 10" photographs in a television style folder manufactured by the Donald Art Company.

HOWDY DOODY TWIN ICE CREAM SANDWICH

Manufactured by the Rivers Ice Cream company. This sandwich was eligible for prize redemption from the Doughnut Corporation's Prize Doodle List in 1954 – 1955.

HOWDY DOODY TWIN POP WATER ICE

Manufactured by Rivers Ice Cream Co. This water ice was eligible towards a premium from the Doughnut Corporation's Prize Doodle List in 1954 – 1955.

HOWDY DOODY TWO-IN-ONE BALLOON

A 1955 double balloon from the Van Dam Rubber Co. sold for $.19.

HOWDY DOODY UKE

A ukulele manufactured by Emenee Industries. A premium from the Howdy Doody's Big Prize Doodle list. It could be obtained for 20 specially marked ice cream bags and $.80 shipping or 400 bags without money. Playing instructions were included.

HOWDY DOODY WALL CLIMBER

A toy introduced on the show July 1955.

HOWDY DOODY WALLET

Vinyl 3" x 7½" blue wallets; contained three connected pictures from the Howdy Doody Magic Trading Card series on the front.

HOWDY DOODY WATER RING

A 15½" inflatable yellow floatable water toy manufactured by the Ideal Toy & Novelty Co. in the 1950s.

HOWDY DOODY WESTERN TIE & HOLDER

A premium from the Howdy Doody's Big Prize Doodle list. It could be had for 10 specially marked ice cream bags and $.25 shipping, or 125 bags and no money.

HOWDY DOODY WONDER BALLOON PARADE

The theme of an album for collecting and affixing Wonder Bread end labels. Sixteen different labels were required to complete the collection.

HOWDY DOODY WONDER CIRCUS ALBUM

A four-page cardboard album for collecting and affixing Wonder Bread end labels. Sixteen different labels were required to complete the collection.

HOWDY DOODY WONDER WALKING TOY

Plastic Howdy figure with a suction cup motor that would walk on any non-porous surface. Sold for $.49 in the 1950s.

HOWDY DOODY WONDERLAND COSTUME

Costumes manufactured by the Bland Charnos Company in the 1950s.

HOWDY DOODY WRIST WATCH

Watches made by Ingraham, Ideal Watch Co., or the Patent Watch Company in 1950s.

HOWDY DOODY'S 3-RING CIRCUS

A 1950 game manufactured by Harett-Gilman, Inc.

HOWDY DOODY'S ADVENTURE GAME

A 1950s Milton Bradley boxed game.

HOWDY DOODY'S BIG PRIZE DOODLE LIST

Four-page 1954 – 1955 Doughnut Corporation brochure for redeeming ice cream wrappers for premiums. Sixteen prizes were offered of which eight were Howdy Doody tie-ins. The Howdy Doody prizes were a ukulele, beach ball, a sailor's hat, Magic Talking Pin, western tie & holder, Clarabell tee-shirt, and a Sun Ray camera. The offer expired on September 30, 1955.

HOWDY DOODY'S BIG TOP

Set backdrop unveiled on August 3, 1948, and made by Scott Brinker. The backdrop was designed to place Howdy in a circus mode.

HOWDY DOODY'S BOWLING GAME

A 1950s Parker Brothers, Inc. game.

HOWDY DOODY'S CHRISTMAS

A 1951 Castle Film. Howdy, Buffalo Bob, and Clarabell rescue Santa who was mistakenly captured by Ugly Sam.

HOWDY DOODY'S CHRISTMAS PARTY

An RCA Victor Little Nipper 45 rpm record #WY442 originally sold for $2.10 and a 78 rpm record #Y442 originally sold for $2.31 with story and songs by Edward Kean; orchestra conducted by Norman Leyden.

HOWDY DOODY'S CIRCUS

Little Golden Book #99 published in 1950, written by Edward Kean and illustrated by Liz Dauber and Dan Gormley.

HOWDY DOODY'S CLARABELL & PESKY PEANUT

A 1950s Whitman Tell-A-Tale book.

HOWDY DOODY'S CLARABELL AND THE MERRY-GO-ROUND

A Whitman Tell-A-Tale book #2558, written by John Barron and illustrated by Mel Crawford in 1955.

HOWDY DOODY'S COMIC CIRCUS ANIMALS

A 1954 Poll Parrot Shoe premium. This 6½" x 8½" toy allowed the user to turn the inside paper wheel to generate hundreds of animals through a circus tent window.

HOWDY DOODY'S CRYSTAL BALL

An RCA Victor record #EYA-43 with story and song by Edward Kean originally sold for $1.13 in 45 rpm and $2.20 in 78 rpm.

HOWDY DOODY'S DO'S AND DON'TS

An RCA Victor record with the story and song by Edward Kean originally sold for $1.13 in 45 rpm and $2.20 in 78 rpm.

HOWDY DOODY'S DRINKING MUG

An Ovaltine premium; a red plastic mug with a label showing Howdy's picture saying "Howdy Doody.../Be Keen — Be Keen/Drink/Chocolate Flavored/Ovaltine!" Ovaltine used this premium with a number of other programs (e.g. Captain Midnite and Little Orphan Annie).

HOWDY DOODY'S ISLAND ADVENTURE

A 1955 Cozy Corner book #2410, illustrated by Robert Gribbrock, originally sold for $.29.

HOWDY DOODY'S LAUGHING CIRCUS

Two 78 rpm RCA Victor story vinyl records, #Y-414 originally sold for $2.31 and a 45 rpm record #WY414 originally sold for $2.36. Howdy introduced us to all his laughing animals with a four-page brochure in 1950. The story and songs were written by Edward Kean; orchestra conducted by Norman Leyden.

HOWDY DOODY'S LUCKY TRIP

Little Golden Book #171 published in 1953; written by Edward Kean and illustrated by Harry McNaught.

HOWDY DOODY'S MAGIC JUKE-BOX

An RCA Victor record EYA-42 with story and song by Edward Kean.

HOWDY DOODY'S OLD-TIME SILENT MOVIE

A story in a March 1953 Dell comic.

HOWDY DOODY'S OWN GAME

A 1949 Parker Brothers game.

HOWDY DOODY'S OWN SAILOR HAT

A premium from the Howdy Doody's Big Prize Doodle list. It could be obtained for one specially marked ice cream bag and $.35 shipping, or 175 bags without money.

HOWDY DOODY'S POLL PARROT EASY AS A-B-C COLORING BOOK

A 1950s premium from Poll-Parrot shoes; designed by Ken Giles.

HOWDY DOODY'S SHAKE-UP MUG

An Ovaltine premium; a red plastic mug with cap so user could add Ovaltine and milk and mix like a cocktail. Ovaltine named this process Shake-A-Doodle. The cup had a label with Howdy's picture saying "Howdy Doody../Be Keen — Be Keen/Drink/Chocolate Flavored/Ovaltine!" Like the above Howdy Doody Drinking Mug, Ovaltine used this same premium with a number of other programs.

HOWDY DOODY'S SUN RAY CAMERA

A premium from the Howdy Doody's Big Prize Doodle list. It could be obtained for 15 specially marked ice cream bags and $.35 shipping, or 175 bags without money. The camera came with four rolls of film and developing papers.

HOWDY DOODY'S TV GAME

A 1954 game with a miniature TV studio and four playing pieces sold for $2.00. Milton Bradley product #4240.

HOWDY DOODY'S WONDERLAND GAME

11¾" x 13¾" Wonder Bread premium. Sixteen spaces were provided for bread end label seals in this geography game.

HOWDY GETS READY FOR SCHOOL

Stori-View set #603 consisting of six slide cards.

HOWDY SHARES HIS TOYS

Slide #1 from Stori-View slides.

HOUR CLASSIC COLLECTIBLES

Company that manufactured a 26" clock in 1976 and various blister packaged wrist watches.

HUFF, MR.

Manager of the circus starting in February 1948. A Frank Paris puppet and the predecessor of Mr. Bluster; he was pulled from the show in early 1948 concerning a merchandising dispute along with Elmer (Howdy #1); destroyed in the RCA Building in December 1955.

HULTGREN, BOB

Program director replacing Bob Rippen when Rippen was promoted to associate producer. Hultgren co-directed the program with Howard Davis and both alternated directing *The Gabby Hayes Show*. He remained with the show until 1960.

HYDE

A marionette conceived by Howard Davis in 1954; one of two bear cubs found in the snow. Main character in a Golden Book story.

I'D LIKE CLARABELL TO VISIT ME BECAUSE . . .

A written entry contest; mid-1952. The winner was Linda Dolan of West Virginia, daughter of a coal miner. Clarabell visited the Dolan family in September 1952. An entire show was dedicated to showing film clips of the trip.

I'M FOR HOWDY DOODY PIN

The first Howdy Doody premium. This 1¼" button was created for the 1948 election; pictures the Frank Paris "Elmer" Howdy.

I'M THE INSPECTOR

Song written by Edward Kean.

IDEAL NOVELTY & TOY CORP.

Company that manufactured numerous Howdy Doody items including:
#5751 Swimming Ring, 20" diameter
Pool Floatation Toy
Wading Pool 40" x 50" x 8"
Howdy Doody Ventriloquist Dolls in 1950 18" ($2.95), 20" ($4.95), and 24" ($7.95) tall; and in 1953 a 20" ($5.98) and 24" ($9.98). Words "Ideal Toy" were embossed on the necks. The dolls are bootless, and wear a neckerchief that says "Howdy Doody."
Howdy Doody wrist watch
Character hand puppets
Howdy Doody Sand Forms (1952)
Howdy Doody Sand Set (1954)

IDEAL WATCH COMPANY, INC.

Manufacturer of a 1950s Howdy Doody Wrist Watch; packaged in a plastic stand with a Howdy Doody figure holding the watch.

IKKY

An Eskimo Howdy and Dilly meet in a 1950 Dell comic adventure.

INDUSTRIA ARGENTINE

An Argentinean company that manufactured a toy truck with the picture of Flub-A-Dub on one side. The truck was constructed out of Pepsi cans with Asian writing on it.

INGRAHAM

Manufacturer of a 1954 Howdy Doody Wrist Watch.

INSIDE STORY OF GOLDILOCKS AND THE THREE BEARS

A Halo Shampoo cartoon commercial aired in November 1949.

INSPECTOR, THE

See: Fedoozle, John J.

INSTANT TOUPEE

An invention created by Chief Thunderthud; September 1958.

INTERNATIONAL SHOE COMPANY

A St. Louis, Missouri, company that manufactured Poll Parrot Shoes in their Roberts, Johnson & Rand Division.

INVISIBLE MAN

Resident of Always Always Land; appeared on a June 1960 show.

©Bob Smith, from the Scott Brinker Collection

Buffalo Bob, Howdy, Mr. Bluster, and Clarabell

©Bob Smith, from the Scott Brinker Collection

Clarabell and Howdy for the March of Dimes project.

ISLE OF JUMBO JANGLE

A tropical island where Pow, a native, is discovered; July 1955.

IT'S HOWDY DOODY TIME, IT'S HOWDY DOODY TIME

1. Theme song of the Howdy Doody show; words written by Edward Kean and Robert Smith. Played to the tune *Ta-Ra-Ra-Boom-De-Ay*.
2. Little Golden Book #223 published in 1955; written by Edward Kean and illustrated by Art Seiden.

IT'S MR. BLUSTER TIME

The new name of the show song Mr. Bluster would use should he be elected President of all the Kids in 1950.

IZBING, MRS.

A March 1956 character who tried to kidnap Heidi.

J.C. PENNEY

Sold 19" Howdy and Clarabell dolls in their 1977 Christmas catalog. The dolls had vinyl heads and cloth bodies.

JABONGA TRIBE

A no-good Indian tribe mentioned by Chief Thunderthud in a January 1954 program.

JACK & JILL

Children's magazine; January 1960 cover story pictured Clarabell, Howdy, and Buffalo Bob.

JACKPOT OF FUN COMIC BOOK

A 1957 premium from the Doughnut Corporation of America. The prizes were offered similar to their 1954 – 1955 Howdy Doody Prize Doodle List.

JANEX CORPORATION

Manufactured a 1974 talking alarm clock in Taiwan and distributed it through their Eatontown, New Jersey, offices.

JA-RU

A Jacksonville, Florida, company that manufactured numerous blister packaged toys in 1987. Toys included:
#2300 Play Light with Battery
#2304 Jackpot Game
#2306 Sparkler
#2307 Watch Set
#2310 Target Set
#2311 Power Tool — Saw or Drill
#2312 Pinball Game
#2314 Sparkle Game
#2316 Doctor Kit
#2318 Spurs
Western Set

JARVIS, NANCY

From Philadelphia, Pennsylvania; one of four winners of the 1951 TV Digest Howdy Doody Coloring Contest.

JAUDI DUDI

See: DUDI, Jaudi

JAY FRANKO COMPANY

Manufactured a series of beach towels, 1987.

JAYSTIX SALES COMPANY

Manufactured the Howdy Doody Wonder Dancer toy; 1952.

JEEVES

Mr. Bluster's personal butler in a March 1953 Dell Comic.

JERRY

A giraffe in the Doodyville circus; pictured on a 1951 Howdy Doody Magic Trading Card.

JERSEY JIM

Played by Jimmy Blaine; one of the replacements for Buffalo Bob during his February 1949 vacation.

JEWELED TRICYCLE

Highlighted in a February 1956 series.

JIM VICTORY TELEVISION, INC.

Distributeed The New Howdy Doody revival TV series; 1976.

JINGLE

Circus giant in the book Howdy Doody and Clarabell; 1951.

JINGLE JUNGLE JUMPING BEANS

Beans found only on the Isle of Jingle Jungle.

JOHN J. FEDOOZLE

A 1955 78 rpm Little Golden Record #R220B; was the flip side of *The Laughing Song*; manufactured by the Sandpiper Press, distributed by Simon & Schuster.

JOHNNY GENIE

May 1955 genie from Dilly Dally's wishing bottle. Helped Buffalo Bob in September 1959.

JOHNNY JUPITER

See: JUPITER, Johnny.

JOSE

A toucan bird from the *Rough and Ready* show who visited Doodyville; August 1959.

JOY CO.

Manufactured two types of Howdy cloth patches in 1971. One patch read "Howdy Doody for President."

JUMBO

An elephant in the Howdy Doody circus; from a Dell comic story.

JUMP

One of three kangaroo puppets manufactured by Margo Rose in 1953. Buffalo Bob discovers that he can't jump in July 1955.

JUPITER, JOHNNY

A program on the Dumont Network 1953 – 1954 and the name of the main character from the planet Jupiter. The Johnny Jupiter marionette visited the Howdy Doody Show in 1953. Props for this program were manufactured by the Brinkers.

K. K. PUBLICATIONS

Published the *Howdy Doody News* for a Poll-Parrot Shoe Store giveaway.

KADOODLE, CAPTAIN

Character that the Princess and Chief Thunderthud met after using the Time-A-Tub in April 1955. He captured the Princess.

KAGRAN

Company formed by NBC and Lehman Brothers to license and market the Howdy Doody characters. The name was derived from the names of Lehman Brothers' executive Frank Mannheim's children, Katherine and Grant. It was created in 1950, becoming effective January 1, 1951. They ended their licensing of Howdy Doody in December 1954 when NBC purchased all unowned shares from Marty Stone. NBC created their own licensing company, California National Productions, to market Howdy Doody images.

KAHN, E.J., COMPANY

A Chicago firm that manufactured the 1950s Magic Electric Lapel Pin.

KANGAROO TOM

Fun Book character.

KARP, MARVIN

Howdy Doody writer; 1949.

KEAN, EDWARD

First writer of the show, 1947 – 1954. He was responsible for most of the story plots, series, and characters. Created the Buffalo Bob name and story. Created Chief Featherman, Mr. Bluster, Dilly Dally, Princess Summerfall Winterspring, and other characters. Created the idea of nominating Howdy Doody for President of all the Kids in the United States in 1948. Created the famous exclamation "Cowabunga." Wrote numerous short stories such as "Howdy Doody's Halloween Party" in Dell Comics. Wrote Howdy Doody stories for the Big Golden Book series. Wrote the Little Golden books *Howdy Doody's Circus, Howdy Doody and Clarabell, Howdy Doody and the Princess, Howdy Doody's Lucky Trip, Howdy Doody in Funland, Howdy Doody and Santa Claus, It's Howdy Doody Time*, and *Howdy Doody and His Magic Hat*. He also wrote the Tell-A-Tale Book *Surprise for Howdy Doody*. Wrote the story and music to the RCA Victor Little Nipper records such as *Howdy Doody's Christmas Party, Howdy Doody's Laughing Circus, Howdy Howdy's Do's and Don'ts, Howdy Doody and You, Howdy Doody's Magic Juke-Box, It's Howdy Doody Time*, and *Howdy Doody and the Air-O-Doodle*. He wrote the copy for the comic strip for 1½ years. His songs included *Clarabell, The Popcorn Song, Cross the Street with Your Eyes, Meatballs and Spaghetti, The Friendship Song, I'm The Inspector*, and many more. In February 1954 he became the program supervisor. He was liaison for the Canadian and Cuban Howdy Doody shows.

KEESHAN, ROBERT (1928 –)

Started working as an NBC pageboy in 1944. Met Buffalo Bob after two years of military service. Ran errands for Buffalo Bob and was eventually assigned to carry props on stage. Buffalo Bob dressed him as a clown in 1948 and he was the first Clarabell Hornblow (1948 – 1952). He also played Chief Featherman and Oscar. After Howdy Doody, he was Corny the Clown on ABC's *Time for Fun* (September 1953), performed on *Tinker's Workshop* (1954), and became Captain Kangaroo (October 3, 1955) on the long running CBS program.

KELLOGG'S®

Cereal company sponsor in the early 1950s. Collectible items include:
 Cereal Boxes with Howdy's picture
 Clarabell Dingle-Dangle
 Rice Krispies ads from *Life* magazine.

KELLOGG'S® RICE KRISPIES

Cereal product advertised on the show, promoted Marshmallow Crispy Squares treats in their *Life* magazines advertisements; 1951. They ads were:
 Howdy, Wild Bill Hickok, Jingles: You'll go for Marshmallow...
 Howdy, Jingles, Wild Bill Hickok: Well, Smack my Lips Here's...
 Howdy: Howdy Doody's Favorite Treat...9 Minute Marshmallow...

KEN GILES TUK-A-TAB TOYS

A Poll-Parrot 1950s premium series which included:
 Howdy Doody Campaign Hat
 Detective Disguises (6 different).

KENNEDY, PAT

Stage manager of the Howdy Doody show; sister of the late President, married to actor Peter Lawford.

KICK WAY

The Myercord Co. brand of Howdy Doody decals.

KID-O CO.

Marketed a Howdy Doody Modeling Compound, 1957.

KING ARTHUR'S COURT

Mythical place visited by Clarabell, using the Time-A-Tub, November 1955.

KING DO DO

See: DO DO, King.

KING LAZEE

See: LAZEE, King.

KING NEPTUNE

See: NEPTUNE, King.

KING SEELEY THERMOS COMPANY

Norwich, Connecticut, company that manufactured the 1977 Howdy Doody & Pals plastic lunch box with a dome thermos.

KING YORDICK

See: YORDICK, KING.

KING ZOOM ZOOM

See: ZOOM ZOOM, King.

KING, MICHAEL (1923 – June 1, 1992)

Puppeteer on the Howdy Doody show; husband of Lee Carney.

KLAGES, BILL

Lighting director of the Howdy Doody show for several years.

KNICKERBOCKER

Toy company, manufatured a 30" Howdy Doody doll in 1971.

KOHNER PRODUCTS

A New York, New York, company that manufactured 1950s Howdy Doody string push up toys, generally 2½" x 5½" made of wood and plastic. Pressing the base made the character collapse; releasing restored the figure to its previous shape. Characters included:
 Howdy Doody with microphone
 Princess Summerfall Winterspring
 Flub-A-Dub
 Clarabell.

KOWABUNGA

See: COWABUNGA.

KOWACHICKEN

Greeting used by Chief Thunderchicken.

KRANTZ, STEVE

Wrote several show scripts. He is a TV producer and husband of author Judith Krantz.

KRISPY KAN

Luce Manufacturing Company's brand of containers.

KUNKEL'S HOWDY DOODY QUICKSHINE

Self-shining shoe polish in assorted colors; manufactured by the American Kunkel Distributing Co., Inc.

KUNKEL'S HOWDY DOODY SHOE POLISH

Shoe polish in assorted colors; manufactured by the American Kunkel Distributing Co., Inc.

LA HORA DE JAUDI DUDI

The name of the Mexican version of the Howdy Doody Show beginning in April 1953.

LABADIE

Leader of the Osage Indians; January 1959.

LAFFALOT, SIR

Character in an August 1960 show who is made invisible by Merlin the Magician; later restored by Buffalo Bob.

LALA-PALOOZA

Device invented by Howdy in 1950. Had switches, dials, and a microphone; used to introduce the Old-Time Movies on the program. Scott Brinker redesigned the Lala-Palooza to become the Scope-Doodle.

LAMB, GIL (June 14, 1904 –)

Dancer who became the second Clarabell for two weeks in June 1952. Since he was noticeably taller than Bob Keeshan, Edward Kean devised the Clownstretcher for the transition. He was replaced by Robert Nicholson when Lamb broke several ribs during a rehearsal. Prior to Howdy Doody, he performed in the Broadway shows *The Show Is On* (1936), *Hold on to Your Hats* (1940), and *Sleepy Hallow* (1948); the movies *The Fleet's In* (1942), *Star Spangled Rhythm* (1942), *Riding High* (1943), *Practically Yours* (1944), *Rainbow Island* (1944), *Hit Parade of 1947* (1947), and *Her Wonderful Lie* (1950); the TV show *Window on the World* (March 1949) on the Dumont Networks, and on the *Hollywood Theater Time* (October – December 1950).

LANG, MARK

April 1956 Grand Winner in the Howdy Dooer campaign. His prizes were a radio, bicycle, and books.

LANKY LOU

A 1949 – 1952 character played by Dayton Allen. An extremely talkative cowboy. If he knew the answer to a question, he took five minutes to answer; questions to which he did not know the answer, he took three minutes. Sometimes the only way to stop him from talking was to ask him a question such as "How old are you?"

LANKY LULU

The name used by Dayton Allen's mother when she made a guest appearance on the show in 1949.

LARSON E. GRAND

See: GRAND, Larson E.

LAUGHING SONG, THE

A 1955 78 rpm Little Golden Record #R220A, written by Willie Gilbert, Jack Weinstock, and Robert Nicholson. It was recorded by the Sandpiper Press and distributed by Simon & Schuster.

LAUGHING-CRYING JUICE

Liquid that Clarabell purchased in May 1955 and used on Sandy McTavish; made people laugh and then cry.

LAZEE, KING

He turned Mr. Bluster into stone in January 1956.

LBZ

West German company that manufactured a 1970s mechanical top.

LEADWORKS, INC.

Manufactured a number of 1988 Howdy Doody products including:
Rodeo clock
Howdy Doody Bobbing Head Figure
Howdy Doody Lamp
Howdy vinyl pen.

LECO ELECTRIC MFG. CO.

Distributed a 1955 Howdy Doody Nite Lite.

LECORNEC, BILL (1915 –)

Hired to operate Dilly Dally and be his voice in 1949, taking the responsibility from Rhoda Mann. He also played live characters Chief Thunderthud, Doctor Singasong, Oil Well Willie, Signore DoReMeFaSoLaTiDo, and Larson E. Grand. LeCornec was also the voice of Happy Tooth in the Colgate commercials.

LEE, STAN

Drew the syndicated Howdy Doody comic strip in 1949 for several months; later became the creator of Spider-man, created The Incredible Hulk in 1962, and appeared in the movie Comic Book Confidential in 1988. He is currently the chairman of the board of Marvel Entertainment, Inc.

LEFF, PINCUS (1908 – April 3, 1993)

Entertainer known as Pinkie Lee. Appeared as a substitute on the Howdy Doody Show after Bob Smith suffered a heart attack. When his own Saturday program went off the air, it was replaced by the Howdy Doody Show. Aside from the Howdy Doody Show, he appeared on *Hollywood Premiere* in October 1949; and had his own fast-paced slapstick comedy shows: *The Pinky Lee Show* from April 5 to November 9, 1950; *These Two* from November 26, 1951 to April 24, 1953; and again the *Pinkie Lee Show* from January 4, 1954 through May 11, 1956. He appeared in two movies: *Lady of Burlesque* (1943) and *In Old Amarillo* (1951).

LEFTON CORPORATION

Manufactured a Howdy Doody planter. The 5" x 5" x 6½" item depicts Howdy seated on a barrel.

LEHMAN BROTHERS

A New York financial instution and partners with NBC in licensing the Howdy Doody characters under the Kagran name.

LEMON, DOC

A magician in the book *Howdy Doody and the Princess*, 1952. Stole the Princess' magic necklace and then disguised himself as Lorenzo the Great.

LEO

1. A leprechaun that regularly visited Doodyville causing problems, March 1957. Visited Doodyville again in March 1960 to march in the St. Patrick's day parade. Witches stole his pot of gold.
2. A lion tamer in the circus in a 1953 Whitman Fun Book.

LESLEE PRODUCTIONS

Produced the Goldberger 1970s *Be a Ventriloquist* LP.

LETTER-GETTER

A mailbox used on the show from 1948 through July 1955.

LEYDEN, NORMAND

Conducted the orchestra for RCA Victors' *Howdy Doody's Christmas Party*, *Howdy Doody's Laughing Song* albums, and Little Golden records' *Look! Look!*

LIBERTY STEEL CHEST CORPORATION

Manufactured a 1950s Ranch House Toolbox and 1956 Howdy Doody Official Outdoor Sports Box.

LIDO TOY COMPANY

Manufactured several tie-in items from their New York offices. They include:
 Howdy Doody character bubble pipes (plastic)
 Howdy Doody television films
 Howdy Doody key chain.

LINDERMAN, CARL

Cameraman on the Howdy Doody show, and later a vice president of NBC sports.

LINEMAR

1950s manufacturer of:
 6½" tin litho Clarabell squeeze action cable doll
 5" wind-up Clarabell Clown figure.

LIONA

Heidi's jungle girlfriend that visited Doodyville, February 1957.

LITTLE GOLDEN BOOKS

A series of children's books published by Simon & Schuster in the 1950s and originally sold for $.25. They were published in French under the Un Petit Livre D'or label. The Howdy Doody titles included:
99. *Howdy Doody's Circus* (1950)
#121. *Howdy Doody & Clarabell* (1951)
#135. *Howdy Doody and the Princess* (1952)
#171. *Howdy Doody's Lucky Trip* (1953)
#172. *Howdy Doody in Funland* (1953)
#184. *Howdy Doody and his Magic Hat* (1954)
#204. *Howdy Doody and Mr. Bluster* (1954)
#223. *It's Howdy Doody Time* (1955)
#237. *Howdy Doody and Santa Claus* (1955)
#252. *Howdy Doody's Animal Friends* (1956)

LITTLE GOLDEN RECORDS

Simon and Schuster label used on the 1950s Howdy Doody 78 RPM records. Among them were:
R220 *The Laughing Song*/John J. Fedoozle (1955)
R261 *Charles Dickens' A Christmas Carol Cowabunga*/Big Chief (1955)

LITTLE NIPPER

Howdy Doody songs and stories were published on this RCA Victor 45 rpm label.

LITTLE ONE, LEAN ONE

A 78 rpm Little Golden Record.

LITTLELANDIA

Country with no animals, disclosed by Heidi in December 1955; location of a series of programs.

LOLLIPOP SONG, THE

Written by Edward Kean.

LOOK! LOOK!

A 1955 78 rpm Little Golden Record #R219A originally sold for $.25 and written by Grean and conducted by Norman Leyden. The flip side was *Will My Dog Be Proud of Me?*

LOOK-A-CROOK MACHINE

Criminal detection machine the Inspector brought from England. Feeding clues into the machine produced pictures of the crook.

LORENZO THE GREAT

A disguise for Doc Lemon, the magician, in a 1952 Little Golden Book.

LOST AND LONESOME LAGOON

Mysterious location where the Arkadoodle became stuck and where Pitty-Pat, the dinosaur is discovered, December 1955.

LUCE MFG. CO

Groton, Connecticut, company that manufactured the Howdy Doody Cookie-Go-Round under the Krispy Kan label; they patented the Blue Magic Dri-Nob.

LUCKY CHARM KEY CHAINS

A Lido Company key chain display holding 12 plastic Howdy Doody replicas, each holding an NBC microphone puzzle.

LUCKY LEFT LEG OF THE LIMA LLAMA

Object of an early 1950s series of shows; Sir Archibald was searched for the Five L's.

LUDEN'S

Show advertiser in 1952 for their product Wild Cherry Cough Drops.

MACLEAN, QUENTIN

Musician, played the organ on the Canadian Howdy Doody show; started November 1954.

McTAVISH, SANDY

Conceived by Howard Davis; he was a Scotsman involved in several adventures in Doodyville, such as building a kippered herring plant in August 1954.

MAD MAGAZINE

Monthly humor periodical that printed a Howdy Doody parody December 1954.

MAD MEANY

Friend of Trigger Happy who made a show appearance in October 1958.

MADAME ALEXANDER

Famous doll manufacturer; manufactured three Clarabelle [sic] Clown dolls from 1951 to 1953; the cloth dolls measured 19", 29", and 49".

MADEMOISELLE FROM ARMENTIERES

Music score used for the Clarabell theme song.

MAGIC BOOK

Howdy's book; center of a July 1955 group of shows.

MAGIC FOREST

Forest where the magician hid the Princess' Magic Necklace in late 1952.

MAGIC GOLDEN TREE

Planted in Doodyville in June 1955.

MAGIC KEY

Used to help save Hobby, the pony; August 1955.

MAGIC MANUSCRIPT PAPER

The actual paper that Howdy used for writing his 1948 Presidential theme song *Howdy Doody for President*.

MAGIC NECKLACE

A possession of Princess Summerfall Winterspring that enabled her to fortell the future. Neckless was stolen by an evil magician in late 1952, and recovered in the Magic Forest.

MAGIC TOOLIE-STICK

Given to Silly Sally by Princess Summerfall Winterspring; June 1955.

MAGIC WISHING SCARF

Central plot revolving around this scarf in a 1955 show involving Dilly Dally.

MAGIC-BOX TRICK

A magic trick Clarabell learned in June 1957. The magic-box made people disappear!

MAHARAJA

A character in a December 1955 series, owned Mambo the dancing elephant.

MAHARAJA OF M'YOOR

Visited Doodyville in May 1955.

MAKE YOUR HOWDY DOODY PUPPET SHOW

An activity book published in the early 1950s; cardboard punch-out cards of six show characters that could be strung as puppets.

MAMBO

Dancing elephant introduced in December 1955. Mambo became part of the circus.

MANGLE WURZEL

A brillo pad attached to a piece of cardboard, used as a hex. When superimposed over a character, the characters behaved irrationally; controlled by Mr. Bluster. The series was discontinued because parents complained their children were afraid of being placed under a spell by it.

MANN, CONRAD

Known on the show as Con Man, he was always duping the residents of Doodyville. In April 1958 he tricked Phineas T. Bluster into validating phony diplomas. In June 1960 he sold straw to Mr. Bluster and in September 1960 he invited in a Buffalo Bob look alike to appear on the show.

MANN, LARRY D.

Voice of Flub-A-Dub and the live Capt. Scuttlebutt in the Canadian Howdy Doody show from November 1954. Aside from Howdy Doody, he was Marty Warren on *Accidental Family* from September 15, 1967, to January 5, 1968; and Lt. Jack Gorden in *Dr. Simon Locke* from 1971 – 1973.

MANN, RHODA

Howdy Doody's and the Princess Summerfall Winterspring's puppeteer and the voice for the puppet Princess. Rhoda originally was employed by Frank Paris, and was kept as a member of the crew after he departed. After Howdy Doody, she worked for Terrytoon Cartoons, and in commercials.

MARBLES

A Doodyville unit of currency introduced in 1952.

MARGE, ELIAS

Illustrated the 1954 book *Howdy Doody and Mr. Bluster*.

MARIHUGH, TAMMY LEA

The Hollywood, California, winner of the 1955 Howdy Doody Smile Contest. She won a $1,000 savings bond, color TV, an electric organ, a speed boat, and a set of encyclopedias. She later played Tammy Johnson on *The Bob Cummings Show* in 1959.

MARQUETTE, HAL

Puppeteer for the Canadian Howdy Doody show starting November 15, 1954; husband of Rene Marquette.

MARQUETTE, RENE

Puppeteer for the Canadian Howdy Doody show starting November 15, 1954; wife of Hal Marquette.

MARS CANDY COMPANY

Candy manufacturer and show sponsor starting April 1948. They produced premiums such as:
 Howdy Doody Christmas Cards (Package of seven assorted)
 Howdy Doody Animated Puppet
 Clarabell Animated Puppet
 A magic kit.

MARSH, LINDA

Briefly played Princess Summerfall Winterspring.

MARSHALL, REX

Played Sailor Rex; one of the substitutes for Buffalo Bob during his February 1949 vacation and again in 1954 after Bob's heart attack. Marshall was also the announcer and interpreter on *Kuda Bux, Hindu Mystic* from March 25 to June 17, 1950; the narrator on *Circuit Rider* from March 5 to May 7, 1951; a regular on *The Herman Hickman Show* from October 3, 1952 to March 27, 1954; and performed commercials for Champion Spark Plugs.

MARX TOYS

Manufactured low priced quality toys from 1921 to 1972 when Marx Toys was purchased by the Quaker Oat Company. Manufacturer of Howdy Doody windup toys. The toys were:
  5" high tin Howdy, with movable head, plays the banjo (1950)
  5½" high tin Buffalo Bob plays the piano, Howdy dances (1950)
  2½" hard white plastic figures of Howdy, Dilly Dally, Mr. Bluster, Princess, and Clarabell
  2½" soft green or pink plastic figures as above
  Howdy Doody wind-up Jeep.

MASON COCONUT BAR

Candy company and show sponsor of the Howdy Doody Show from 1949.

MASON, AU & MAGENHEIMER MANUFACTURING COMPANY

Brooklyn, New York, manufacturers of the Mason's Coconut Bar and Mason's Dots; 1949 sponsor of the show.

MASON, MR.

A traveling salesman who visited Doodyville, May 1955.

MATHER, JACK

Voices of Dilly Dally and Percival Parrot in the Canadian Howdy Doody show from November 1954.

MATTY

Circus monkey in a 1953 Whitman book.

McBAIN, CARYL

Played Princess Haida in the Canadian Howdy Doody show from November 15, 1954.

McCUTCHEON, BILL

Played Timothy Tremble from June 1955; he is currently a Broadway actor.

McLAUGHTON, ANDREA (Oct 1947 –)

Performed commercials on the show in 1952 – 1953. She was the youngest regular performer on *Paul Whitman's TV Teen Club* (age of 4).

McNAUGHT, HARRY

Illustrated of the 1953 book *Howdy Doody's Lucky Trip*.

MEATBALLS AND SPAGHETTI

Song written by Edward Kean.

MENDEZ, PRINCE

A magician and an actor on the first *Puppet Playhouse*.

MERLIN

A magician in King Arthur's Court, November 1955. In August 1960, he made Sir Laffalot invisible.

MEWS, PETER

Played Timber Tom in the Canadian Howdy Doody show from November 15, 1954.

MIDNIGHT STUDIO

Company who manufactured a Howdy Doody rubber stamp.

MIGHTNIGHT CAVE

Location of a Howdy and Dilly Dally adventure in a 1951 Whitman book.

MIGHTY

Midget in the circus in the 1951 book *Howdy Doody and Clarabell*.

MILLER, LEWIS M.

Held show cue cards from 1959 – 1960.

MILLER, MAXINE

Played Princess Hilda, married to writer John Gerard.

MILLER, MITCH AND ORCHESTRA

Band leader and orchestra who performed and recorded the music for Simon & Schuster Howdy Doody records.

MILLIE

1. First name of wife of Bob Smith
2. Tattooed lady in the Val Carney 1958 circus.

MILTON BRADLEY COMPANY

Toy and game manufacturer from Springfield, Massechussets; produced several Howdy Doody toys in the early 1950s:
#4240 Howdy Doody's Adventure Game
#4312 Howdy Doody Paint Set
Howdy Doody's TV Game.

MIRROR LAND

Adventure location for Gumby in a July 1956 show.

MO MO

Martian that Dilly Dally and Heidi met in October 1955.

MONKEY BUSINESS

Name of a monkey in the circus, appeared in a 1950 Whitman Coloring Book.

MONSIEUR FONTAINEBLEAU

See: FOUNTAINEBLEAU, Monsieur.

MORSHEN, BERNIE

Property manager for the show from 1949 through the 1950s. In December 1952, he briefly played Clarabell after the departure of Bob Keeshan.

MOTHERGOOSE LAND

Location for a July 1955 series of programs. Show characters were magically turned into Mother Goose characters and then back to their original characters.

MR. BLUSTER BULLETIN

Name that Mr. Bluster intended to call the Poll Parrot Howdy Doody News should he be elected President of all the Kids in 1950.

MR. BLUSTER'S SURPRISE

Tru-Vue film card #T-6 manufactured in 1955. Mr. Bluster attempted to ruin Howdy's party.

MR. TOOTH DECAY

See: DECAY, Mr. Tooth.

MR. X SHOW, THE

Name of the show after Mr. Bluster took over the circus for two days in June 1952.

MUDDLE TOWN

Vacation community for Buffalo Bob in July 1955 show.

MUIR, NICHOLSON

A producer played by Bill LeCornec in 1976. The character was named for Roger Muir and Robert Nicholson.

MUIR, ROGER (1919 –)

Executive producer of the Howdy Doody show; also produced the Gumby Show.

MULTIPLE PRODUCTS CORPORATION

Manufactured the 1951 Howdy Doody Quiz Show action guidewheel.

MUKI

Character in a February 1956 African adventure.

MUNSON BOOK CO.

Published the Howdy Doody Simon & Schuster series of books in Toronto, Canada, 1952.

MURGATROID

A taffy eating fish in an October 1955 show.

MUSCLE-BERRY JUICE

A juice that makes the drinker stronger. Pesky the Clown used it in October 1957 show.

MUSCLES

A strong man in the circus in the 1951 book *Howdy Doody and Clarabell*.

MUSIC IS FUN WITH HOWDY DOODY

Songbook produced by Childrens Songs, Inc. in 1949.

MYERCORD CO.

Manufactured the Kwick Way brand Howdy Doody decals.

MYSTERY OF THE FIVE L'S

See: LUCKY Left Leg of the Lima Llama.

©Bob Smith, from the Scott Brinker Collection

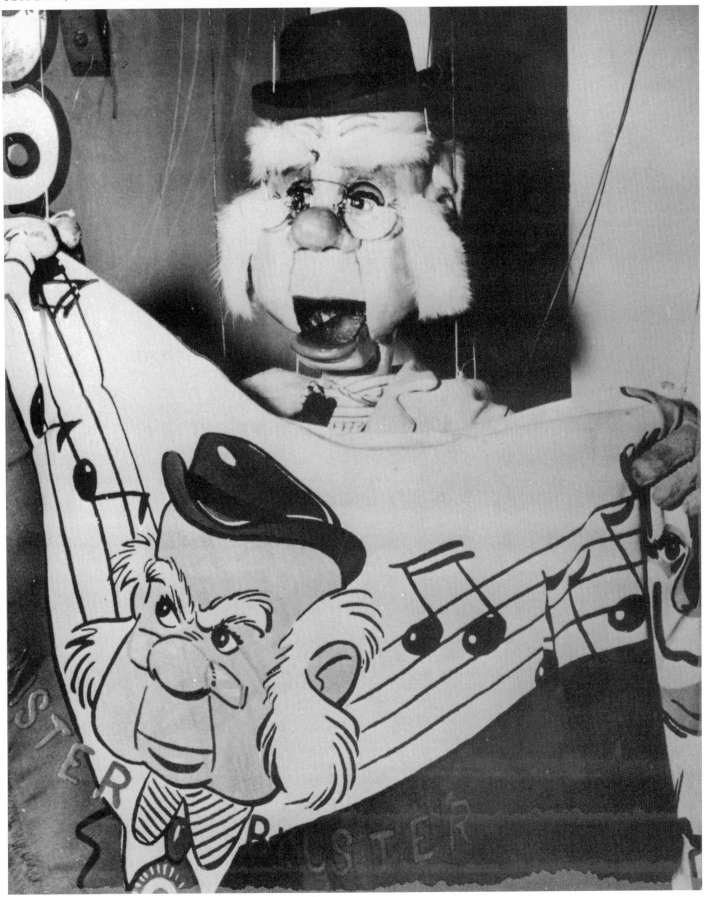

Phineas T. Bluster displaying the Mr. Bluster Neckerchief.

MYSTIC-RIDDLE ANIMALS

Riddles in a May 1955 show that enabled Buffalo Bob to prove was is a Pioneer.

NABISCO

Cereal and cookie manufacturer that created tie-in premium items:
Character mask premiums on the back of Shredded Wheat boxes
Coloring cards for the Canadian market.

NABISCO HOWDY DOODY DOODLES OF FUN

Coloring cards with related stories about the characters written in English and French; created for the Canadian market.

NAME THE TUG BOAT CONTEST

Sponsored by Colgate-Palmolive. The contestant had to create a three word name for the boat and write it on the back of a box of Colgate Dental Creme or Halo Shampoo label with their name, address and age. Prizes were 48 color TVs and 672 other prizes. Prizes were awarded according to the age of the winner. Reuben H. Donnelley Corp. judged this contest that ended on November 26, 1955.

NASIUN, DIAMOND JIM

Person who hired Capt. Windy Scuttlebutt to take him and his treasure to the Tennis Sea on a July 1960 show.

NATIONAL BABY INSTITUTE AWARD

Awarded to Bob Smith for his "outstanding contribution to children's entertainment" in 1949.

NATIONAL PARENT-TEACHER MAGAZINE

Endorsed and recommended the Howdy Doody show for children's viewing, June 1950.

NEIL, MILT (1914 –)

Artist of the Howdy Doody program. He replaced Nino, the Sketch Artist, in 1948. He helped design Mr. Bluster, Flub-A-Dub, Dilly Dally, and other puppets. Introduced on the November 7, 1949, show when Howdy announced a new Sunday newspaper comic strip. Designed the ADCO Liberty Howdy Doody Lunch Box in 1955; played Fletcher the Sketcher in the 1976 revival series.

Before the Howdy Doody Show, he worked for Walt Disney Studios and The Unique Art Manufacturing Company. He was also employed by the Milton Bradley Co.

NEPTUNE KING OF THE SEAS

Captured Howdy and Mr. Bluster in October 1955 show.

NEW HOWDY DOODY SHOW, THE

Name of the 1976 revival series (130 shows) written by Robert Nicholson and Willie Gilbert.

NEW YORK NEWS

Newspaper publisher; published the Howdy Doody color funnies in the Sunday News. The cartoon was started in November 1949 and illustrated by Milt Neil and Chad Grothkopf. A promotional button was manufactured for the occasion (October 1949).

NICHOLSON MUIR

See: MUIR, Nicholson.

NICHOLSON, ROBERT (Nick)

(1918 – September 23, 1993)

Musician hired in October 1952 to assist with the music for the TV and radio programs. Introduced as the third Clarabell in a Changing Island episode in January 1953 and played that role until March 15, 1955. He performed the voice of Dilly Dally until Bill LeCornec was rehired. He was the show's musical director and the orchestra leader on *The Bob Smith Show* television program in 1954. He played Cornelius Cobb, Sandra Witch, Pesky the Clown, and Mr. Nick, the mayor of Clown Town. He composed and directed the *Howdy Doody Suite* with a 25-piece orchestra on the show in April 1955. When Allen Swift departed the program in May 1956, he performed the voices of Flub-A-Dub, Mr. Bluster, Captain Windy Scuttlebutt, and John J. Fedoozle. In 1976, he helped write *The New Howdy Doody Show*. He also hosted *The Gumby Show*.

NICK, MR.

Played by Bob Nicholson. Mayor of Clown Town; introduced on the March 16, 1955 show.

NINO

Sketch artist on early programs.

NOISE ABATEMENT WEEK

A week in April 1959, when everyone tried to be as quiet as possible! The quietest person won an award.

NORTHEAST NAUTICALS

Manufactured a 7" plastic figure night lights.

NYLINT TOOL & MANUFACTURING COMPANY

Formed in 1937 in Rockford, Illinois, by D. Nyberg and B. Klint; started producing toys in 1946 specializing in steel reproductions; produced two types of Howdy Doody Pumpmobiles.

O'TOOLE, TILLIE

School teacher who taught spelling with riddles and rhymes in a 1953 Whitman book.

OFFICIAL CHIEF & PRINCESS KIT

Leather kits produced by the Connecticut Leather Company under the Coleco division label between 1951 and 1954. The kits were advertised for "Braves and Squaws," "make them for mom and dad," and for "hours of fun and years of wear." The Adult Moccasin Kit came in three men and two women's sizes. The moccasins were prebeaded with rubber insoles. Other kits were:
Children's Moccasin Kit
Leather Craft Project Set (Consisting of a wallet, change purse, comb holder, and key chain)
Indian Headdress
Princess Handbag Kit.

OFFICIAL PL'A-TIME COSTUME

Halloween costumes of Howdy, Princess Summerfall Winterspring, Dilly Dally, Clarabell, or Flub-A-Dub manufactured by Collegeville Products in the early 1950s. All the packages had a cut-out Howdy Doody mask on the box front.

OGLIVIE FLOUR MILLS CO., LIMITED, THE

Distributed Howdy Doody Play Money via their oats, cake mixes, and flour packages in 1953. A BSA bicycle was redeemable for $1 million of the money through June 1, 1954.

OHMS V. WATTS

See: WATTS, Ohms V.

OIL WELL WILLIE

Doodyville's warm-hearted prospector played by Bill LeCornec. Oil Well Willie always searched for oil, but never discovered any.

OLD MOTHER EARTH

Helped Mr. Bluster in November 1955.

OLD-TIME MOVIES

From a library of old silent movies that NBC purchased from Warner Brothers for $50,000. As the movies played, Buffalo Bob narrated his own version of the story.

OLTMAN, BILLY

Winner of the 1950 Howdy Doody Look-Alike contest. He won 500 prizes and gave 250 to his friends and the other 250 to the New York Foundling Hospital, Charleston Hospital of Schenectady, and the St. Charles Hospital in Long Island, New York. He returned to Doodyville for the 10th Anniversary show in December 1957.

ONEIDA

Printing company; printed the 1950s Poll Parrot premium Howdy Doody jigsaw puzzle envelopes.

OORAGNAK

Chief Thunderthud's Indian tribe; spells kangaroo backwards.

OSAGE INDIANS

Presented Buffalo Bob with an all-wool blanket in January 1959 made on the reservation. Woven into the blanket was a picture of Thunderbird, the Indian rain god.

OSCAR

Played by Bobby Keeshan. He never said a word except his own name.

OUTER ORBIT

A 1976 talking puppet flying saucer with voice by Robert Nicholson.

OVALTINE

A beverage company that began advertising their drink mix on the show in April 1948. Their premiums included:
Howdy Doody Drinking Mug
Howdy Doody Shake-Up Mug.

PADDLE

A gnu conceived by Willie Gilbert and Jack Weinstock and

built by Margo Rose; discovered by Howdy on a mysterious mountain in November 1955. Became a member of the circus.

PAPOOSE GINA RUNNINGWATER

See: RUNNINGWATER, Papoose Gina.

PAPOOSE HATTAHEELA

See: HATTAHEELA, Papoose.

PARIS, FRANK (– 1984)

Created the original "Mortimer Snerd" type Howdy Doody puppet on a freelance basis for NBC for $500. He withdrew the puppet from the program after a royalty dispute. He wanted to use the "Elmer" Howdy Doody character, but was barred from doing so by the courts. He also performed on the show *Toby and the Circus,* and was one of the early acts on the *Puppet Playhouse.* After leaving the *Puppet Playhouse,* he started his own rival program *Peter Pixie* on WPIX, New York, from 5 to 6 PM.

PARKER BROTHERS, INC.

Toy and game manufacturer; manufactured Howdy Doody games such as:
Howdy Doody's Own Game
Howdy Doody's Bowling Game.

PARROCUTE, JACK

Poll Parrot's cousin in Parrotown; operated a cracker factory, and was nicknamed "Cracker" Jack.

PAT THE PURP

A toy and the name of Howdy Doody's Balloon Zoo Animal.

PATCH, MARILYN

Played Happy Harmony in the 1976 revival program.

PATENT WATCH CO.

Manufactured a 1954 Howdy Doody Wrist Watch with moveable eyes.

PATTERN #156,587

Design pattern number awarded to Howdy Doody. First puppet to receive such a number.

PEABODY AWARD

Started in 1940 as an award for excellent broadcasting in various categories. The George Foster Peabody Broad-casting Award was presented to the Howdy Doody Show for 1948 by the University of Georgia.

PEANUT

Circus elephant in the Whitman Tell-A-Tale books *Howdy Doody's Clarabell Clown and the Merry-Go-Round* in 1955 and *Howdy Doody's Clarabell and Pesky Peanut.*

PEANUT GALLERY

The seating stands on the show; originally sat 40 children; it was increased to accomodate 250 children and parents in the 1976 revival series. Tickets were always very difficult to obtain and parents wrote to NBC for them years in advance.

PEANUT PUZZLER

Quiz part of the program in 1948.

PEANUTS

What the children in the Peanut Gallery were called; Charles Schultz adopted the name for his comic strip.

PECKY

Woodpecker brought to Doodyville in February 1958 show by Professor Whipporill.

PEDDLER PETE

Character in a May 1955 episode that sold a wishing lamp to Dilly Dally.

PEPPER

A pied piper that visited Doodyville in October 1955. His piccolo charmed all the Doodyville animals; February 1956. After charming Flub-A-Dub, Pepper tries to sell the Flub.

PEPPERMINT FOREST

Adventure location for a January 1956 program.

PEPPI MINT

Character introduced in December 1956 played by Marti Barris. She started as Hazel Witch's maid.

PEPSI-COLA CO.

Beverage company; in 1976, Pepsi planned to sponsor a series of Howdy Doody drinking glasses. Sample sets were manufactured and distributed to area reps for evaluation. The project was canceled. Only four samples of these glasses are known to survive. They picture Howdy, Flub-A-Dub, Mr. Bluster, and Clarabell.

PERCIVAL PARROT

Sidekick of the Canadian version of Clarabell who could interpret Clarabell's gestures. His voice was performed by Jack Mather from November 1954.

PERFECTLY FLAWLESS

A March 1956 show character who saved Heidi from Mrs. Izbing and Bruno.

PESKY

Played by Robert Nicholson; a clown that was in Doodyville from May 1957. Generally aligned himself with Mr. Bluster's schemes.

PESKY PEANUT

An elephant in the 1950s Tell-A-Tale book *Howdy Doody's Clarabell and Pesky Peanut.*

PETER PUPPET PLAYTHINGS, INC.

A Long Island City, New York, company that manufactured marionettes designed by Raye Copelan. There were several versions of Howdy wearing various shirts, eye types, scarves, and belts. The marionettes were:
Howdy 17½" tall, originally sold for $3.49.
Clarabell was 15½" (39.4cm) tall.
Princess Summerfall Winterspring was 14½" tall.
Mr. Bluster was 13" tall.
#361 Flub-A-Dub, 7" tall, originally sold for $2.98.
Dilly Dally was 13" tall.
They also manufactured:
22" x 28" Peter *Puppet Playhouse* with roll-up curtain.
1950s Howdy Doody Character set in Scope Doodle boxes.
Howdy Salt & Pepper Shakers.
Hand puppets.

PETERSEN, KARL, JR.

Bob Smith's personal chauffeur, 1955 – 1960; a Production Assistant, 1956 – 1960.

PIED PIPER

Tried to take away the Doodyville kids to Funland in a June 1957 show.

PHYLLIS

1. First name of the wife of producer Roger Muir.
2. Snake charmer in the 1958 Val Carney circus.

PIERRE, THE CHEF

Dayton Allen played this circus chef, 1948 – 1951; he was constantly concocting new delicacies. Pierre returned for the 10th anniversary program; December 28, 1957.

PIGGY BANK

A new bank in Doodyville; September 1959.

PIGGY, I.M.

Arrived in Doodyville in September 1959 to open the Piggy Bank.

PINKIE LEE

See: LEFF, PINCUS

PIONEER SCIENTIFIC

First sponsor of the Howdy Doody show. The Polaroid Television Filters were screens to be placed over the TVs to reduce glare.

PIONEER VILLAGE

Name of studio built in Bob Smiths' New Rochelle, New York, home in 1954 to film the show while Bob was recovering from a myocardial infarction; broadcast from January 17, 1955 to September 7, 1955.

PITTY-PAT

A dinosaur discovered on the Lost and Lonesome Lagoon in December 1955; became part of the circus.

PIXIE-MIXIE PIE POT

A pie making machine invented by Buffalo Bob; January 1958.

PLACEMATTERS

Manufactured the 1955 Howdy Doody TV Merrimat.

PLAN TWEEDLE-DEEDLE

A Mr. Bluster and Clarabell plan to unmask an impostor in an August 1955 show.

PLATINUM PLAYPUS

A very rare animal whom Buffalo Bob searches for in 1953 for two weeks. The search was also his vacation.

PLATTER, SPIN

A disc jockey in Doodyville; July 1959.

PLAYROOM PORTRAITS

Six Blue Bonnet® premiums 3¼" x 3½" close up color illustrations from the reverse side of margarine boxes. The portraits were of:
 Howdy Doody — 2 types
 Mr. Bluster
 Princess Summerfall Winterspring
 Dilly Dally
 Flub-A-Dub
 Clarabell
 Chief Thunderthud
 Oil Well Willie
 The Inspector
 Captain Scuttlebutt

POINTS, PAN

Played by Toby Tarnow in the Canadian version of Howdy Doody.

POKEY

Plasticine clay horse and friend of Gumby; created by Art Clokey and introduced on the Howdy Doody show in "The Adventures of Gumby," 1956.

POLL PARROT

The logo and emblem for Poll Parrot brand shoes copyrighted in 1925 by Paul Parrot. Poll Parrot was featured with Howdy in many premiums. Scott Brinker manufactured a Poll Parrot marionette in 1950 who appeared on the show; voice and manipulation by Dayton Allen.

POLL PARROT MAGIC EYE PICTURE

A large cardboard picture of Howdy with changeable eyes.

POLL PARROT'S HOWDY COMIC BOOK

A premium from Poll Parrot shoes; created two comics in the 1950s:
#2 Howdy, Dilly, and Poll Parrot being chased
#4 Howdy & Dilly in Italy (1951)

POLL PARROT'S HOWDY DOODY FLICKER KEY CHAIN

A Poll Parrot premium similar to the flicker ring. The key chain had a 3-D image that flickered between a picture of Howdy Doody and Poll Parrot.

POLL PARROT'S HOWDY DOODY FLICKER RING

A Poll Parrot premium. The ring had a 3-D image that flickered between a picture of Howdy Doody and Poll Parrot. There were two styles of the ring, one in a TV set type frame, and one without the frame.

POLL PARROT'S HOWDY DOODY PHOTO ALBUM

An 8-page premium album; 8½" x 11" with four pages of photographs of Howdy and friends.

POLL PARROT'S HOWDY DOODY SNAP-A-WINK

A 1953 Poll Parrot Shoe premium. This Tiddly Wink type game required the player to send the wink through the open mouth of a Clarabell portrait.

POLL PARROT SHOES

Sponsor and source of numerous premiums in 1950s; premiums included:
 Howdy Doody Flicker Ring
 Howdy Doody Flicker Key Chain
 Howdy Doody For President Flip-up Badges (2 different)
 Snap-A-Wink game
 Howdy Doody Jumble Joy Book (1955)
 3-D Character Face masks (6 different)
 Comic Books (2 different)
 Detective Disguises
 Howdy Doody News (1950)
 Photo Album with photos
 Howdy Doody's Comic Circus Animals (1954)
 Howdy Doody Easy as A-B-C Coloring Book
 Magic Eye Picture

POLL PARROT'S HOWDY DOODY DETECTIVE DISGUISES

A 1950s premium designed by Ken Giles in the "Tuk-A-Tab" mask series. Assorted eyes, hair, noses, and mouths could be punched out and worn. There are six different cards.

POLL PARROT'S HOWDY DOODY NEWS

A giveaway from the Poll Parrot shoe stores published by K.K. Publications. This newspaper/comic book reported on the Howdy Doody circus. Howdy was the Editor-in-Chief, Bob Smith the Managing Editor, Clarabell in charge of games and pictures, Flub-A-Dub wrote society and animal news, Mr. Bluster was the office boy, and Dilly Dally was the pencil sharpener.
#1 May 1950 — "Howdy Starts Newspaper" (Small Size)
#2 July 1950 — "Howdy Stars in Circus"
#3 1951
#4 1951

POLLY

A parakeet that Dilly Dally sings to in a September 1955 show.

POOBAH

Played by Allen Swift, he was the Hindu twin of Bahpoo.

POOFINWHIFF

A bird in shows from August 1958 that laid various types of magical eggs.

POPCORN SONG, THE

A 1951 RCA Victor 45 rpm record #5324, written by Edward Kean; on the flip side of *A Howdy Doody Christmas*.

POT O' GOLD

Owned by Tim the Leprechaun and found by Howdy and the Inspector in a September 1955 show.

POW

An unhappy caveman discovered by Timothy Tremble on the Isle of Jingle Jungle in a July 1954 show.

PREMIUM ASSOCIATES

New York, New York, company that distributed the Howdy Doody Talking Pins for th Standard Ice Cream Company.

PRESIDENTIAL CAMPAIGN 1948

Howdy's platform consisted of three Christmas days every year, larger allowances, 5-cent banana splits with four balls of ice cream, more pictures in history books, free circus and rodeo admissions. Campaign pins were offered in March 1948 and created a landslide of requests. Ballots were printed on the end seals of Wonder Bread. Howdy received 68,000 votes, more than Henry Wallace, the Progressive Party Presidental candidate for the U.S.

PRESIDENTIAL ELECTION 1952

Mr. Bluster was the spokesman for Mr. X. Princess Summerfall Winterspring went into a trance to discover the identity of Mr. X, but her magic necklace was not helpful.

PRETTY BOY BURT

See: BURT.

PRINCE HOWL VAL

See: VAL, Prince Howl.

PRINCE MENDEZ

See: MENDEZ, Prince.

PRINCESS FRYINGPAN BOTTLEWASHER

See: BOTTLEWASHER, Princess Fryingpan.

PRINCESS HAIDA

See: HAIDA, Princess.

PRINCESS HILDA

See: HILDA, Princess.

PRINCESS MAKE-IT-YOURSELF CHILDREN'S HANDBAG KIT

A 1950s leather shoulder bag kit originally sold for $1.98.

PRINCESS MAKE-IT-YOURSELF MOTHER & DAUGHTER HANDBAG KIT

A 1950s matched leather shoulder bag kit originally sold for $4.98.

PRINCESS RAYO DE LUNA

See: DE LUNA, Princess Rayo.

PRINCESS SUMMERFALL WINTERSPRING

See: WINTERSPRING, Princess Summerfall.

PRIZE DOODLE LIST

See: Howdy Doody's Big Prize Doodle List.

PRODUCTION COSTS

The first show, December 1947, was estimated at a cost of $600. Estimated production costs of the Howdy Doody show per 30 minutes were:
1951 $2,000
1952 $6,800
1954 $4,170

PROFESSOR BUBBLESCHMIDT

See: BUBBLESCHMIDT, Prof.

PROFESSOR FITZNOODLE

See: FITZNOODLE, Prof.

PROFESSOR FORTISSMO

See: FORTISSIMO, Prof.

PROFESSOR JACQUIN DEBOX

See: DEBOX, Prof. Jacquin.

PROFESSOR TORO

See: TORO, Professor.

PROFESSOR VON SPUTNICK

See: VON SPUTNICK, Prof.

PROFESSOR WHIPPORILL

See: WHIPPORILL, Prof.

PUPPET PLAYHOUSE

Original TV name of the Howdy Doody Show; started December 27, 1947; the name was changed to The Howdy Doody Show in 1948.

PUPPET THEATER

Incorrect listing of the *Puppet Playhouse* in the *NY Times* December 27, 1947.

PURINTON POTTERY COMPANY

Shippenville, Pennsylvania, company that manufactured a 9¾" Howdy Doody cookie jar.

QUACKENHAM, CHESTER Q.

New York City confidence man that cheated Mr. Bluster out of the money he made from selling Doodyville in a December 1955 show.

QUEEN GREAT GRANDMOTHER

Introduced several candidates for Princess Summerfall Winterspring in late 1954; she arrived again in Doodyville in June 1955 with seeds for the Magic Golden Tree.

QUEEN MOTHER OF THE TINKA TONKA TRIBE

Created in October 1953 as a means for Judy Tyler to leave the show; promotion from princess to queen.

QUEEN TINA

See: TINA, Queen.

QUIBBLE BIBBLE QUESTION QUASHER SQUASHER

A 1952 machine that could answer any question asked. The user wrote the question on the Bibble Board, inserted the board in the Question Squasher and the answer appeared on a large ticker tape.

RABBIT SNATCHER

An invention created by Mr. Bluster; used to catch Easter bunnies in an April 1955 show.

RADIO CORPORATION OF AMERICA

Produced Howdy Doody records on the RCA Victor label. Owned by NBC at the time.

RAINBOW MISH-MUSH

A February 1955 series of shows where the rainbow's colors were captured by the professor's invention, and accidentally mixed up the colors of trees and things in Doodyville.

RANCHER ROBB

See: ROBB, Rancher.

RAND SHOE COMPANY

St. Louis, Missouri, corporation that manufactured Poll Parrot brand shoes.

RCA VICTOR

Label of the Radio Corporation of America. Single 45 rpm Howdy Doody records. Titles included:
#5324 *A Howdy Doody Christmas/The Popcorn Song* (1951) — 45 rpm
EYA-23 *Howdy Doody's Christmas Party* — 45 rpm
EYA-41 *Howdy Doody and You* — 45 rpm
EYA-42 *Howdy Doody's Magic Juke Box* — 45 rpm
EYA-43 *Howdy Doody's Crystal Ball* — 45 rpm
Y-397 *Howdy Doody and the Air-O-Doodle* (1949) — 78 rpm
Y-414 *Howdy Doody's Laughing Circus* (1950) — 78 rpm
Y-442 *Howdy Doody's Christmas Party* — 78 rpm
WY-397 *Howdy Doody and the Air-O-Doodle* (1949) — 45 rpm
WY-414 *Howdy Doody's Laughing Circus* (1949) — 45 rpm
WY-442 *Howdy Doody's Christmas Party* — 45 rpm
It's Howdy Doody Time
Howdy Doody's Do's and Don'ts
Howdy Doody and Mother Goose
Howdy Doody and the Musical Forest
Howdy Doody and Santa Claus — 45 rpm

RENE, HENRI

Conducted the orchestra for the RCA Victor album *Howdy Doody and the Air-O-Doodle* in 1949.

RINGLING BROS. BARNUM & BAILEY CIRCUS

Howdy Doody joined this U.S. circus for guest appearances in 1950.

RIPP, HEINO

Technical director for the show in 1948; he later became technical director for the Sid Caesar *Your Show of Shows*.

RIPPEN, ROBERT (1919 –)

Directed the show from 1948 and produced it from 1952; retired from the show in May 1956. He later became head of Rutgers University TV Department (NJ).

RIVERS ICE CREAM CO.

Manufactured the Howdy Doody Twin Ice Cream Sandwich, Howdy Doody Fudge Bar Milk Sherbet, Howdy Doody Ice Cream, Howdy Doody Twin Pops, and Howdy Doody Chocolate Covered Ice Milk from their Chicopee Falls, Massachusettes, offices. The bags were eligible for premiums from the Doughnut Corporation's Prize Doodle List in 1954 – 1955.

ROALEX COMPANY

A New York company that manufactured the 1950s Howdy Doody and His Friends Slide Puzzle Game; originally sold for $.39.

ROBB, RANCHER

Cousin of Cornelius Cobb; introduced in February 1956.

ROBIE

Robot invented by Professor Toro; January 1956.

ROBINSON, HUBBELL

CBS programming chief in 1950 when he negotiated with Bob Smith unsuccessfully to move the show from NBC to CBS.

ROCK CANDY MOUNTAIN

Location where Sidney Scarecrow rescued Howdy in a January 1956 show.

ROCKEFELLER CENTER

New York location of NBC where the Howdy Doody Show originated. Howdy, Buffalo Bob, and Clarabell lit the annual Christmas Tree there in 1953.

ROCKGLAS CORP.

New York City company who manufactured the Howdy Doody sunglasses.

ROCKET DOODLE

A 1951 rocketship that Howdy used to fly from Doodyville to the North Pole to rescue Santa.

RODEO RAY

Played by Ray Forrest. He was one of the early substitutes for Buffalo Bob after Bob's 1954 heart attack.

RAE, CLAUDE

Was the voice of Howdy Doody, Mr. Bluster, and Mister X in the Canadian Howdy Doody show from November 1954.

RONNIE

A toy reindeer and the name of Howdy Doody Balloon Zoo Animal.

ROSE, MARGO

A puppeteer on the show from December 1952; the wife of Rufus C. Rose. She controlled Heidi Doody, Buzz Beaver, Hop, Skip, Jump, Grandpa Doody, Petey Bluster, Mike Hatchet, Tom Turtle, and Paddle.

ROSE, RUFUS C. (– 1975)

Hired as puppeteer in December 1952. He introduced the puppets: Capt. Windy Scuttlebutt, Photo Doody, Hyde, Zeke, and Tizzy. Kept the Howdy, Mr. Bluster, Heidi Doody, Dilly Dally, and Flub-A-Dub at his Waterford, Connecticut, home; he was the voice of the Bloop. Rufus Rose wrote the definition of the word "puppet" for the 14th edition of the *Encyclopedia Britanicia*.

ROYAL COLORING CARDS

The back panel of Royal Pudding boxes; had a series of cards that could be cut out and colored. They were:
2 Princess and a seal
5 Mr. Bluster
7 Howdy Doody
#11 The Bloop.

ROYAL ELECTRIC COMPANY

Manufactured 1950s Howdy and Santa plastic 14" tall wall lights.

©BOB SMITH, FROM THE SCOTT BRINKER COLLECTION

The first Princess Summerfall Winterspring. This puppet was replaced by Judy Tyler. This costume was sold at the June 18, 1995, Christie's auction for $1,265.00.

ROYAL PUDDINGS

A product of Standard Brands, Inc. and a Howdy Doody sponsor and premium maker. Premiums included:
 Trading card set
 Masks
 Coloring Cards
 Packages with Howdy's picture on the front.

ROYAL PURPLE COW

A Welch's promotion in early 1952 to introduce a half grape juice, half milk drink. Advertising agents concocted a story about a cow who loved to eat the same kind of grapes that went into grape juice. Howdy, Buffalo Bob, and Clarabell appeared with a cow, dyed purple, for the live promotion. The cow was injured in the first appearance. Test marketing of mixing milk and grape juice with children was a flop and the promotion was canceled.

ROYAL TRADING CARDS

A set of 15 cards cut from the backs of Royal brand desserts. The cards were:
 1. Howdy Doody
 2. Mr. Bluster
 3. Flub-A-Dub
 4. Dilly Dally
 5. The Inspector
 6. Don Jose Bluster
 7. Buffalo Bob
 8. Clarabell
 9. Lanky Lou
 10. Doctor Singasong
 11. Pierre, the Chef
 12. Sir Archibald
 13. Princess Summerfall Winterspring
 14. Oil Well Willie
 15. Chief Featherman.

ROYAL, JOHN F.

NBC's first Vice President of TV in 1947 when the Howdy Doody show went on the air. In 1944 he acquired the rights to the Army Signal Corps footage and created the show: *The War as it Happens*.

RUNNINGWATER, PAPOOSE GINA

Played by Gina Genardi; she was introduced on the show on January 26, 1954. She later became the third Princess Summerfall Winterspring.

RUSHTON COMPANY

An Atlanta, Georgia, company that manufactured a Windy the Dog plush animal wearing a Howdy Doody Navy hat.

RUSSELL MANUFACTURING CO.

Manufactured the 1955 Howdy Doody Card Game in Leicester, Massechusettes. The card game sold for $.19.

S.S. WISHY-WASHY

Capt. Scuttlebutt's ship.

SAILOR REX

Played by Rex Marshall; one of the replacements for Buffalo Bob during his February 1949 vacation.

SALAMI SAM

Played by Dayton Allen. When the meat industry objected to the name, it was changed to Ugly Sam.

SALLY

A seal in the circus whom Howdy taught to juggle; appeared in a 1950 Whitman coloring book.

SALTED PEANUTS

What Chief Thunderthud called the Peanut Gallery after Mr. Bluster confused him in a February 1955 show.

SAM, SLAPSY

A clown town figure who employed Clarabell in August 1959.

SANDY McTAVISH

See: McTAVISH, Sandy.

SANDPIPER PRESS

Division of Simon & Schuster that designed and produced the Big Golden Books and Little Golden Records.

SANDRA

Marionette witch; voiced by Rufus Rose and introduced in April 1958, from Always Always Land. She generally caused mayhem with the Doodyville residents.

SANTA VISITS HOWDY DOODY'S HOUSE

A Christmas coloring book.

©Bob Smith, from the Scott Brinker Collection

Phineas T. Bluster, mayor of Doodyville.

SARABELL

Played by Lee Carney, she was a female Clarabell.

SARNOFF, ROBERT

Son of General Sarnoff. He participated in the decision of which rendering would be the second Howdy Doody in 1949, the first advertising salesperson for the program; he became president of NBC.

SARNOFF, DAVID

Chairman of NBC. He believed that the Howdy Doody show was responsible for the sale of more TV sets than any other two shows combined.

SAYERS, HENRY

Wrote the music to *Ta-Ra-Ra-Boom-De-Ay*. The melody was later used as the theme for the Howdy Doody Show. Edward Kean and Bob Smith wrote the words to *It's Howdy Doody Time*.

SCARECROW, SIDNEY

A January 1956 character that rescues Howdy and then the Storybook Princess.

SCARF-SNATCHER

A Mr. Bluster invention designed to steal a magic scarf from Dilly Dally in February 1955.

SCHAFFEL, HAL (d.1993)

Howdy Doody producer in the 1950s.

SCHLENGEL, BERTHA

The name of an actress christened by Buffalo Bob in the Old-Time Movies. The name was actually that of a friend of Buffalo Bob's mother.

SCHLOSSLER BROTHERS, INC.

Manufactured the Howdy Doody Chocolate Covered Ice Cream bar at their Plymouth, Indiana, factory. The bags were eligible for premiums from the Doughnut Corporation's Prize Doodle List in 1954 – 1955.

SCHWICTENBERG, CHARLIE

An actor's name christened by Buffalo Bob in the Old-Time Movies. The name was also that of a friend of Buffalo Bob.

SCOPEDOODLE

An early Doodyville invention built by Scott Brinker. It was a vertical machine with a fold-down front consisting of dials. The Scopedoodle was used to show the Old-Time Movies.

SCOPP, ALFIE

Played Clarabell in Canadian version of the Howdy Doody show from November 1954.

SCREAMING MIMI

Hazel Witch's invisible bird who became a menace to Doodyville; June 1959.

SCUTTLEBUTT, CAPTAIN WINDY

1. A puppet introduced in January 1953, voice by Allen Swift; he was a jolly sea captain with a large dog, later voiced by Robert Nicholson. He now resides with Margo Rose.
2. CANADA: Live character played by Larry Mann on the Canadian version of the Howdy Doody show from November 1954.

SECRET SEVEN SOLUTION

Howdy Doody's June – July 1958 contest to find the best way to spend a summer vacation.

SECRET TREASURE, THE

A Tru-Vue film card #T-5 manufactured in 1955. In this adventure, Howdy finds a treasure map.

SEIDEN, ART

Artist who drew the Howdy Doody pictures in the Big Golden Books of 1952. Illustrated the pictures for the Little Golden Books *Howdy Doody in Funland, Howdy Doody and Clarabell, Howdy Doody and the Princess, Howdy Doody and His Magic Hat, It's Howdy Doody Time, Howdy Doody's Animal Friends,* and *Howdy Doody and Santa Claus.*

SHAKE-A-DOODLE

Ovaltine's advertising used to sell their product and the Shake-Up Mugs.

SHAW, MEL (b.1914)

Original co-inventor and co-designer of the second Howdy Doody with Robert Allen.

SHURA-TONE PRODUCTIONS INC.

A Brooklyn, New York, company that produced five models of record players during the Kagran period; they were called "Phono-Doodle."

SIGAFOOSE

Indian tribe from which Buffalo Bob and Buffalo Tom were descended.

SIGNORE DoReMiFaSoLaTiDo

See: DoReFaSoLaTiDo, Signore.

SILVER-RICH CORP.

A Long Island City, New York, company that manufactured:
Sun-Ray Camera
Camera Films (4 pre-exposed per package)
   #1 Howdy Doody at the Zoo.

SIMON & SCHUSTER

Publisher of Howdy Doody books under the Little Golden Book and Big Golden Book labels as well as Howdy Doody records under the Little Golden Records label.

SIMON SLY

See: SLY, Simon.

SIMON, SIMPLE

New York city pie maker who wanted to buy the Pixie-Mixie Pie Machine from Buffalo Bob in January 1958.

SIMPLE SIMON

See: SIMON, Simple.

SINGASONG, DR.

Live character played by Bill LeCornec; this character dressed in a high black hat and a mourning suit; he spoke as if he were singing and provided musical entertainment. He was the circus doctor who sang all the time. He believed that singing would make is patients feel much better, although it frequently had the reverse effect.

SIR ARCHIBALD

See: ARCHIBALD, Sir.

SIR LAFFALOT

See: LAFFALOT, Sir.

SKIP

One of three kangaroo puppets manufactured by Margo Rose in 1953.

SLAPSY SAM

See: SAM, Slapsy.

SLATER CORP.

Manufactured It's Howdy Doody Time! buttons.

SLIPPERDOODLES

Poll Parrot slippers with the Doodyville characters on the instep. When the characters were squeezed, squeaking noises were emmited.

SLY, SIMON

An African hunter in a February 1956 diamond mine adventure.

SMILE CONTEST

Photo contest from November 11 to December 1, 1957.

SMILEY, TOM

Technical director of the show from 1949 to 1955.

SMITH, DICK

Make-up artist in the early years of the program; designed Clarabell. He won an Academy Award for his work in *Amadeus*.

SMITH, Mr.

Played by Robert E. Smith. Dressed as an explorer, wearing a pith helmet; he became Buffalo Bob in late 1949.

SMITH, ROBERT E. (November 27, 1917 –)

Musician/actor; professionally a radio personality since 1933, starting at station WBEN, Buffalo, NY. Formed Hi Hatters male trio, sang on the *Kate Smith Show* 1935 – 1936. He played the piano, organ, drums, and most brass and reed instruments. In 1946 he was hired by NBC to emcee the Bob Smith early morning radio show, 6:00 – 9:00 AM. Created the Howdy Doody character on the Triple B Ranch Radio Show, Saturday mornings in March 1947 while on WEAF Radio, NY. On December 27, 1947, he hosted the first *Puppet Playhouse* TV Show – later called *The Howdy Doody Show*. The character Elmer was Bob's friend who was so shy, he hid in his desk. He developed the Howdy Doody character successfully into the TV phenomenon it later became. Bob Smith retained the rights for the Buffalo Bob character. From 1970 – 1976, he appeared at over 300 colleges, where the Howdy Doody Alumni wanted to "relive their happy, carefree, childhood days." From 1972 he appeared with Clarabell in shopping malls. Currently he appears regularly at antique shows, malls, television commercials, and in parades throughout the country.

SMITH, VICTOR

Stage name: Buffalo Vic. Buffalo Bob's deceased brother. Appeared with Buffalo Bob for a few performances in May 1950. Was Howdy's voice while Buffalo Bob was recovering from his heart attack; replaced by Allen Swift.

SNAP-A-WINK

See: POLL Parrot's Howdy Doody Snap-A-Wink.

SNAPPER, GINGER

An assistant whom the Inspector brought from England; October 1956.

SNICKERS

A product of the Mars Candy Company and an advertised product on the program. Snickers had a 1950s 13" Princess dancing puppet premium.

SNICKERSDOODLE

A 1950 contest. Promoting Snickers Candy Bar.

SOCIETY FOR GIVING FLUB-A-DUB ICE CREAM

Flub-A-Dub used his membership in this group as his qualifications for being the society editor of the Poll Parrot Howdy Doody news.

SOUND-O-DOODLE

An April 1956 invention that could reproduce any sound.

SOUTHWARD, HO, HO!

An adventure story in the March 1953 issue of Howdy Doody comics.

SPECIALTY ADVERTISING SERVICE

A New York company who manufactured:
 Howdy Doody set of 42 Trading Cards (1951)
 Howdy Doody Play Money (1952 & 1953)
 Howdy Doody TV Merrimat (1952)
 Poll Parrot "Howdy Doody Snap-A-Wink" (1953).

SPELLING BEE

An insect that made honey that Buffalo Bob searched for in a December 1955 show.

SPIN PLATTER

See: PLATTER, Spin.

SPINLAND

Community where Pepper the Piper tried to sell Flub-A-Dub; February 1956 show.

SPINNER

A spider who worked with Merlin at King Arthur's Court; November 1955 show.

SPLINTERS

A wooden man manufactured by Howdy Doody and brought to life by Sandra Witch; April 1958 show.

SQUEAKIE

A character that Howdy and Heidi met in Underworld in November 1955.

STADLIN, IRA (1924 –)

Stage name: Allen Swift. Replaced Dayton Allen as the voices of the Bluster brothers, Flub-A-Dub, and others from December 1952. He played Chief Thunderchicken (Spring 1953), Professor Bellringer (January 1955), Carnival Cal (April 1955), Abra K. Dabra (June 1955), Monsieur Fontainebleau, Poobah, and his twin, Boopah. During Buffalo Bob's absence from his heart attack in 1955, he voiced Howdy Doody. Swift left the program in May 1956; subsequently he hosted *The Popeye Show*. He still performs commercials as the "man of 1,000 voices" and writes Broadway plays.

STAHLWOOD CO.

Manufactured 1950s Howdy Doody in an airplane rubber squeeze figure, 5" x 7".

STANDARD BRANDS INC.

Manufacturers of Royal Brand Puddings and Blue Bonnet Margarine. They were a sponsor of the Howdy Doody Show.

STANDARD ICE CREAM CO.

Manufactured Howdy Doody fudge bars in early 1950s.

STARE, FRED A.

Developed the whammy eye that made things disappear in October 1959.

STICK MEN

Cultivators of Caboose Cabbage in September 1959.

STONE, FRANK

Father of Marty Stone; made appearances as Buffalo Frank in stores and malls for Kagran.

STONE, MARTIN

Had his own TV programs. Met Bob Smith in December 1947 and became his agent. He created the Sigafoose Indian story to introduce the Buffalo Bob name. Conceived the idea of Princess Summerfall Winterspring to appeal to girls for marketing merchandise. Stone was the moving force behind the mass marketing of the Howdy Doody name. He also produced the NBC program *Author Meets the Critic*, 1950 – 1951, directed by Howard Davis.

STORI-VIEWS

A product of Church Craft Pictures, Inc., produced in the early 1950s. Stori-Views were individual cards; each slide card had two identical color photos to be seen in the left and right sides of a 3-dimensional viewer, with an accompanying story on the card. Stories consisted of either 6 or 12 cards. Kits originally sold for $2.50, viewers alone sold for $1.50, 12 card sets for $1.00, and 6 card sets for $.50. Available Howdy Doody card sets were:
#601 Howdy Doody and His Pals (12 cards)
#602 Do's & Don't's on Manners (12 cards)
#603 Howdy Gets Ready for School (6 cards)
#605 The Howdy Doody Show (6 cards)
#606 Howdy Doody Explains TV (6 cards)
#K-60 Junior Kit — 1 Stori-Viewer and card set #601.

STORY OF HOWDY DOODY'S PEANUT GALLERY

A 1976 record album.

STORY PRINCESS

Played by Arlene Dalton. Brought onto the program at the start of show's color production from the Ziegfield Theater, September 12, 1955. She told stories to the children in the Peanut Gallery.

STRACO

Brand of the 1987 Howdy Doody Play Tool Set and felt-covered plastic Mr. Bluster, Howdy, and Clarabell banks distributed by the F.J. Strauss Co., Inc.

STRAUSS CO, F.J.

Distributed the Straco brand 1987 Play Tool set and felt Howdy, Mr. Bluster, and Clarabell banks that were manufactured in Hong Kong.

SUN-RAY CAMERA

Brand of premium camera that came with 4 films and 6 developing papers manufactured by the Silver-Rich Corp. Among the pre-processed films available were:
#1 Howdy Doody at the Zoo
Howdy Doody at the Rodeo.

SUNNY

Aided Mr. Bluster in February 1956 by organizing a mayoral parade for him.

SUNNY CLOUD, PAPOOSE

Character in May 1955 show; one of the potential replacements for the second Princess.

SUPER TALK-O-SCOPE

A monitor with gadgets that enabled kids to see characters and people anywhere they were; used on the show in June 1955. The scope was originally designed by Scott Brinker as the Lala-Palooza and used to introduce the Old-Time Movies.

SUPRIS POUR HODY DODY

An Un Petit Livre D'Or French version of *Surprise for Howdy Doody*.

SURPRISE FOR HOWDY DOODY

A Tell-A-Tale Book #832 published in 1951; written by Edward Kean.

SQUIRREL-WAR

A cartoon series aired on the program in October 1955.

SUTTON'S

Manufactured the 1970s Fingertronic Puppet Theater.

SWIFT, ALLEN

See: STADLIN, Ira

TALUN, WALTER

Played a giant in a July 1951 program. He also performed as Goliath in the 1951 movie *David and Bathsheba*.

TA-RA-RA-BOOM-DE-RAY

Tune of the Howdy Doody theme song.

TAGG, ELMER

Set designer for the show in the early 1950s.

TARNOW, TOBY

Played Pan Points in the Canadian version of Howdy Doody in 1957.

TAYLOR, SMITH & TAYLOR

Manufactured the 1950s Howdy Doody ceramic plate, cup, and bowl.

TELOPTISCOPE

A 1952 device that rotated and pointed to direction it wanted to go.

TEE-VEE TOYS, INC.

A Roxbury, Massachusettes, company that manufactured a 1950s Howdy Doody Birthday Cake Decoration Set. They also manufactured a 1950 set of 4" plastic mono-colored figures of Howdy, Princess Summerfall Winterspring, Mr. Bluster, Dilly Dally (with moveable mouths), and Clarabell (with a whistle). The same pieces were also available painted in individual television-like boxes encouraging one to put on his own show. A Flub-A-Dub was also available in an individual box.

TELE-PERISCOPIC CAMERA

Howdy's device that allowed the Peanut Gallery to follow far away adventures on the S.S. Wishy-Washy in July 1955.

TELEVISION'S FAMOUS HOWDY DOODY COLORING BOOK

A Whitman Publishing Co. title #2093 and #2176 produced in 1950 and originally sold for $.25.

TELEVISION'S FAMOUS HOWDY DOODY FUN BOOK

A Whitman Publishing Company title from 1953 illustrated by Jack Crowe and originally sold for $.25.

TELEVISION'S FAMOUS HOWDY DOODY STICKER FUN

A Whitman Publishing Company activity book produced in 1951 and originally sold for $.25.

TELL-A-TALE BOOKS

A series of children's books published by Whitman Publishing Co. in the 1950s and originally sold for $.15 each. Titles included:
#832 or #2573 *Surprise for Howdy Doody* (1951)
#902 *Howdy Doody and the Monkey Tale* (1953)
#934 *Howdy Doody's Clarabell & Pesky Peanut*
#944 *Howdy Doody and the Magic Lamp* (1954)
#2558 *Howdy Doody's Clarabell Clown and the Merry Go Round* (1955)
Howdy Doody Famous TV Star.

TENNIS SEA

Location of a July 1960 treasure show with Windy Scuttlebutt and Diamond Jim Nasium.

THEODORE

A matador that who visited to Doodyville in an October 1959 show.

THERMOS

Manufactured a 1977 plastic dome lunch box with matching bottle.

THOMAS, LOWELL, JR.

Son of newsman Lowell Thomas; he was a cameraman, world traveler, and lecturer who showed adventure films on the program starting September 12, 1955.

THOMAS, THELMA

A west coast Walt Disney artist hired to create a new face for the Velma Dawson Howdy Doody.

THREE FLYING GONKLETWERPS

See: GONKLETWERPS, Three Flying.

THREE MUSKETEERS

A chocolate confection candy bar manufactured by Mars Candy Company, an advertised product on the show.

THUMB, TOM

Midget in the circus and in a Dell comic.

THUNDERBIRD TRIBE

Western Canadian tribe from where Princess Haida originated.

THUNDERCHICKEN, CHIEF

Played by Allen Swift. He was a rival of Chief Thunderthud and was introduced to the show in early 1953 as a replacement for Chief Featherman. He spoke with a New York accent.

THUNDERTHUD, CHIEF

Played by Bill LeCornec; he was conceived as a rival for Chief Featherman. Thunderthud was a member of the Ooragnak (kangaroo backwards) tribe and always shouted "Kowabonga" in both greeting and anger.

TIM

A leprechaun freed by Clarabell in August 1955, and the object of a series of shows searching for his pot o' gold. Falls from a balloon with Howdy Doody in February 1956.

TIMBER TOM

Played by Robert Goulet (actor); he was the Canadian version of Buffalo Bob, a forest ranger with a vast amount of outdoor information; started November 15, 1954.

TIME-A-TUB

A time machine invented by Buffalo Bob; April 1955.

TINA, QUEEN

The Queen of Littlelandia; December 1955. Mr. Bluster attempted to become her king.

TINKA-TONKA PRINCESS

Gina Genardi's role until she became the new Princess Summerfall Winterspring, February 24, 1955.

TINKA-TONKA TRIBE

The tribe of Princess Summerfall Winterspring and Chief Featherman.

TIZZY

A dinosaur puppet conceived by Willie Gilbert and Jack Weinstock, built by Margo Rose, and introduced in 1955. His voice described as being a cross between Sir Archibalds' and Eleanor Roosevelts'.

TOBY TYLER AT THE CIRCUS

Performed on the *Puppet Playhouse* starting in December 1947; a Frank Paris 13-part puppet series about a boy who ran away from home and joined a circus. Toby Tyler was made into a 1960 Disney movie wth the same name.

TODD, A.O.

Offered a prize to the first Doodyville resident to go around the world the fastest; October 1957.

TOGO

A clown visited Doodyville in September 1956 turning everything topsy turvy.

TOM TURTLE

See: TURTLE, Tom.

TONS OF FUN

A fat threesome (named Buffalo Vic, Buffalo Clint, and Buffalo Bullets) so named by Buffalo Bob as performers in the Old-Time Movies.

TOOTH, HAPPY

A Colgate toothpaste charactar, voice by Bill LeCornic, always under attack by Mr. Tooth Decay.

TOOTSIE POPS

A lollipop candy with a chewy chocolate center advertised on the show and manufactured by Tootsie Roll Industries.

TOOTSIE ROLL

A chocolate chewy candy advertised on the show and manufactured by Tootsie Roll Industries.

TOOTSIE ROLL INDUSTRIES

A Chicago, Illinois, corporation. They sponsored the show advertising Tootsie Rolls and Tootsie Pops. They also owned the Mason's candy lines who were show sponsors.

TORO, PROFESSOR

Inventor of Robie, a Robot; January 1956.

TOY NOVELTY ASSOCIATES

Imported the 1950s Howdy Doody Trapeze toy from the Arnold Toy Company in West Germany.

TRAMMELL, NILES

President of NBC when Howdy Doody show began airing in 1947.

TRAPPER TYRONE

Played by Lew Anderson; he was an woodsman who helped Buffalo Bob look for his dog on an island in a June 1955 show.

TREMBLE, TIMOTHY

Played by Tim McCutcheon. Arrived in Doodyville in June 1955 as a friend of Mr. Bluster. Involved in plots to fool Howdy, chopped down the magic golden tree; disguised as an Indian Princess and a tree doctor.

TRICK OF FIRE

A wizard trick that initially trapped Howdy and Mr. Bluster in a December 1955 program.

TRIGGER HAPPY

A western bad man who came to Doodyville in October 1958 and spent time in the Doodyville jail.

TRIPLE B RANCH

Stood for Big "Brother Bob." Bob Smith's original half hour children's quiz show in 1947 on the NBC radio program with Elmer (later Howdy Doody).

TRU-VUE CO.

A Beaverton, Oregon, company that manufactured Howdy Doody 3-D Film Cards with viewer and 35 mm boxed film strips; 1954.

TRU-VUE FILM CARDS

Seven different full color three-dimensional pictures on 4" x 5½" cards in envelopes manufactured by the Tru-Vue Co. in the 1950s sold for $.29 each and a viewer sold for $1.49. Viewer cards included:
T-4 Howdy Doody and Clarabell the Clown (1954)
T-5 Howdy Doody in The Secret Treasure (1955)
T-6 Howdy Doody in Mr. Bluster's Surprise (1955).

TRU-VUE FILM STRIPS

Small 35mm black and white adventure film strips produced in the early 1950s. Titles included:
#235 A Visit to the Howdy Doody Show.

TRUTH WATER

A special kind of water brought to Doodyville in February 1957 by Liona. After drinking it, a lie caused the teller to hop on one foot until he told the truth.

TUCK-A-TAB MASK

See: POLL Parrot's Howdy Doody Tuck-A-Tab Mask.

TURTLE, TOM

A marionette conceived by Willie Gilbert and Jack Weinstein, built by Margo Rose, and voiced by Lew Anderson; discovered during a December 1955 Arkadoodle adventure; became part of the circus. He now resides with Margo Rose.

TV DIGEST

A pre-national TV guide with a Howdy Doody related cover story on two issues:
November 17, 1951 (Thanksgiving theme)
December 27, 1952 (Christmas theme).

TV DIGEST COLORING CONTEST

A contest ending in December 1951. There were four winners announced: Rickie Boysen, Nancy Jarvis, Patricia Cusack, and Ronald Hatt. All received their prizes on the December 30th program. There were over 10,000 entries. There were 196 additional prize winners who were awarded prizes of Ice Follies tickets, Howdy Doody TV Game, Howdy Doody Coloring Set, and Howdy Doody Coloring Book in January 1952.

TV GUIDE MAGAZINE

Weekly periodical; television guide that featured a Howdy Doody cover story the week of June 25 – July 1, 1954 in the national edition, and cover stories in the regional editions July 26, 1948, September 2, 1948, and November 23, 1951.

TYLER, JUDY

See: HESS, Judith

U.S. PACKAGING CORPORATION

A Bridgeport, Connecticut, company who manufactured the Frosty Snow Spray.

UGLY SAM

A 1949 – 1952 character played by Dayton Allen; he was a poor wrestler who always lost his matches, wore a striped suit, and was dim-witted.

UN PETIT LIVRE D'OR

The French version of Little Golden Books. Titles included:
#71. *Howdy Doody Au Pays Des Jeux* (1953)
Supris Pour Howdy Doody (1951).

UNDERLAND

A place at the bottom of a rabbit hole in a November

1955 series. Heidi landed there after hearing the Alice in Wonderland story.

UNIQUE ART MANUFACTURING COMPANY

Produced metal toys from 1916 through 1952 until they were acquired by Marx Toys. A Newark, New Jersey, sponsor of Howdy Doody show, 1950. They manufactured:
Howdy Doody and Buffalo Bob Smith at the Piano wind-up (box title was Doin' the Howdy Doody) toy
Metalic Howdy Doody Bank.

UNITED WORLD FILMS

Sold 8mm and 16mm Castle Films brand Howdy Doody movies from their New York office. Prices ranged from $1.95 to $21.75.

UPA

Cartoon production company that produced the cartoon "Howdy Doody and His Magic Hat" in 1954.

URLI

Village in Tibet that was the home of King Yordik in May 1958.

VAC-U-FORM

Produced 1950s Howdy and Santa Christmas decorations. The decorations were 14" x 10" x 1". They included:
Howdy in the chimney with Santa next to him
Howdy on Santa's knee in front of the fireplace.

VAH, PRINCE HOWL

Turkish prince who came to Doodyville looking for a doctor to take back with him to Turkey. He captured Howdy Doody and Princess Summerfall Winterspring; February 1959.

VAN DAM RUBBER CO.

Manufactured the 1955 Howdy Doody Two-in-One balloon in New York City.

VAN RIP DER FLUGEL, WENDELL

Played by Allen Swift; he visited Doodyville in January 1955 with his twin brother, Winkle.

VAN RIP DER FLUGEL, WINKLE

Played by Allen Swift; he visited Doodyville in January 1955 with his twin brother, Wendell.

VANDOR

Salt Lake City, Utah, company who manufactured:
1970s 10" Howdy winking cookie jar
1988 Howdy bumper car salt & pepper shakers
1988 8½" Howdy bumper car cookie jar
wall plaque
bookends
spoon rest
bank.

VANISHING WATER

A special water that made the drinker disappear. Clarabell used it in August 1957.

VICTORY, JIM

Marketed the 1976 revival program for NBC.

VIGRAN, HERB

Was the voice of some of the puppets in the 1950s. Aside from Howdy Doody appearances, Vigran played criminals on *The Adventures of Superman* in the 1950s and Ernest Henshaw on *The Ed Wynn Show* from September 25, 1958 to January 1, 1959.

VON SPUTNICK, PROF.

The name Buffalo Bob used when he disguised himself as a famous balloonist in an April 1958 show.

WADE, WARREN

One of the programming heads of NBC in 1947 who brought the Howdy Doody Show to TV; participated in the decision of which rendering would become the second Howdy Doody in 1949.

WALLENDAL, GARY

Winner in the adult division of the 1978 Milwaukee, Wisconsin, Howdy Doody Look-Alike Contest.

WALLWORTH, CHARLES

Designed premiums such as the Howdy Doody masks.

©Bob Smith, from the Scott Brinker Collection

Clarabell and Howdy check out a Scott Brinker invention.

WARBURG, FELICIA

Stage manager for the Howdy Doody show.

WATTS, OHMS V.

An electric man who came to Doodyville in January 1958 with the circus. Became involved with a Mr. Bluster plot.

WAYNE, RONALD

The producer of the show during the revival series in 1976 – 1977; filmed in Miami, Florida. He formerly produced *The Jackie Gleason Show*.

WEAF RADIO

Broadcast Buffalo Bob's radio program in 1946. It started the Triple B Ranch in March 1947. Was broadcast six times per week from 6:00 – 9:00 AM. The program ended in 1954 after Bob Smith's heart attack. WEAF became WNBC.

WEATHER-WIFFER-SNIFFER

Device to predict the weather. Invented by Buffalo Bob in July 1955.

WEINSTOCK, JACK

Contract writer for the show with Willie Gilbert for Howard Davis, and then as head writer. Together they conceived marionettes and characters such as Tiz, Mike Hatchet, Tom Turtle, Paddle, Sandra and Hazel Witches, Peppi Mint, and Petey Bluster. Before Howdy Doody, Weinstock wrote for the *Captain Video* program;. He wrote *The Laughing Song* with W. Gilbert and R. Nicholson. He co-authored the Broadway show *How to Succeed in Business Without Really Trying* with Gilbert and Abe Burrows; Weinstock directed the show. They won the 1962 Pulitzer Prize and the 1961 – 1962 New York Drama Critic's Circle Award for the show.

WELCH'S GRAPE JUICE COMPANY

A Westfield, New York, company and 1950s Howdy Doody sponsor from December 2, 1950 until August 1955; they were responsible for numerous premiums and advertising products:
Welch's Howdy Doody Cook Book (1952)
Grapeade and Grape Jelly Jars Howdy Doody lids (1953, 1954)
Grape Juice Bottles with Howdy Doody photo
Frozen Grape Juice Howdy Doody Cans
Howdy Doody Climber.

WELCH'S HOWDY DOODY COOKBOOK

A 34-page cookbook printed in March 1952 containing 78 recipes using grape juice. The book was produced under the direction of Barbara Collyer for the Welch's Grape Juice Co.

WELCH'S JELLY JARS/GLASSES

Two series of jelly jar/glasses were produced. On the bottom of each glass was the image of a character: Howdy Doody, Dilly Dally, Princess Summerfall Winterspring, Flub-A-Dub, Clarabell, Mr. Bluster, or no image (caused by a filled die). Among them, a total of 243 different glasses possible for collection.

Series 1 (1953): Glasses were printed in seven colors, with six sayings and seven bottom image types (147 different glasses are possible). All text begins with "Hey Kids!.."
Printed in blue, orange, or pink:
..Ding Dong Dell, Ring for Welch's, You'll Like It Swell!
..Hip Hip Hooray, Welch's Leads the Parade
..Come on Along Your Welch's Sure Helps Make You Strong!
Printed in green, red, yellow, and white:
..What a Shot, Just Like Welch's, It Hits the Spot
..On Land or Sea, Welch's Taste Best We All Agree!
..Wherever We Eat, Welch's Is Our Favorite Treat!

Series 2 (1954): Glasses were printed in six colors, with six sayings and the seven bottom images (126 different glasses are possible):
Printed in green, red, or yellow:
Drinking Grape Juice is Seals' Favorite Act
Here Comes Music for Doodyville Circus
Doodyville Elephant Squirts Clarabell
Printed in pink, orange, or blue:
Dilly Dally is Circus Big Shot
Clarabell Gets a Kick Out of Circus Mule
Clarabell Tries Tiger Trick.

WESTERN PRINTING & LITHOGRAPHING CO.

A Racine, Wisconsin, company who designed and produced Howdy Doody comic books and the printed the Big Golden Books of 1952. Their Wolf Printing Company division produced the Poll Parrot comics.

WHAMMY EYE

Developed in October 1959 by Fred A. Stare to make things disappear by staring at them.

WHEATIES

Cereal manufactured by General Mills; produced Howdy Doody cut-out masks on the backs of their boxes.

WHIPPLE, DOC

The program organist from 1948 – 1960.

WHIPPORILL, PROF.

A bird expert who spoke in Doodyville; February 1958.

WHITE GOLD ENTERPRISES

The company that marketed Howdy Doody Eggs from Lakewood, New Jersey; 1950.

WHITE MANE

Film serial shown in December 1955.

WHITMAN PUBLISHING CO.

A Racine, Wisconsin, company that manufactured Howdy Doody tie-ins such as books under the Tell-a-Tale Books and Cozy Corner book labels; coloring and activity books, Frame Tray puzzles and coloring books. Among their products sold under the Whitman label were:
#1188 Howdy Doody And Clarabell Coloring Book (1955)
#1410 Howdy Doody Follow the Dots (1955)
#2018 Howdy Doody Coloring Book
#2080 Television's Famous Howdy Doody
#2093 Television's Famous Howdy Doody Coloring Book (1950)
#2111 Howdy Doody Show Punch Out Book (1952)
#2158 Howdy Doody Sticker Fun (1953)
#2165 Howdy Doody Fun Circus (1955)
#2169 Howdy Doody Fun Book (1951)
#2176 Television's Famous Howdy Doody Coloring Book
#2187 Television's Famous Howdy Doody Fun Book (1953)
#2195 Television's Famous Howdy Doody Sticker Fun (1951)
#2918 Howdy Doody Coloring Book (1954)
#2953 Howdy Doody Coloring Book (1957).

WIDGEON, LULIE BELLE

A marionette and the owner of the Chicapoodle in 1952.

WIEN, LYNDA

One of the writers during the revival series.

WILDCAT WILBUR

Replacement for Buffalo Bob in July 1955. Offended most Doodyville residents. Replaced by Bison Bill.

WILL MY DOG BE PROUD OF ME?

1955 78 rpm Little Golden Record #R219B originally sold for $.25 and the lyrics were written by Howard Davis and music by Robert Nicholson. The flip side was Look! Look! by Steve de Baum.

WILLIAM MORRIS AGENCY

Contracted Buffalo Bob for NBC.

WILLIE WINKUM

See: WINKUM, Willie.

WINDER-FINDER

A machine introduced in July 1957. It found missing people.

WINDY

Enormous English sheep dog, companion of Capt. Windy Scuttlebutt.

WING DING

A 1952 prop built by Scott Brinker, designed to measure cheers and applause for the Presidential candidates. (Forerunner of the applause meter on Queen For a Day show?)

WINKUM, WILLIE

A May 1956 character that decided to build a hotel in Doodyville.

WINTERSPRING, PRINCESS SUMMERFALL

She was introduced as a puppet, and the first female character on the program, in October 1950. She was suggested by Martin Stone, named by Edward Kean, designed by Milt Neil, and constructed by Scott Brinker, with voice and controls performed by Rhonda Mann. Like Chief Featherman, she was from the Tinka-Tonka Tribe; on the day she was born there was summer sun, fall leaves, winter snow, and spring flowers at the same time; her costume reflected this. Her magic-power necklace allowed her to forsee the future.
The second princess came to life in July 1952. Played by Judy Tyler. The live princess was created and cast by Roger Muir. One of the decisions to make the marionette come alive was the poor marketing response of the puppet. This second princess was promoted to Queen Mother of the tribe. The third Tinka-Tonka Princess was crowned as Princess Summerfall Winterspring on February 24, 1954, and played by Gina Genardi.

WIRECRAFT INC.

Manufactured Sun-Ray developing papers and a series of six Howdy Doody negatives that could be used with the camera.

WISHELL

A magic whistle that can grant wishes; used in a June 1956 show.

WISHY-WASHY

See: S.S. Wishy-Washy.

WISKER-FRISKER-DOODLE

Demonstration given to Gabby Hayes by Clarabell in October 1955.

WITCH HAZEL

Was not allowed to march in the Easter parade with a football helmet. April 1960 show.

WITCHCRAFT CO.

Long Island City company selling Howdy Doody Sun-Ray brand pictures and extra developing papers in the 1950s.

WIZARD

Center of a series of December 1955 programs where he played tricks on Doodyville residents; returned in February 1956.

WIZARD OF WHAT

Character introduced in September 1958 to counter activities of Sandra Witch.

WOLF PRINTING COMPANY

A division of Western Publishing Company and the printers of the Poll Parrot Comics.

WOLLENSCHLAGER, ADOLF

An actor so christened by Buffalo Bob in the Old-Time Movies. The name was also that of a friend of Buffalo Bob.

WONDER BREAD

A division of Continental Baking Company. They were a sponsor and premium maker. Their premiums included:
 American History end seal album
Flip-Up Badges (2 sizes)
 Paper Hat — "Howdy Doody says eat Wonder Bread, it's my favorite"
 Bread End Seals and Album
    Series 1 - Howdy Doody Wonder Balloon Parade for 16 seals
    Series 2 - Howdy Doody Circus Album for 15 seals
    Series 3 - Howdy Doody's Wonder-Land Game for 16 labels
 Cardboard character puppets with and without loafs of bread in their hands
 President of all the kids in the United States end seal ballots (1948).

WONDERLAND COSTUMES

Manufactured a Clarabell Playsuit.

WONG, MR.

Judge in the September 1958 Doodyville camera contest.

WORTHINGTON WORM

An October 1955 arrival in Doodyville.

WUZZY

A pygmy who stowed away in a case of bananas sent to the Howdy Doody circus. He became an attraction in the Museum of Natural History African Village.

X, MR.

1948: Was Double Doody running against Howdy for president. Never spoke, but his campaign manager, Heffleseniffer Booglegut, stated that Mr. X wanted 100 days of school a week and ice cream once every five years, his platform included the abolishment of comic books. In 1952, Mr. X was played by John J. Fedoozle.
CANADA: Claude Roe was his voice in the Canadian version of the Howdy Doody show from November 1954.

XENON

The planet Dilly Dally dreamed about in a Dell comic. He and Howdy were captured as spies. They were rescued by Flub-A-Dub, who had been left there in a previous dream.

YODSTIK, KING

King in Urli, Tibet, that called on Howdy and Buffalo Bob to solve a mystery in May 1958.

YORKIN, BUD

Stage manager for the Howdy Doody show in 1949, and later the producer of *All in the Family*. He won two Emmy awards; in 1959 in Best Writing of a Single Musical or Variety Program for "An Evening with Fred Astaire"; and in 1960 in Outstanding Directorial Achievement for "The Jack Benny Hour Specials." He directed several movies: *Best of Spike Jones* Vol. 1 & 2 (1954), *Start the Revolution Without Me* (1970); *The Thief Who Came to Dinner* (1973); *Twice in a Lifetime* (1985); and *Arthur 2: On the Rocks* (1988).

ZEKE

Conceived by Howard Davis in 1954; one of two bear cubs found in the snow. Main character in a Golden Book story.

ZINGO-CYCLE

A large unicycle that Clarabell rode. Appeared on a 1951 Howdy Doody Magic Trading Card.

ZIPPY

Chimpanzee who met the Howdy Doody cast at a Kellogg's convention in New Orleans at the end of 1952. Zippy took a strong dislike to Mr. Bluster and attacked the puppet each time he saw him. He competed with Flub-A-Dub as the Doodyville Number One Animal star on the show (January 1955).

ZOOM ZOOM, KING

Character in a November – December 1955 series. He owned a magic drum.

ZOOMO

The Human Cannonball in the circus; appeared in a 1950 Whitman Coloring Book.

ZUCONIC, DOROTHY

Created the bandaged Howdy Doody puppet to replace the Elmer (Howdy #1) version withdrawn from the program by Frank Paris in mid-1948.

Time Line

Programs and event dates are inconsistant, e.g. there are three different dates attributed to program #2000 in different works. Later show information has been gathered from *TV Guide*. The missing show numbers are unknown at this point.

December 27, 1947 Show #1: Howdy Doody shown on TV as the *Puppet Playhouse* at 5PM EST. *It's Howdy Doody Time* theme song was played and became the theme for all future shows. Acts included Nino, a sketch artist; the Gaudschmidt Brothers Poodle act; and a magician, Prince Mendez. The Peanut Gallery consists of eight children.

January 3, 1948 Show #2: Bob Keeshan's first appearance on the show as a stage hand. Another episode of "Toby Tyler at the Circus."

January 10, 1948 Show #3: Doc Whipple's first show playing an organ.

January 17, 1948 Show #4: The Frank Paris Howdy Doody makes his first appearance.

March 4, 1948 Show #11: Howdy reads the constitution and decides he is qualified to run for president. He asks viewers for campaign suggestions. The program begins a Tuesday, Thursday, and Saturday schedule from 5:00 – 6:00 PM.

March 6, 1948 Show #12: Howdy's presidential campaign begins. Other puppet characters deride the decision.

March 9, 1948 Show #13: Howdy departs to Staten Island on a secret mission. He writes his theme song *Howdy Doody for President* on Magic Manuscript Paper.

March 23, 1948 Show: Buffalo Bob offers the viewing children free "I'm For Howdy Doody" campaign buttons. Only 5,000 buttons have been ordered.

March 25, 1948 An NBC press release states that 6,304 requests for campaign buttons have been received from the New York City area.

March 26, 1948 An NBC press release states that 26,000 requests had been received for the Howdy Doody campaign buttons.

May 22, 1948 Norman Blackburn hires Velma Dawson to produce a Howdy Doody puppet.

June 1, 1948 Velma Dawson ships the new Howdy Doody puppet to NBC in New York.

June 7, 1948 NBC announces to the press that the new Howdy Doody would be appearing on the program.

June 8, 1948 Show: Cosmetic surgery bandages are taken off Howdy presenting the Dawson puppet to the public.

August 3, 1948 Show: The show has a new background set with a circus motif of bright colors. The new set is called "Howdy Doody's Big Top."

August 15, 1948 Howdy Doody starts five day/week programming.

September 2, 1948 *Gulf Road Show Starring Bob Smith* begins on NBC.

September 24, 1948 Howdy, Buffalo Bob, Clarabell, and Rhoda Mann made a personal appearance at the Jordan Marsh department store in Boston, MA. They stayed four hours seeing thousands of children and parents.

October 1, 1948 Unique Art Manufacturing Company begins sponsoring 15 minutes of the Howdy Doody Show.

November 2, 1948 Show: Howdy Doody elected president.

November 24, 1948 Show: Howdy rides a bicycle to promote bike safety.

November 30, 1948 Show: Howdy Doody's Orchestra.

December 22, 1948 Howdy Doody sings *All I Want For Christmas Is My Two Front Teeth* on the *Gulf Road Show Starring Bob Smith*.

January 14, 1949 Show: Howdy Doody inaugurated "President of all the Kids in the United States." Ben Grauer swears Howdy into office.

February 16, 1949 Show: Buffalo Bob embarks on a South American cruise to locate and bring back a Flub-A-Dub.

February 26, 1949 Howdy, Buffalo Bob, Clarabell, and Rhoda Mann make a personal appearance at Macy's department store in New York, Howdy Doody products are sold out.

May 15, 1949 Howdy, Buffalo Bob, and Clarabell in Washington, DC for I Am An American Day.

June 4, 1949 U.S. Patent applied for Howdy Doody puppet by Robert Y. Allen and Melvin Shaw.

June 17, 1949 Show: Famous fathers are hosted with their children, including Paul Winchell, Morey Amsterdam, and Bennett Cerf.

June 23, 1949 Show: First split screen broadcast with Howdy and Clarabell transmitted from Chicago and Buffalo Bob in New York.

June 30, 1949 *Gulf Road Show Starring Bob Smith* final program.

July 6, 1949 Show: Howdy Doody's July Birthday.

July 21, 1949 Show: Howdy is being forced to pay Mr. Bluster 500 marbles per day. 9,990 marbles are required to keep the Flub-A-Dub in Doodyville. Howdy negotiates a trade of a new "tie-in" scarf for that day's marbles.

October 25, 1949 Show #400: Dilly Dally introduced.

November 7, 1949 Show: A wrap up of the Giddy-Giddy Water Fountain series and an end to the Bluster Brother Circus. A Halo Shampoo commercial "The Inside Story of Goldilocks and the Three Bears" is shown. Buffalo Bob announces that this is the first day that the program is shown in 12 new viewer markets including Greentree, Charlotte, Atlanta, and Birmingham. Howdy announces that Milt Neil and Chad Grothkopf will produce a Sunday newspaper comic in two weeks and the artists are introduced.

November 20, 1949 Howdy Doody Sunday Comics begins in the papers; strip is drawn by Milt Neil and Chad Grothkopf, copy by Edward Kean and Chad Grothkopf.

December 15, 1949 Sales of Howdy Doody related merchandise for 1949 top $11 million.

December 30, 1949 Show: Wrestlers Primo Carnera and Antonino Rocca visit the show to promote television matches and to teach Clarabell how to wrestle.

January 3, 1950 Howdy Doody awarded U.S. Patent #156,587.

March 17, 1950 Show #500: The Howdy Doody Boy of 1950 look alike contest is launched.

March 25, 1950 Mason Candy Bar premium brings in 250,000 responses. A response required a Mason's Coconut Candy bar wrapper and a dime.

May 20, 1950 Victor Smith appears with Buffalo Bob for several shows.

June 12, 1950 Show: Gil Lamb starts as the second Clarabell.

June 26, 1950 Show: Bob Keeshan returns as Clarabell.

July 13, 1950 Show: Norman Shelly from the *Peter Pan* Broadway cast dressed as Nan the dog, visits the program on behalf of the ASPCA.

December 31, 1950 Howdy Doody Show generates $15 million in licensed items for the year 1950.

January 1, 1951 Kagran now owns the Howdy Doody puppets, names, likenesses, and trademarks with the exception of Buffalo Bob. They begin licensing under the Kagran name.

February 22, 1951 Princess Summerfall Winterspring introduced as a new puppet.

March 1, 1951 Videodex rates the Howdy Doody Show as third most popular program on TV with a 23.7% rating, reaching 2,407,000 homes with six sponsors and a cost of $1,000/minute.

March 4, 1951 Show: Dr. Roy K. Marshall is the guest from his own show *The Nature of Things* to present the first partial eclipse of the sun on TV at 5:45 PM.

December 8, 1951 *TV Digest* Howdy Doody Coloring Contest closes.

December 22, 1951 The Howdy Doody program begins broadcasting for one hour Saturday mornings on NBC radio. The script is written by Bob Cone and guests are Milton Berle and Gabby Hayes.

December 30, 1951 Show: Winners of the *TV Digest* Howdy Doody Coloring Contest are introduced and awarded prizes.

January 28, 1952 Show #989: Clarabell is about to be inducted into the Ooragnak Tribe; Chief Thunderthud, objecting to it, plots to stop it.

February 12, 1952 Show #1000: A one hour special. The second Howdy Doody two way cross country broadcast. Rhoda Mann, Dayton Allen, Flub-A-Dub, and Howdy were in Los Angeles with the rest of the cast in New York. There was a live broadcast with Kukla, Fran, and Ollie from Chicago, the first program to reach the thousand broadcasts level. Buffalo Bob and Clarabell entertain 2,000 children in the Peanut Gallery. Guests are Ed Wynn, Milton Berle, Jack Carter, and Dave Garroway.

April 1, 1952 Show: Mr. Bluster goes to Mexico to meet Mr. X.

April 4, 1952 Show: The Inspector waits outside a cave in Mexico for Mr. Bluster and Mr. X to come out.

April 5, 1952 Show: Super Talk-O-Scope picks up Mr. Bluster talking to Mr. X and then the Talk-O-Scope blows a tube. Princess Summerfall Winterspring sings *Easter Parade*.

April 7, 1952 Show: Super Talk-O-Scope has been repaired. The Inspector is still outside the cave, but Mr. Bluster and Mr. X have left by another exit.

June 10, 1952 Show: Mr X shares his secret password with the Peanut Gallery. Clarabell supports Mr. X in the campaign. Buffalo Bob promotes bicycle safety.

June 16, 1952 Show: Buffalo Bob receives a letter from Big Ben. The letter says that the circus will be torn down and the land converted into a gravel dump.

June 17, 1952 Show: The club house must be moved to a new location. Mr. Bluster, unaware of the situation, is given control of the circus, the one thing he has always wanted.

June 18, 1952 Show: Mr. Bluster, proud of his new acquisition, renames the Howdy Doody Show, the "Mr. X Show."

June 20, 1952 Show: To Mr. Bluster's dismay, the circus is torn down and the gang moves their clubhouse.

June 23, 1952 Show: The gang has taken up residence in their new clubhouse. Mr. Bluster starts to scheme to obtain four rooms for himself.

June 1952 Bob Keeshan, Dayton Allen, Bill LeCornec, and Rhoda Mann depart from the show in a pay dispute.

June 1952 Rufus Rose starts as puppet master on the program.

July 20, 1952 Howdy Doody syndicated in Mexico and Cuba as Judi Dujdi.

August 1, 1952 Buffalo, New York, declares this day as Buffalo Bob Smith Day.

August 28, 1952 Show: Secret of the Bongo-Bongo Tree. Adventure in determining the identity of Mr. X, with appearances from Lanky Lou, Oil Well Willie, and Oscar the Professor.

November 3, 1952 Show: With Mr. X in the lead of the counted election ballots, Chief Thunderthud finds them and takes them out of town. Buffalo Bob pursues them.

November 4, 1952 Show: Howdy recruits Flub-A-Dub Jr. to help find the ballots.

November 5, 1952 Show: The ballots are recovered, and Howdy is re-elected President of all the Kids in the United States. First appearance of J. Cornelius Cobb.

June 16, 1953 Show: Capt. Scuttlebutt discovers an impostor on board his ship, Signore DoReFaSoLaTiDo and Monsieur Fontainebleau have an argument.

June 26, 1953 Show: Program test transmitted in color.

July 6, 1953 Show: Princess, Inspector Mystery.

August 28, 1953 Show: Princess with the Marble Grabber.

November 28, 1953 Blue Bonnet Sue and Howdy Doody Mystery Picture Coloring Contest ends.

December 11, 1953 Howdy and Buffalo Bob light Christmas tree at Rockefeller Center.

January 24, 1954 Show: The search is on for a new Princess. Gina Ginardi is introduced as Papoose Gina Runningwater.

January 27, 1954 Show: The search for the magical papoose continues. Thunderthud wants to punish Clarabell for placing a cactus in the Chief's bed.

January 28, 1954 Show: Papoose Hattaheela is introduced on the show.

May 28, 1954 Show #1598: Clarabell leaves Doodyville on an important mission.

May 31, 1954 Show #1599: Long absent Flub-A-Dub makes his appearance with Buffalo Bob.

June 1, 1954 Show #1600: Papoose Sunny Cloud and a performing dog try to teach Windy the dog some new tricks. Ogilive Flour Company, Limited's, Howdy Doody Play Money exchange for a BSA Bicycle expires.

June 2, 1954 Show #1601: At the Peanut Gallery, kids are given ukuleles. Buffalo Bob leads them all in a song that may bring Windy the dog back to Doodyville.

June 3, 1954 Show #1602: With Windy the dog still missing, Mr. Bluster sends a mysterious telegram to try to get the dog back for his circus.

June 4, 1954 Show #1603: The Magician, Abra-Ra-Dab, Mr. Bluster's pal, does some tricks for the Doodyville gang.

June 7, 1954 Show #1604: The Magic of Abra-Ra-Dab makes all the animals of Doodyville appear before us, Windy the dog is still missing.

June 8, 1954 Show #1605: The voices of Howdy and Mr. Bluster are all mixed up. Windy is seen through the magic crystal ball.

June 9, 1954 Show #1606: Dilly Dally writes a song to coax Windy the dog back to Doodyville.

June 10, 1954 Show #1607: Chief Thunderthud makes a Fly-Away Machine to take him high in the sky. He wants to get a bird's-eye view of Doodyville.

June 11, 1954 Show #1608: Clarabell continues the trip to the Tinka Tonka Reservation. His antics are seen through a super Talk-A-Scope.

June 14, 1954 Show #1609: The Peanut Gallery meet a new Doodyville character, Timothy Tremble.

June 15, 1954 Show #1610: The Queen Great Grandmother arrives. She brings seeds for a magic golden tree.

June 16, 1954 Show #1611: Mr. Bluster tries to give prunes instead of the magic golden tree.

June 17, 1954 Show #1612: The magic golden tree is planted.

June 18, 1954 Show #1613: Timothy Tremble disguises himself as a tree doctor when the magic golden tree becomes ill.

June 21, 1954 Show #1614: Clarabell returns from his trip to the Tinka Tonka Reservation. Buffalo Bob introduces him to the magic golden tree.

June 22, 1954 Show #1615: Timothy Tremble dresses up as an Indian princess to help Mr. Bluster fool Howdy and the gang.

June 23, 1954 Show #1616: Mr. Bluster plots with Timothy Tremble to chop down the magic golden tree.

June 24, 1954 Show #1617: Clarabell and Buffalo Bob unmask the fake Indian princess and once again upset Mr. Bluster's scheme.

June 25, 1954 Show #1618: The big event arrives. Princess Summerfall Winterspring returns to Doodyville.

June 28, 1954 Show #1619: The Princess gives Dilly Dally a magic Tooley-Stick. Buffalo Bob gets a mysterious letter from Mother Goose Land.

June 29, 1954 Show #1620: Clarabell and Howdy discover that the Tooley-Stick works surprise magic. Mr. Bluster plots to get the letter.

June 30, 1954 Show #1621: Mr Bluster helps Buffalo Bob decode the mysterious letter. The Bloop is scared away by the Tooley-Stick.

July 1, 1954 Show #1622: A search party looks for Mr. Bloop. Mr. Bluster gets a letter from Buffalo Bob. Clarabell's trick is spoiled.

July 2, 1954 Show #1624: Buffalo Bob reads the mystery letter that starts him on a trip to Mother Goose Land. Howdy and Dilly search for the missing Mr. Bloop.

July 5, 1954 Show #1624: Buffalo Bob searches for boys and girls who have visited Mother Goose Land.

The Bob Smith Show begins on TV.

July 6, 1954 Show #1625: Songs about Mother Goose characters.

July 7, 1954 Show #1626: Buffalo Bob continues his search as Clarabell acts up again.

July 8, 1954 Show #1627: Dilly Dally visits the popular corner of Little Jack Horner.

July 9, 1954 Show #1628: The Magician puts a spell on Howdy's magic book. Dilly Dally disappears on a trip to Mother Goose Land.

July 12, 1954 Show #1629: Clarabell comes to the rescue of Dilly Dally and discovers that his friend has turned into Little Boy Blue.

July 13, 1954 Show #1630: His magic still working backwards, Abra-Ka-Dab turns Clarabell into Old Mother Hubbard while Dilly Dally is tricked by Mr. Bluster.

July 14, 1954 Show #1631: Howdy and the gang plan to get the magic book from Mr. Bluster. They want to rescue Clarabell.

July 15, 1954 Show #1632: Timothy Tremble tricks Mr. Bluster. Bluster turns into the Farmer in the Dell.

July 16, 1954 Show #1633: Howdy gets the magic book back, rescues Clarabell and Mr. Bluster, and returns in time to hear Buffalo Bob report from San Francisco.

July 19, 1954 Show #1634: Buffalo Bob and the circus discover that Jump the kangaroo can't jump. Buffalo Bob brings Howdy a wall-climber for all the Peanut Gallery to see.

July 20, 1954 Show #1635: When Buffalo Bob goes to fill a prescription, Clarabell does a disappearing act with the prescription blank.

July 21, 1954 Show #1636: Timothy Tremble gets directions for a trip to the Isle of Jumbo Jangle, and forgets where he put them.

July 22, 1954 Show #1637: Capt. Scuttlebutt gets the S.S. Wishy-Washy ready for the voyage. Clarabell tries to prove that he should be a ship's captain.

July 23, 1954 Show #1638: Clarabell stows away aboard ship as Buffalo Bob follows the start of the voyage through Howdy's Tele-Periscopic Camera.

July 26, 1954 Show #1639: A new papoose comes to visit Buffalo Bob and the Doodyville gang, who are trying to find a song that will help the ailing kangaroo jump again.

July 27, 1954 Show #1640: The crew of the good ship Wishy-Washy lands on a mysterious island and Timothy Tremble meets Pow, an unhappy caveman.

July 28, 1954 Show #1641: The guests of the Peanut Gallery receive Howdy televiewers to help them find a clue to the mysterious Jingle Jungle Jumping Beans.

July 29, 1954 Show #1642: Clarabell's new idea for a jumping-bean song turns out to be the trick. All that Buffalo Bob and Howdy find is the Last Chord.

July 30, 1954 Show #1643: The ship Wishy-Washy docks in Doodyville. Timothy Tremble's on board with the Jingle Jungle Jumping Beans but has misplaced them.

August 2, 1954 Show #1644: The princess brings a rocking-horse pony to Doodyville. Buffalo Bob and Howdy discover a mystery hidden in the pony.

August 3, 1954 Show #1645: Buffalo Bob and Howdy meet Doughface Dobbin, who wants to take Hobby the pony away from Doodyville.

August 4, 1954 Show #1646: Chief Thunderthud brings an Indian wampum wagon, which is supposed to supply the marble that will save Hobby. Clarabell plays a trick on Doughface.

August 5, 1954 Show #1647: The Doodyville gang has a ceremony.

August 6, 1954 Show #1648: Mr. Bluster teams up with Doughface to get the Princess's pony; Dilly Dally warns everyone of the thickening plot.

August 9, 1954 Show #1649: Mr. Bluster plots to get the Princess but Clarabell plays a trick on him.

August 11, 1954 Show #1650: Howdy is sure he can save the pony, but can't find the magic key.

August 12, 1954 Show #1651: Clarabell tries to find the magic key, and Flub-A-Dub has a riddle that is no help to Buffalo Bob.

August 13, 1954 Show #1652: Buffalo Bob and Howdy try to get enough marbles to save the pony from being taken away from Doodyville.

August 16, 1954 Show #1653: A birthday party for Mr. Bluster turns into a real surprise.

August 17, 1954 Show #1654: Howdy reveals news about an amazing chemical that has been discovered by Uncle Louie Bluster.

Friday, 1-22-54

1

Well HD,boys & girls - &
tell me,kids,what time is
it?
HD
Yes kids,it's HD time in
Cinci,Detroit,Bklyn,S.F.
here in H'wood & every-
where - so kids,let's go.

LUDEN'S #1

Well kids from coast to
coast,here we are in
H'wood - it's many
thousands of miles from
DV,but gee the funniest
thing happened this

2

morning -
(R) Yes kids...& why?
STING
(R) Because...mystery.
Yes kids - many times big
mysteries have darkened
our doorstep in DV - & it
seems like the Mystery
Bug has followed us to
Calif.
(TO BOB)
Kawa Mystery. Kawa
Mystery Bug. Kawa Bug
Mystery. Mystery Kawa
Bug-Bug.
No, Ch Thud.
Don't interrupt me. I say

3

Kawa Mystery.
Yes Ch,I know,I just said
it,but calm down - Kids,
that Thud is so silly -
anyway kids, the Mystery
Bug has followed us here
& we have to find -
Kawa Mystery Bug. Kawa
Bug. Kawa Mosquito.
Kawa Mystery Bug, Kawa
Mystery Mosquito. 'MM'
I like that - ha.ha ha MM.
Owww - & kids,we have
to find the Mystery
Mosquito,oww I mean we
have to -
Kawa Mosquito. Kawa

4

Caterpillar. Kawa
Cacoon. Kawa Cuckoo
Cacoon. Kawa Ladybug,
Kawa Darning Needle,
Kawa Doodlebug,Kawa...
Mystery Bug. What is the
Mystery,BB, tell us..
what you stalling for,
tell us.
I-stalling? Thud,you
haven't given me a chance
to say a word. Now if
you'll promise to be
quiet, (CARD) I'll show
the Mystery to you & the
kids.
Good. I promise be quiet.

5

CB: JOINS. BOT BEHIND-
FOR THUD
Hy,C B.
How,MU clown.
Now here's the story kids-
this card has two words
on it - words we don't
understand - words we
never heard of -
DINGLESPIEL SESS-
KANIRP
Kawa DS S?
Yes - 2 mystery words.
Kawa Mystery words.
Kawa words for the birds.
Kawa Birds. Kawa
Flamingo. Kawa Yellow-

6

Bellied Sap Sucker.
(TOSSES) Kawa Pelican,
I likum pelican,his beak
hold more than his belly
can. Kawa Woodpecker,
Kawa (TOUCHES) Bald
Eagle, Kawa Cuckoo, ha
ha, Kawa Seagull-Seagull
like to be near the water.
Seagull cry 'Caw,caw,
give me water,caw,caw,
give me water,caw'.
CB: SQUIRTS.
(PUFFED - GRUNTS)
Thanks,C B - for once
your seltbot followed
orders usefully,but

Cue Cards. These six cards are the opening of the January 22, 1954 show, and are quite representative of the show.

©BOB SMITH, FROM THE SCOTT BRINKER COLLECTION

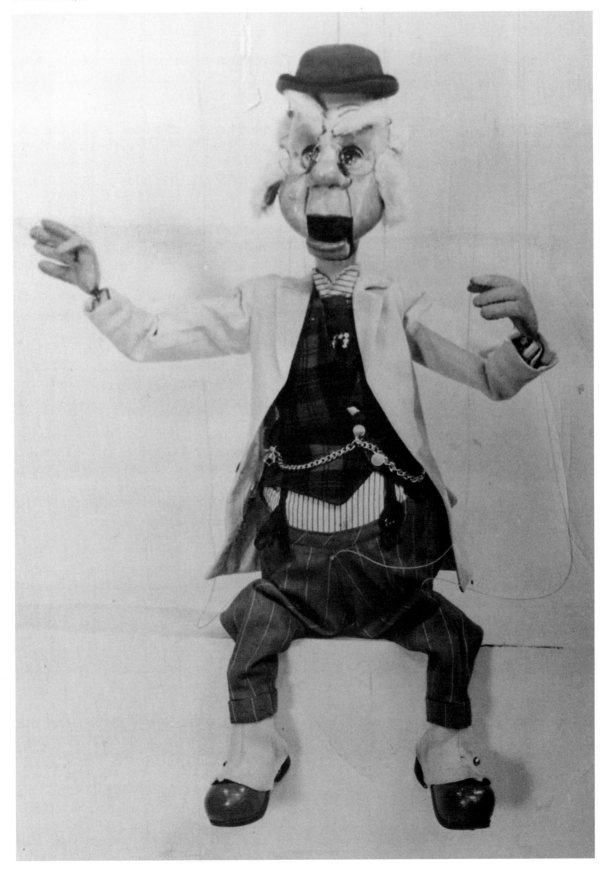

Mr. Bluster speaking to the peanuts.

August 18, 1954 Show #1655: The Battle of the Blusters begins when Clarabell nearly blows up Howdy's circus with his version of the chemical.

August 19, 1954 Show #1656: Clarabell tries with his seltzer bottle to erase the horseshoe imprint on Buster B. Bluster.

August 20, 1954 Show #1657: The Battle of the Blusters finds Don Jose Bluster looking for Uncle Louie Bluster in Hawaii. The Peanut Gallery tries to guess the properties of the mystery chemical.

August 23, 1954 Show #1658: Phineas T. Bluster and Clarabell try Plan Tweedle-Deedle in an effort to prove Bluster is an impostor.

August 24, 1954 Show #1659: Dilly Dally is promised lots of ice cream for helping Phineas with the mystery chemical.

August 25, 1954 Show #1660: Howdy, Oil Well Willie, and the kids attend a new radio show, "Bluster's Baloney Bonanza."

August 26, 1954 Show #1661: Don Jose Bluster teaches the hula to an ostrich and Buster B. Bluster makes a startling announcement.

August 27, 1954 Show #1662: All the Doodyville gang are amazed when they learn the nature of the mystery drug.

August 30, 1954 Show #1663: A stranger comes to town with plans to build a factory in the center of Doodyville Park.

August 31, 1954 Show #1664: Clarabell and Howdy try to prevent the stranger from taking over the park.

September 1, 1954 Show #1665: Buffalo Bob and Chief Thunderthud each tell a story to prove ownership of Doodyville Park. They call Grandpa Doody out in California.

September 2, 1954 Show #1666: Mr. Bluster teams up with the stranger. Buffalo Bob reaches Grandpa Doody.

September 3, 1954 Show #1667: Buffalo Bob finds a magic stick that may save Doodyville Park or spoil everything.

September 6, 1954 Show #1668: Cornelius Cobb hosts the program; Bob Smith suffered a heart attack that morning. With the danger to Doodyville Park growing, Buffalo Bob goes to Paris, France, to find the missing history book.

September 7, 1954 Show #1669: Buffalo Bob's search takes him to Arabia. Howdy, at home, finds the missing history book.

September 8, 1954 Show #1670: The Inspector has a surprise for Howdy and Buffalo Bob. Grandpa Doody has an adventure.

September 9, 1954 Show #1671: Chief Thunderthud gets tricked into an unexpected trip to Bavaria.

September 10, 1954 Show #1672: Mr. Bluster wins and loses, at the same time, his claim to Doodyville Park.

September 20, 1954 Show #1678: Happy Felton is in charge of Doodyville while Buffalo Bob is ill. Capt. Scuttlebutt builds an ark to store new animals for the circus.

September 21, 1954 Show #1679: Hepzibah the goat pays a visit to Happy Felton and Gabby.

September 22, 1954 Show #1680: Mr. Bluster plots to become the skipper of the ark.

September 23, 1954 Show #1681: Construction continues on the ark.

September 24, 1954 Show #1682: The Doodyville gang sing their own version of *Polly Wolly Doodle*.

September 27, 1954 Show #1683: Ted Brown hosts.

September 28, 1954 Show #1684: Ted Brown hosts.

September 29, 1954 Show #1685: Ted Brown hosts.

September 30, 1954 Show #1686: Ted Brown hosts.

October 1, 1954 Show #1687: Ted Brown hosts.

October 4, 1954 Show #1688: Ted Brown continues as the big wheel in Doodyville. A new papoose comes to town.

October 5, 1954 Show #1689: Mr. Bluster decides that he'll get the circus animals before Howdy can. Ted Brown is in charge of Doodyville.

October 6, 1954 Show #1690: Captain Scuttlebutt unveils the model of a new boat and appoints himself captain.

October 7, 1954 Show #1691: Mr. Bluster promises Clarabell a starring roll in his new circus. Ted Brown hosts.

October 8, 1954 Show #1692: Clarabell learns to become an animal trainer; Doodyville plans an election.

October 11, 1954 Show #1693: Ted Brown and Gabby Hayes host.

October 12, 1954 Show #1694: Ted Brown and Gabby Hayes host. Paul Winchell and Jerry Mahoney visit Gabby Hayes on the program.

October 13, 1954 Show #1695: Ted Brown and Gabby Hayes host.

October 14, 1954 Show #1696: Ted Brown and Gabby Hayes host.

October 15, 1954 Show #1697: Ted Brown and Gabby Hayes host.

October 18, 1954 Show #1698: Ted Brown and Gabby Hayes host.

October 19, 1954 Show #1699: Ted Brown and Gabby Hayes host.

October 20, 1954 Show #1700: Ted Brown and Gabby Hayes host.

October 21, 1954 Show #1701: Ted Brown and Gabby Hayes host.

October 22, 1954 Show #1702: Ted Brown and Gabby Hayes host.

October 25, 1954 Show #1703: Clarabell makes Gabby Hayes watch a Wisker-Frisker-Doodle demonstration.

October 26, 1954 Show #1704: Chief Thunderthud sends five pounds of fresh water taffy to Murgatroid the fish.

October 27, 1954 Show #1705: The crew eats a magic dinner.

October 29, 1954 Show #1706: Bison Bill finds the reducing machine.

November 1, 1954 Show #1707: The Princess returns to Doodyville and joins the search for the mysterious flying Gnu. The Princess is Gina Ginardi. Gabby Hayes heads the show.

November 2, 1954 Show #1708: Mr. Bluster gets caught in a storm.

November 3, 1954 Show #1709: Howdy contacts the Arkadoodle and learns of the great tidal wave.

November 4, 1954 Show #1710: The gang on the Arkadoodle explores the mysterious mountain and meets up with "Paddle the Gnu."

November 5, 1954 Show #1711: Bison Bill and Howdy tackle the puzzle of the argyle socks for Paddle the Gnu.

November 11, 1954 Show #1715: Mr. Bluster flies backwards on Boomer Zoomer.

November 12, 1954 Show #1716.

November 15, 1954 Show #1717: Gabby Hayes has a fantastic dream about two talking bears.

November 15, 1954 First performance of the Canadian Howdy Doody show, from Toronto.

November 16, 1954 Show #1718: Clarabell finds mysterious footprints in the snow.

November 17, 1954 Show #1719: Howdy meets amazing animal bear cubs, Hyde and Zeke.

November 18, 1954 Show #1720: Gabby Hayes and Bison Bill learn about King Zoom Zoom and his magic drum.

November 19, 1954 Show #1721: Mr. Bluster runs off with Howdy's circus animals.

November 22, 1954 Show #1722: Gabby Hayes is still part of the Doodyville gang.

November 23, 1954 Show #1723: Clarabell's antics delight the Peanut Gallery.

November 24, 1954 Show #1724: Bison Bill continues to substitute for Buffalo Bob.

November 25, 1954 Show #1725: The Doodyville gang continues its adventures on the Arkadoodle.

November 26, 1954 Show #1726: Mr. Bluster continues to upset the plans of Howdy and his gang.

November 29, 1954 Show #1727: While aboard the Arkadoodle, Gabby Hayes finds a mysterious box in the middle of the ocean.

November 30, 1954 Show #1728: The Arkadoodle heads for India in search of a dancing elephant.

December 1, 1954 Show #1729: Clarabell spoils a Bluster trick. Gabby Hayes meets a maharaja.

December 2, 1954 Show #1730: Mambo the elephant is introduced as Dilly Dally returns to Doodyville.

December 3, 1954 Show #1731: Mr. Bluster tries to deceive Howdy and Bison Bill by pretending to help get Mambo back to Doodyville.

December 6, 1954 Show #1732: Mr. Bluster flies to the Marahaja's palace to take the dancing elephant from Howdy and Gabby Hayes.

December 7, 1954 Show #1733: Mambo the elephant disappears. Howdy and Bison Bill head the search.

December 8, 1954 Show #1734: Clarabell plays a trick on Howdy. The mystery of Mambo is solved.

December 9, 1954 Show #1735: The search continues for an unusual present for the Maharaja. Gabby gets an idea for a surprise gift.

December 10, 1954 Show #1736: The Maharaja must decide whether the elephant can join Howdy's circus. The Arkadoodle sets out to find a mysterious new animal.

December 13, 1954 Show #1737: Howdy, Captain, and Dilly discover that the Arkadoodle is trapped in the Lost and Lonesome Lagoon.

December 14, 1954 Show #1738: Clarabell plays a trick on Howdy and Bison Bill. Mr Bluster flies the Boomer Zoomer to the Lost and Lonesome Lagoon.

December 15, 1954 Show #1739: Dilly Dally finds that he must return to Doodyville in a hurry. Mr. Bluster gets the dinosaur.

December 16, 1954 Show #1740: The Princess tries to help Howdy and Dilly Dally charm the dinosaur.

December 17, 1954 Show #1741: Dilly Dally saves the dinosaur for Howdy's circus and the Arkadoodle starts back to Doodyville.

December 20, 1954 Show #1742: All the new animals: Paddle the Gnu, the bears Hyde and Zeke, Tom Turtle, Mambo the Elephant, and Pitty-Pat the Dinosaur are so happy to be in Doodyville that they sing a song.

December 21, 1954 Show #1743: Howdy brings his preparations for Christmas. Clarabell brings him a mysterious tree.

December 22, 1954 Show #1744: Mr. Bluster plots to spoil Howdy's Christmas.

December 23, 1954 Show #1745: Howdy and Bison Bill try to get Mr. Bluster to wish everyone a Merry Christmas.

December 24, 1954 Show #1746: Howdy and all the Doodyville gang hold their annual Christmas party.

December 27, 1954 Show #1747: Howdy invents a New Year's eve game. Clarabell seems to have disappeared.

December 28, 1954 Show #1748: Howdy and Bison Bill try to solve the mystery of Clarabell's disappearance. Gabby Hayes hosts.

December 29, 1954 Show #1749: Clarabell returns as Howdy and Gabby discover a Bluster scheme.

December 30, 1954 Show #1750: Howdy's New Year's game is played by the Doodyville circus, and there's a surprise winner.

December 31, 1954 Show #1751: Howdy starts his eighth year with a New Year's party.

January 3, 1955 Show #1752: The Princess sings the new *Howdy Doody Mambo* as the new mystery begins.

January 4, 1955 Show #1753: Flub-A-Dub and Zippy the chimpanzee compete for the title of Doodyville's number one animal star.

January 5, 1955 Show #1754: Eleven suspects turn up in the double alphabet-alphabet mystery-mystery.

January 6, 1955 Show #1755: Winkle Van Rip der Flugle and his twin Wendell make a surprise appearance.

January 7, 1955 Show #1756: Dr. Singasong is the 16th suspect in the giant Doodyville mystery.

January 10, 1955 Show #1757: The alphabet mystery delivers four clues by parachute.

January 11, 1955 Show #1758: Clarabell & the dinosaur join the hunt for the mystery hero.

January 12, 1955 Show #1759: The Bluster Bounce is introduced in Doodyville.

January 13, 1955 Show #1760: The mystery gadget is all assembled but no one is able to solve the identity of the mystery hero.

January 14, 1955 Show #1761: The mystery hero turns out to be a very welcome surprise guest.

January 17, 1955 Show #1762: From his camp up in Pioneer Village, Buffalo Bob comes in to catch up on the Doodyville goings. Here to welcome him back are Howdy and the old gang, and the new faces of Bison Bill, the Tinka Tonka Princess, and a host of animal additions.

January 24, 1955 Show #1767: Mr. Bluster plots to find Buffalo Bob's secret hideaway and Professor Bellringer returns to Doodyville with a mysterious suitcase.

January 25, 1955 Show #1768: Howdy learns of the professor's new invention as he tries to solve the mystery of the suitcase.

January 26, 1955 Show #1769: Clarabell plays a trick on a new arrival.

January 27, 1955 Show #1770: Buzz Beaver plots against the Doodyville gang, but Mr. Bluster's plans backfire. Buffalo Bob appears in a remote from Pioneer Village.

January 28, 1955 Show #1771: Buffalo Bob and Bison Bill try out the professor's invention; Mr. Bluster makes an important decision.

January 31, 1955 Show #1772: Buffalo Bob, from Pioneer Village, reveals a plan to keep Buzz Beaver in check.

February 1, 1955 Show #1773: The weather report from Buffalo Bob at Pioneer Village predicts a rainstorm.

February 2, 1955 Show #1774: Chief Thunderthud gives an Indian head-dress to each member of the Peanut Gallery as part of a special ceremony.

February 3, 1955 Show #1775: Howdy Doody and Bison Bill help Buffalo Bob to give Buzz Beaver the surprise of his life.

February 4, 1955 Show #1776: Mr. Bluster prepares a trick plan and a rainbow comes to Doodyville. Will the invention work?

February 7, 1955 Show #1777: The professor's invention brings colors down from the sky.

February 8, 1955 Show #1778: Buffalo Bob and Howdy have a plan, but Clarabell's trick turns everything upside down in Doodyville.

February 9, 1955 Show #1779: Chief Thunderthud has a surprise, and Doodyville is all mixed up: grass is purple and the trees are pink.

February 10, 1955 Show #1780: Bison Bill's hair turns a new hue as the Princess tries Indian magic. Mr. Bluster gets a big surprise. Buffalo Bob is seen in a split screen from Pioneer Village.

February 11, 1955 Show #1781: Buffalo Bob and Howdy solve the rainbow mish-mush, and Dilly Dally makes a mystifying discovery.

February 14, 1955 Show #1782: The ancient Tinka-Tonka crown disappears and Dilly Dally finds a scarf with a mysterious message written on it.

February 15, 1955 Show #1783: Buffalo Bob sings a song of advice: *Keep your Sunny Up.* The scarf is discovered to have magic qualities.

February 16, 1955 Show #1784: Bison Bill asks Dilly Dally to return the magic scarf before Mr. Bluster and Buzz Beaver can carry out a plan to steal it.

February 17, 1955 Show #1785: Mr. Bluster has hilarious results when he works some magic on Chief Thunderthud.

February 18, 1955 Show #1786: Clarabell and Mambo the Elephant do a dance. Buffalo Bob tells the kids about Daniel Boone.

February 21, 1955 Show #1787: The Doodyvillers realize that the Princess has no name.

February 22, 1955 Show #1788: Chief Thunderthud says "How!" to the "salted peanuts" in the gallery.

February 23, 1955 Show #1789: Mr. Bluster is up to his old tricks, but Clarabell gets in the way.

February 24, 1955 Show #1790: The Princess is still hoping to be crowned Princess Summerfall Winterspring.

February 28, 1955 Show #1791: Princess Summerfall Winterspring's gown is blown away.

March 1, 1955 Show #1792: Buffalo Bob tells Dilly Dally to return the scarf but Dilly discovers that it can bring him all the lollipops he wants.

March 2, 1955 Show #1793: Mr. Bluster and Buzz Beaver team up to get the magic scarf.

March 3, 1955 Show #1794: Clarabell joins Mr. Bluster and Buzz Beaver when Mr. Bluster turns Chief Thunderthud into a puppy.

March 4, 1955 Show #1795: Mr. Bluster invents a magic scarf snatcher.

March 7, 1955 Show #1796: Mr. Bluster's invention snatches the scarf, but Dilly gets it back.

March 8, 1955 Show #1797: Capt. Scuttlebutt tricks Dilly into giving up the scarf. From his home in Pioneer Village, Buffalo Bob comforts Dilly.

March 9, 1955 Show #1798: Clarabell, disguised as Mr. Dinkelweather, fools Howdy, Buffalo Bob, and Bison Bill.

March 10, 1955 Show #1799: Mr. Bluster pretends to be friendly, but Buffalo Bob and Howdy see through the ruse.

March 11, 1955 Show #1800: Buffalo Bob pretends to be a fortune teller and persuades Dilly to give up the magic scarf.

March 14, 1955 Show #1801: Dilly Dally resigns as mayor.

March 15, 1955 Show #1802: Clarabell behaves so badly in his campaign for mayor that Buffalo Bob calls on a mysterious stranger for help.

March 15, 1955 Bob Nicholson's last performance as Clarabell.

March 16, 1955 Show #1803: The stranger turns out to be none other than Mr. Nick, mayor of Clarabell's home town.

March 16, 1955 Lew Anderson starts in the role of Clarabell.

March 17, 1955 Show #1804: Clarabell disappears. Mr. Bluster and Tizzy the Dinosaur run for mayor.

March 18, 1955 Show #1805: Bison Bill takes the candidates to Clown Town to learn to behave.

March 21, 1955 Show #1806: Dilly Dally has to be rescued by Paddle the Gnu when he floats away.

March 22, 1955 Show #1807: Mr. Nick writes a campaign song. Clarabell learns a lesson in Clown Town.

March 23, 1955 Show #1808: Mr. Bluster rejects both campaign songs and sets about writing one himself. The race for mayor gets hotter and hotter!

March 24, 1955 Show #1809: There's a big parade that includes the Peanut Gallery as the campaign enters its final stretch.

March 25, 1955 Show #1810: The new mayor of Doodyville is announced. Bison Bill departs Doodyville.

March 28, 1955 Show #1811: Although he loves Doodyville, Mr. Nick announces that he plans to leave Doodyville to form an orchestra.

March 29, 1955 Show #1812: Buffalo Bob finds a 25-piece orchestra and sends it off to Doodyville. Buffalo Bob appears from his home in Pioneer Village.

March 30, 1955 Show #1813: Clarabell is so excited about the presents he gives to Howdy, Mr. Nick, and Chief Thunderthud he falls into a big pie.

March 31, 1955 Show #1814: A blizzard prevents Buffalo Bob from getting musical notes through to Doodyville. Happy Talk must get them.

April 1, 1955 Show #1815: Clarabell tries to disrupt the performance of the orchestra led by Buffalo Bob and Mr. Nick. The actual 25-piece studio orchestra plays the *Howdy Doody Suite* for the audience. The children's concert will become a monthly feature.

April 4, 1955 Show #1816: Mayor Bluster forbids the wearing of Easter bonnets and declares open season on Easter bunnies.

April 5, 1955 Show #1817: Buffalo Bob and Mr. Nick try to protect the rabbits. Tizzy the Dinosaur and the Princess wear bonnets.

April 6, 1955 Show #1818: Mr. Bluster invents a rabbit snatcher and puts Clarabell in charge of the hutch.

April 7, 1955 Show #1819: Buffalo Bob sends a fresh supply of pork eating rabbits in from Pioneer Village.

April 8, 1955 Show #1820: Mr. Nick and Buffalo Bob seem successful in saving the bunnies. Princess Summerfall Winterspring sings *Easter Parade*.

April 11, 1955 Show #1821: Capt. Scuttlebutt finds a bottle with a note inside. It tells of buried treasure.

April 12, 1955 Show #1822: Howdy tells Buffalo Bob to build a time machine.

April 13, 1955 Show #1823: Mayor Bluster orders Paddle the Gnu to start a rainstorm and hold up work on the Time-a-Tub.

April 14, 1955 Show #1824: Clarabell sneaks into the Time-a-Tub.

April 15, 1955 Show #1825: Clarabell lands in the stone age.

April 18, 1955 Show #1826: The Princess and Chief Thunderthud meet Yankee Doodle.

April 19, 1955 Show #1827: Capt. Kadoodle captures the Princess.

April 20, 1955 Show #1828: Buffalo Bob plans to rescue the Princess.

April 21, 1955 Show #1829: Chief Thunderthud finds Mr. Bluster's ancestor, Thaddeus, imprisoned in a pillory in early Doodyville.

April 22, 1955 Show #1830: An attempt is made to rescue the Princess and find the hidden treasure.

April 23, 1955 Show #1831: Carnival Cal is hired to manage the Doodyville Fair.

April 26, 1955 Show #1832: The fair opens — and all the lights go out.

April 27, 1955 Show #1833: When another disaster occurs at the fair, Doodyville suspects Chief Thunderthud.

April 28, 1955 Show #1834: As Clarabell engages in more high jinx at the fair, there's another mishap.

April 29, 1955 Show #1835: Buffalo Bob tries to solve the mystery.

May 1, 1955 Show #1836: A generous stranger named Harvey Hotplate offers to sponsor a Doodyville invention contest.

May 3, 1955 Show #1837: Mr. Bluster plots with Buzz Beaver and Clarabell to keep Tizzy the Dinosaur from winning the invention contest.

May 4, 1955 Show #1838: Mr. Nick and Dilly Dally have strange results when they try out their invention on Mr. Bluster.

May 5, 1955 Show #1839: Mr. Bluster demonstrates his Great Grandfather Gravity Loser, and thanks to Howdy Doody and Chief Thunderthud, has a high time.

May 6, 1955 Show #1840: Buffalo Bob and Harvey Hotplate decide on the winner of the Doodyville invention contest. Buffalo Bob appears from his home in Pioneer Village.

May 9, 1955 Show #1841: Chief Thunderthud, the Princess, Harvey Hotplate, Sandy McTavish, and Clarabell visit Buffalo Bob at his Pioneer Village home.

May 10, 1955 Show #1842: Mr. Bluster claims that Buffalo Bob isn't a pioneer. He, Phineas Bluster is the true grandson of Buffalo Tom.

May 11, 1955 Show #1843: Buffalo Bob tries to prove he's a real Pioneer by guessing the mystic-riddle animals.

May 12, 1955 Show #1844: Mr. Bluster asks the Inspector for help. Clarabell and Chief Thunderthud set off for Africa.

May 13, 1955 Show #1845: The last mystery animal is a catfish with one glass eye. Buffalo Bob tries to catch it.

May 16, 1955 Show #1846: The fishing contest continues with Princess Summerfall Winterspring and Chief Thunderthud performing rain dances.

May 17, 1955 Show #1847.

May 18, 1955 Show #1848: Nick and Howdy commission Capt. Scuttlebutt.

May 19, 1955 Show #1849: Everyone in Doodyville is busy fishing. Clarabell falls into the lake.

May 20, 1955 Show #1850: Buffalo Bob makes a find.

May 23, 1955 Show #1851: Peddler Pete sells Tizzy a wishing lamp.

May 24, 1955 Show #1852: Johnny Genie brings the Princess down.

May 25, 1955 Show #1853: Clarabell buys some laughing-crying juice and gives it to Sandy McTavish. Buffalo Bob appears from his home in Pioneer Village.

May 26, 1955 Show #1854: Chief Thunderthud and Clarabell visit Central Park.

May 27, 1955 Show #1855: Capt. Scuttlebutt plots to steal the lamp.

May 30, 1955 Show #1856: The town is in an uproar — Dilly Dally is stranded on the moon. Buffalo Bob appears from his home in Pioneer Village.

May 31, 1955 Show #1857: Mr. Nick tries to cheer up the Peanut Gallery with a song.

June 1, 1955 Show #1858: Capt. Scuttlebutt steers his boat into a hurricane.

June 2, 1955 Show #1859: Buffalo Bob sends Flub-A-Dub and the Inspector on a rescue mission in the Air-O-Doodle.

June 3, 1955 Show #1860: Johnny Genie says goodbye to the gang.

June 6, 1955 Show #1861: Howdy startles the town with his announcement that he doesn't like Doodyville anymore.

June 7, 1955 Show #1862: Dandy Doody, Howdy's double, turns up with plans to move the gang to Dandyville.

June 8, 1955 Show #1863: Dandy Doody convinces some of the Doodyvillers that Dandyville would be a better place to live.

June 9, 1955 Show #1864: Mr. Nick and Chief Thunderthud discover that there's more to Dandy Doodle's plan than meets the eye.

June 10, 1955 Show #1865: Buffalo Bob learns that Dandyville boasts an even bigger man than he: Elephant Bob.

June 13, 1955 Show #1866: Doodyville's in an uproar. Elephant Bob from Dandyville has come to town.

June 14, 1955 Show #1867: Mr. Nick overhears Capt. Scuttlebutt and Dandy Doody's plot to get him to move to Dandyville.

June 15, 1955 Show #1868: Chief Thunderthud, Clarabell, Flub-A-Dub, Mambo the Elephant, Dilly Dally, and Tizzy the Dinosaur desert Doodyville for a new life in Dandyville.

June 16, 1955 Show #1869: Dilly Dally's report is so frightening that Capt. Scuttlebutt goes off to bring him back.

June 17, 1955 Show #1870: Dandy Doody and Elephant Bob are unmasked. Mr. Bluster has disappeared with Buffalo Bob's pet dog, Happy Talk.

June 20, 1955 Show #1871: Inspector John J. Fedoozle is given one more chance to prove his worth as a private eye. Buffalo Bob is in New York searching for Happy Talk and Mr. Bluster.

June 21, 1955 Show #1872: When the Inspector fails to catch the flower thief, Dilly gets the chance to be a detective.

June 22, 1955 Show #1873: Dilly is busy solving an old mystery. Mr. Nick and Howdy have a problem.

June 23, 1955 Show #1874: The person who discovers the stolen seltzer bottle and horn will be Doodyville's new detective. The show kicks off the Doody Dime-A-Day compaign in support of the March of Dimes. Mr. Bluster steals the map to Pioneer Village's location.

June 24, 1955 Show #1875: Clarabell is running wild with a new seltzer bottle that shoots a mile.

June 27, 1955 Show #1876: Buffalo Bob and Trapper Tyrone are on a desert island. In Doodyville, the search is on for the man who stole Clarabell's horn.

June 28, 1955 Show #1877: Capt. Scuttlebutt pretends to look for Clarabell's horn.

June 29, 1955 Show #1878: Buffalo Bob finds two beachcombers on the island, but neither of them is Happy Talk or Mr. Bluster.

June 30, 1955 Show #1879: The Captain arrives with Clarabell's horn.

July 1, 1955 Show #1880: Buffalo Bob finds Happy Talk; Mr. Nick reveals the real thief.

July 4, 1955 Show #1881: Clarabell finds a letter from the Department of Pioneers in his letter-getter.

July 5, 1955 Show #1882: Wildcat Wilbur prepares to take over as Buffalo Bob leaves for Muddle Town.

July 6, 1955 Show #1883: Mr. Bluster fires Tizzy the Dinosaur and puts Buzz Beaver in the job.

July 7, 1955 Show #1884: The Princess delivers an important note to Mr. Nick.

July 8, 1955 Show #1885: Sandy McTavish is so disgusted with Wildcat Wilbur that he decides to return to Scotland.

July 11, 1955 Show #1886: Chief Thunderthud brings a map to Buffalo Bob in Pioneer Village.

July 13, 1955 Show #1887: Clarabell is fired as Doodyville's clown and Mr. Bluster is asked to take his place.

July 14, 1955 Show #1888: Prof. Bubbleschmidt gives Flub-A-Dub an intelligence test.

July 15, 1955 Show #1889: Howdy and Mr. Nick demand a special mayoral election.

July 18, 1955 Show #1890: Bison Bill returns to Doodyville and takes over the Peanut Gallery. Buffalo Bob is still in his Pioneer Village home.

July 19, 1955 Show #1891: Buffalo Bob builds a Weather-Wiffer-Sniffer.

July 20, 1955 Show #1892: Mr. Bluster can't seem to stop his African eggplant from growing.

July 21, 1955 Show #1893: Capt. Scuttlebutt's African-Awake-A-Week nut keeps Dilly Dally from sleeping.

July 22, 1955 Show #1894: At the picnic, Clarabell and Chief Thunderthud enter a pie eating contest.

July 25, 1955 Show #1895: Buffalo Bob drinks some African Confusy-Doozy juice.

July 26, 1955 Show #1896: Capt. Scuttlebutt and Buzz Beaver plan to steal the Weather-Wiffer-Sniffer.

July 27, 1955 Show #1897: Mr. Bluster receives an African Flutterby.

July 28, 1955 Show #1898: The Princess sings *Echo Song*.

July 29, 1955 Show #1899: The gang says goodbye to Bison Bill.

August 1, 1955 Show #1900: Mr. Nick returns from Clown Town and Mr. Bluster starts a paper called the Bluster Bullet.

August 2, 1955 Show #1901: Mr. Bluster has been printing too many lies, so Howdy decides to start another newspaper. He chooses Buffalo Bob as editor.

August 3, 1955 Show #1902: Mr. Bluster owns the only inkwell in Doodyville. Capt. Scuttlebutt sails for a supply of paper for the Doodyville Bugle.

August 4, 1955 Show #1903: Chief Thunderthud and Sandy McTavish go searching for an inkwell.

August 5, 1955 Show #1904: Capt. Scuttlebutt switches to Mr. Bluster's side in the case of the warring newspapers.

August 8, 1955 Show #1905: Clarabell returns to Doodyville. Sandy McTavish and Mr. Bluster make a deal. Buffalo Bob appears from his camp in Pioneer Village.

August 9, 1955 Show #1906: Buffalo Bob publishes the first edition of the Doodyville Bugle, and Prof. Fitznoodle arrives to try and turn water into ink.

August 10, 1955 Show #1907: The Captain joins Mr. Bluster's side. Sandy McTavish is out to recover his walking stick.

August 11, 1955 Show #1908: All seems lost for Buffalo Bob when the Captain arrives with the paper for the first edition of the Bluster Bullet.

August 12, 1955 Show #1909: Prof. Fitznoodle turns oil into ink and Sandy offers a brand new oil well to Doodyville.

August 15, 1955 Show #1910: Howdy and Dilly Dally try to find out about the secret pets that Sandy brought back from Scotland.

August 16, 1955 Show #1911: Clarabell frees Tim the Leprechaun.

August 17, 1955 Show #1912: Tim the Leprechaun plays tricks.

August 18, 1955 Show #1913: Tim visits Buffalo Bob while Mr. Bluster plots with the Captain.

August 19, 1955 Show #1914: Hyde and Zeke provide the clue that sends Buffalo Bob and Trapper Tyrone in search of the Leprechaun's gold.

August 22, 1955 Show #1915: Buffalo Bob, Trapper Tyrone, and Zippy find a clue to the gold in Dublin.

August 23, 1955 Show #1916: Howdy and Dilly Dally try to solve the second clue, but Clarabell finds the answer.

August 24, 1955 Show #1917: Mayor Bluster fires Clarabell, and appoints Tim the Leprechaun the official Doodyville clown.

August 25, 1955 Show #1918: Prof. Fitznoodle invites Mr. Nick and the Peanut Gallery to his animal farm.

August 26, 1955 Show #1919: There is a clown contest between Clarabell and Tim. Buffalo Bob and Trapper Tyrone lead a band in Germany.

August 28, 1955 Show #1920: Mr. Bluster and Capt. Scuttlebutt go to the North Pole in search of the treasure.

August 30, 1955 Show #1921: Mr. Nick opens a restaurant where Clarabell waits on tables. Dilly Dally solves the next clue.

August 31, 1955 Show #1922: Buffalo Bob, Trapper Tyrone, and Zippy arrive in darkest Africa. The Peanut Gallery sings a song about sound.

September 1, 1955 Show #1923: Chief Thunderthud demonstrates his magic eyes. Dilly Dally sings a song to Polly Parakeet.

September 2, 1955 Show #1924: Buffalo Bob solves the last riddle. Howdy and the Inspector find the Leprechaun's pot o' gold.

September 5, 1955 Show #1925: Buffalo Bob returns to Doodyville with the mysterious stranger who saved him.

September 6, 1955 Show #1926: The mystery man turns out to be a little girl named Heidi.

September 7, 1955 Show #1927: Mr. Bluster and Capt. Scuttlebutt decide that Heidi must go.

September 8, 1955 Show #1928: Mr. Nick leaves Doodyville to start an orchestra. Clarabell and Heidi help him pack.

September 9, 1955 Show #1929: The bouncing Bluster brothers are featured. The Doodyville gang makes plans for the future.

September 12, 1955 Show #1930: The program is now broadcast both in black and white and compatible color from a newly styled set. Gabby Hayes visits on his way to Europe to meet the only known Hayes without a beard. There are two color cartoons: "Ginger Nut Christmas Circus" and a serialized story "Ghost Ship," adapted from the Howdy Doody comic book, begins. The Story Book Princess is introduced and tells the story of Jigsaw, the Puzzle; Lowell Thomas Jr. begins his "Flight to Adventure" series on the program with the help of Zippy the chimp. Heidi is introduced to the kids. Princess Summerfall Winterspring sings *Freddie the Mistreated Teddy Bear* to Hyde and Zeke. Finally, Mr. Bluster announces his intention to rename Doodyville as Blusterville.

September 13, 1955 Show #1931: Watch for the pet shop with live animals, with well stocked cookie jars, a Hatch-A-Hutch, Doodyville Park, and other new spots of interest.

September 14, 1955 Show #1932: Mayor Bluster banishes Heidi from Doodyville.

September 15, 1955 Show #1933: Buffalo Bob prepares to take Heidi back to Africa.

September 16, 1955 Show #1934: In a giant ceremony, Howdy adopts Heidi as his sister.

September 19, 1955 Show #1935: Buffalo Bob and Clarabell give a concert.

September 20, 1955 Show #1936: Grandpa Doody returns to meet Heidi.

September 21, 1955 Show #1937: Buffalo Bob wonders why he can't hear the voice of Doodyville. The Story Princess tells another tale.

September 22, 1955 Show #1938: Mr. Cobb is on Mr. Bluster's side. Grandpa Doody searches for something mysterious.

September 23, 1955 Show #1939: Grandpa Doody is put in jail after being caught in Mr. Bluster's house.

September 26, 1955 Show #1940: Grandpa Doody hides from the Inspector. The new Howdy Doody comic strip begins today.

September 27, 1955 Show #1941: Buffalo Bob and Howdy learn what the Mystery D.C.S. is.

September 28, 1955 Show #1942: Heidi Doody protects her grandfather. There's a comic strip and an animal farm.

September 29, 1955 Show #1943: Mr. Bluster tries to put Grandpa Doody in jail; Howdy comic strips are shown.

September 30, 1955 The Doughnut Corporation's ice cream premium exchange offer ends.

September 30, 1955 Show #1944: The Mystery D.C.S. is found.

October 3, 1955 Show #1945: Howdy and Dilly Dally continue their chase after the magic carpet. Lowell Thomas Jr. shows a film.

October 4, 1955 Show #1946: Chapter 4 in the squirrel-war cartoon and more adventures with the magic carpet as Mr. Bluster almost gets it for himself.

October 5, 1955 Show #1947: Heidi is rescued by Howdy and Dilly Dally.

October 6, 1955 Show #1948: Howdy has a space adventure. The Story Princess tells another story.

October 7, 1955 Show #1949: Howdy and Dilly Dally are on the moon. Buffalo Bob tries to reach them.

October 10, 1955 Show #1950: Heidi and Dilly Dally meet Mo Mo the Martian.

October 11, 1955 Show #1951: Howdy discovers a stowaway aboard the space fish. Mr. Nick and Chief Thunderthud are in Cleveland.

October 12, 1955 Show #1952: Mr. Bluster is captured by King Do Do. Mr. Cobb returns.

October 13, 1955 Show #1953: Capt. Scuttlebutt reports a strange sight on Doodyville Bay.

October 14, 1955 Show #1954: Howdy and Mambo the Elephant take a ride on a submarine.

October 17, 1955 Show #1955: King Neptune causes a sea quake.

October 18, 1955 Show #1956: Howdy and Mr. Bluster are held captive by King Neptune. Buffalo Bob and the Princess sing.

October 19, 1955 Show #1957: Howdy rescues Mambo the Elephant from the seashell castle.

October 20, 1955 Show #1958: A pied piper comes to Doodyville. When he blows his piccolo, the Princess follows him.

October 21, 1955 Show #1959: Mr. Bluster uses the magic piccolo to charm the Doodyville animals.

October 24, 1955 Show #1960: Hyde and Zeke meet a new arrival, Worthington Worm. Howdy and Heidi make friends with a bear. The Story Princess tells a tale.

October 25, 1955 Show #1961: Heidi and the bear look for Hyde and Zeke. Pepper the Piper lures the bear away.

October 26, 1955 Show #1962: The bear is rescued. Buffalo Bob punishes Mr. Bluster.

October 27, 1955 Show #1963: A new story starts. Buffalo Bob and Howdy are in danger.

October 31, 1955 Show #1964: The search for the butterfly continues; Howdy goes to the Valley of the Ants.

November 1, 1955 Show #1965: The butterfly is found.

November 2, 1955 Show #1966: Buffalo Bob tells the story of the Time-A-Tub.

November 3, 1955 Show #1967: Howdy and Mr. Bluster capture the knight.

November 4, 1955 Show #1971: Buffalo Bob tells how Clarabell disappears in King Arthur's court.

November 7, 1955 Show #1972: The falcon drops Howdy into the moat that surrounds King Arthur's, castle; also a cartoon.

November 8, 1955 Show #1973: Howdy goes hunting. Merlin and Spinner the Spider trick Howdy and Mr. Bluster; Clarabell plays a trick on Chief Thunderthud.

November 9, 1955 Show #1974: The Time-A-Tub returns back to Doodyville with Howdy and Mr. Bluster on board.

November 10, 1955 Show #1975: Buffalo Bob reads *Alice in Wonderland* to Heidi. She disappears after she hears the story.

November 11, 1955 Show #1976: Howdy finds Heidi has fallen into a rabbit hole and landed in Underland. A Lowell Thomas Jr. adventure film is shown.

November 14, 1955 Show #1977: Howdy, Heidi, and Squeakie walk past Cave of the Wind.

©BOB SMITH, FROM THE SCOTT BRINKER COLLECTION

Mr. Bluster and the Inspector.

November 15, 1955 Show #1978: Allie the Cat and Mr. Bluster walk cross the boiling lake.

November 16, 1955 Show #1979: Squeakie the Mouse risks his life for Howdy; Old Mother Earth catches Mr. Bluster.

November 17, 1955 Show #1980: Two mysterious strangers turn up in Doodyville complaining that the Inspector and Mr. Bluster are impostors. A new Howdy Doody cartoon is shown.

November 21, 1955 Show #1982: Capt. Scuttlebutt sides with a buzzard.

November 22, 1955 Show #1983: Mr. Bluster goes to Algeria.

November 23, 1955 Show #1984: Howdy saves the day.

November 25, 1955 Show #1985: Carney Cal brings a circus.

November 26, 1955 The Colgate-Palmolive Co. Name the Tug Boat contest ends.

November 28, 1955 Show #1986: Carney Cal's circus opens at last. Benny the Bengal Tiger escapes.

November 29, 1955 Show #1987: Clarabell and Mr. Bluster set a trap for the mysterious man in black.

November 30, 1955 Show #1988: The mysterious man in black reveals his identity. Buffalo Bob sings *Apple on a Stick*.

December 1, 1955 Show #1989: Heidi tells the story of Littlelandia, a country where there are no animals.

December 2, 1955 Show #1990: Mr. Bluster and Howdy go to Littlelandia. There is a Lowell Thomas Jr. adventure film.

December 5, 1955 Show #1991: Mr. Bluster is ready to be crowned king. He's given Queen Tina a donkey, but she thinks it's a kitten. The Story Princess tells a tale.

December 6, 1955 Show #1992: Boris and Mr. Bluster steal a kitten from Howdy and Dilly. There's an Old-Time Film.

December 7, 1955 Show #1993: Buffalo Bob saves the kingdom of Littlelandia. A Gabby Hayes film from England is shown.

December 8, 1955 Show #1994: With Buffalo Bob, Howdy, and the gang, we watch the lighting of the Christmas tree in Rockefeller Center, New York City. Back in Doodyville, a stranger has arrived.

December 9, 1955 Show #1995: Heidi is under a magic spell; the Wizard vanishes with the magic cloth.

December 12, 1955 Show #1996: Howdy and Mr. Bluster escape from the trick of fire.

December 13, 1955 Show #1997: More adventures in the House of Cards; the Wizard turns Mr. Bluster into a goat.

December 14, 1955 Show #1998: Buffalo Bob takes off on a jet to find honey from the spelling bee; also a cartoon.

December 15, 1955 Show #1999: Mr. Bluster plots to take the place of Santa Claus; also a Lowell Thomas Jr. adventure.

December 16, 1955 Show #2000: Mr. Bluster is in Santa's workshop. Buffalo Bob and Howdy celebrate the 2000th Howdy Doody show; first episode of the serial "White Mane."

December 19, 1955 Show #2001: Buffalo Bob arrives in Balgonia to rescue the Inspector and Dilly.

December 20, 1955 Show #2002: Mr. Bluster decides to replace Santa Claus and become Bluster Claus.

December 21, 1955 Show #2003: Howdy proves to the Eskimos that he isn't a fish thief; a visit to Santa's workshop.

December 22, 1955 Show #2004: Mr. Bluster steals the Christmas lists of all the children in the world.

December 23, 1955 Show #2005: Mr. Bluster is defeated at last. Santa Claus visits Doodyville.

December 27, 1955 Show #2007: Mr. Bluster sells Doodyville and sets out to become mayor of New York.

December 28, 1955 Show #2008: Howdy and Heidi discover that Doodyville has been sold to the Army to be used as a site for testing bombs.

December 29, 1955 Show #2009: Chester Q. Quackenham, expert and confidence man, finds Mr. Bluster and Clarabell.

December 30, 1955 Show #2010: Mr. Bluster and Clarabell lose all their money and are stranded in New York.

January 3, 1956 Show #2012: Cactus Carl turns up with news that he has discovered a fountain of youth; a special cartoon.

January 4, 1956 Show #2013: Heidi is missing. Mr. Bluster and Cactus Carl have taken her west; an Old-Time Movie.

January 5, 1956 Show #2014: Buffalo Bob sends Chief Thunderthud after Heidi. Mr. Bluster tells the Ooragnak Tribe that he is Chief Thunderthud; a Gabby Hayes film.

January 6, 1956 Show #2015: Howdy and the Inspector start west in a covered wagon.

January 9, 1956 Show #2016: Buffalo Bob leaves on a secret mission and returns to Doodyville.

January 10, 1956 Show #2017: Howdy and the Inspector arrive at the reservation.

January 11, 1956 Show #2018: A mysterious message from Buffalo Bob.

January 12, 1956 Show #2019: Howdy and Mr. Bluster are in the Peppermint Forest.

January 13, 1956 Show #2020: Howdy gets stuck in Rock Candy Mountain; a scarecrow rescues him.

January 16, 1956 Show #2021: Buffalo Bob goes on a mysterious trip. In Storybook Land, King Lazee turns Mr. Bluster into a stone.

January 17, 1956 Show #2022: Howdy and Sidney Scarecrow rescue the Storybook Princess; Buffalo Bob sends a message; Old-Time Movie.

January 18, 1956 Show #2023: Dr. Doodle arrives with a strange ray that Mr. Bluster uses.

January 19, 1956 Show #2024: Mr. Bluster uses the Doodle to make the general store fly away; an Old-Time Movie is shown.

January 20, 1956 Show #2025: Clarabell finds the Doodle and saves Doodyville. Buffalo Bob sends a message that he'll be back Monday.

January 23, 1956 Show #2026: Mr. Cobb tells the story of Buffalo Bob's trip to see Prof. Toro.

January 24, 1956 Show #2027: Professor Toro's new invention is in evil hands.

January 25, 1956 Show #2028: Buffalo Bob and Howdy climb the mountain.

January 26, 1956 Show #2029: Howdy and Dilly Dally go off to explore the cave.

January 27, 1956 Show #2030: Howdy is in real trouble.

January 30, 1956 Show #2031: Robie obeys the orders of Buffalo Bob; a new cartoon series "The Flying Carpet" begins today.

January 31, 1956 Show #2032: Mr. Cobb's cousin, Rancher Robb, visits Doodyville. Episode 2 in "The Flying Carpet."

February 1, 1956 Show #2033: Mr. Bluster accuses Rancher Rob of stealing the tug boat. Part 3 of "The Flying Carpet."

February 2, 1956 Show #2034: Cobb and Robb have an adventure. Part 4 of "The Flying Carpet."

February 3, 1956 Show #2035: The jeweled tricycle disappears. Part 5 of "The Flying Carpet."

February 6, 1956 Show #2036: Everyone in Doodyville is looking for the jeweled tricycle.

February 7, 1956 Show #2037: The jeweled tricycle is found.

February 8, 1956 Show #2038: A new adventure begins in the jungles of Africa. Simon Sly, a hunter, and his witch doctor pal, Ama, search for the lost diamond mine.

February 9, 1956 Show #2039: Dilly and Heidi crash in the jungle; Simon Sly finds them.

February 10, 1956 Show #2040: On their way to rescue Heidi and Dilly, Howdy and Mr. Bluster get lost.

February 13, 1956 Show #2041: Howdy and Heidi rescue Dilly from a lion; Mr. Bluster has a lucky fall.

February 14, 1956 Show #2042: Simon Sly sets Muki free; Clarabell plays a trick on Mr. Cobb.

February 15, 1956 Show #2043: A new adventure starts as Pepper the Piper arrives in Doodyville; Mr. Bluster has a way to get Flub-A-Dub.

February 16, 1956 Show #2044: Howdy and Dilly meet Don Jose in Venezuela; Pepper wants to sell Flub-A-Dub to a zoo.

February 17, 1956 Show #2045: Abra K. Dabra, the magician, arrives in town; Buffalo Bob goes to help Howdy and Dilly.

February 20, 1956 Show #2046: Buffalo Bob is off to rescue Howdy and Dilly.

February 21, 1956 Show #2047: Pepper goes to Spin-land to sell Flub.

February 22, 1956 Show #2048: A new adventure begins; Mr. Cobb gives Dilly a new toy.

February 23, 1956 Show #2049: The Wizard arrives in Doodyville to perform magic.

February 24, 1956 Show #2050: Howdy and Tim fall out of the balloon onto an iceberg.

February 27, 1956 Show #2051: Howdy, Mr. Bluster, and Mr. Forever decide to run for Mayor of Doodyville.

February 28, 1956 Show #2052: Phineas T. Bluster enlists the aid of Sunny in organizing a parade to start his election campaign.

February 29, 1956 Show #2053: Mrs. Izbing makes preparations to take Heidi back to Sweden.

March 1, 1956 Show #2054: Mrs. Izbing hires Bruno to visit Doodyville and bring Heidi back with him.

March 2, 1956 Show #2055: Perfectly Flawless holds off Bruno and Mrs. Izbing while the election campaign continues; Flub-A-Dub leaves to search for more Flub-A-Dubs.

March 5, 1956 Show #2056: Buffalo Bob goes to Chicago.

March 6, 1956 Show #2057: The big tug of war takes place; an Old-Time Movie is shown.

March 7, 1956 Show #2058: Capt. Scuttlebutt takes the kids on a boat ride; a hurricane arrives.

March 8, 1956 Show #2059: Buffalo Bob flies to Holland to find the kids; Mr. Bluster gets into some mischief.

March 9, 1956 Show #2060: Howdy plugs the dike.

March 12, 1956 Show #2061: The Fib-A-Doodle is in Doodyville. Everyone is worried.

March 13, 1956 Show #2062: The Inspector has a clue as to the whereabouts of Clarabell's secret fun room.

March 14, 1956 Show #2063: Bison Bill is worried about the missing Inspector.

March 15, 1956 Show #2064: Howdy goes to rescue the Inspector.

March 16, 1956 Show #2065: Mr. Cobb disguises himself as Harvey Hotplate.

March 19, 1956 Show #2066: Bison Bill worries about the old magic lamp.

March 20, 1956 Show #2067: Bison Bill and Mr. Cobb return to Fun Rock; Clarabell makes the Genie invisible.

March 21, 1956 Show #2068: Everyone dives underwater to look for the lamp.

April 2, 1956 Show #2074: Doodyville is preparing for the spring festival on Friday.

April 3, 1956 Show #2075: There's a milk snatcher in Doodyville today.

April 4, 1956 Show #2076: The little waif returns.

April 5, 1956 Show #2079: The newcomer to Doodyville adds to the mystery.

April 6, 1956 Show #2080: The mystery is cleared up; a spring festive occurs.

April 13, 1956 Show #2085: Clarabell and Chief Thunderthud argue.

April 16, 1956 Show #2086: Howdy and Dilly act strangely.

April 17, 1956 Show #2087: Howdy is building a machine.

April 18, 1956 Show #2088: The new machine, a Sound-A-Doodle, can reproduce any sound.

April 19, 1956 Show #2089: Clarabell takes the Sound-A-Doodle.

April 20, 1956 Show #2090: Buffalo Bob recovers the machine.

April 24, 1956 Show #2092: Mark Lang wins the Howdy Doody "Dooer" contest.

April 25, 1956 Show #2093: Buffalo Bob and Howdy are melancholy over the disappearances.

April 26, 1956 Show #2094: Dilly Dally and Mr. Cobb join the exodus.

April 27, 1956 Show #2095: Mr. Bluster sets up a new town called Blusterville.

April 30, 1956 Canada: Clarabell is hired by a baseball team; Mr. Bluster wants him to leave Doodyville.

May 1, 1956 Canada: Dilly Dally and Howdy get lost in the woods visiting the stump elevator.

May 2, 1956 Canada: Flub-A-Dub brings Alex back to Doodyville; Timber Tom tries to get maple syrup from Mr. Bluster.

May 3, 1956 Canada: Flub-A-Dub persuades Clarabell to be a super salesman.

May 4, 1956 Canada: Dilly Dally finds Mr. Bluster by going down the stump elevator; Taffy announces the new mayor of Doodyville.

May 7, 1956 Show #2101: Mambo the Elephant falls and hurts his leg.

May 8, 1956 Show #2102: Clarabell uses the Clarabus as a taxi.

May 9, 1956 Show #2103: Buffalo Bob sends for Professor Fortissimo, the world's greatest entertainer.

May 10, 1956 Show #2104: Professor Fortissimo is locked in.

May 11, 1956 Show #2105: Howdy and Dilly get a surprise visit from the Maharaja of M'yoor.

May 14, 1956 Show #2106: Howdy has a plan.

May 15, 1956 Show #2107: Dilly Dally is a detective.

May 16, 1956 Show #2108: Mr. Bluster fails as captain.

May 17, 1956 Show #2109: Everyone wants his old job back; the Story Princess has another tale.

May 18, 1956 Show #2110: Mr. Bluster wants to be mayor.

May 21, 1956 Show #2111: Mr. Bluster and Clarabell change Buffalo Bob's map.

May 22, 1956 Show #2112: Mr. Cobb finds torn pieces of the map.

May 23, 1956 Show #2113: Howdy and Dilly Dally are troubled by a bearded stranger when they camp out.

May 24, 1956 Show #2114: Howdy complains to Buffalo Bob about missing items.

May 25, 1956 Show #2115: Howdy and Dilly attempt to learn the identity of the bearded stranger.

May 28, 1956 Show #2116: Howdy wins a contest. Dilly tells a story.

May 29, 1956 Show #2117: Mr. Mason, a traveling salesman, arrives in Doodyville.

May 30, 1956 Show #2118: Willy Winkum decides to build a hotel. Howdy decides he can't sing.

May 31, 1956 Show #2119: Dilly Dally conducts an orchestra.

June 1, 1956 Show #2120: Buffalo Bob announces a secret; this is the last weekday program.

June 16, 1956 Show #2121: This is the first Saturday morning program. Buffalo Bob gets a wishell, a magic whistle that can grant wishes. The Howdy Doodlers, a musical combo, appears. Gumby is introduced on the program as a regular cartoon.

June 23, 1956 Show #2122: All the children are ready for summer vacation, but Mr. Bluster wants school to stay open all summer.

June 30, 1956 Show #2123: Howdy and Dilly Dally invent a new machine, the Flapadoodle, and everyone in Doodyville tries to figure out what it does. Clarabell gets disguised as a horse to uncover the secret. Today Gumby is also seen as he returns from the moon.

July 7, 1956 Show #2124: Movie maker Farley Flicker comes to Doodyville to cast the title role for his new picture "The Hero"; everyone dresses up to audition for the part.

July 14, 1956 Show #2125: Buffalo Bob hires a boat and everyone in Doodyville is invited to go along except Clarabell and Capt. Scuttlebutt. Today's Gumby adventure takes us to Mirror Land.

July 28, 1956 Show #2127: There is a draught in Doodyville and all the plants are dying from lack of rain. Buffalo Bob invents the "Wetter Weather" machine and makes rain, and everyone is happy except Clarabell and Mr. Bluster, who are in a panic.

August 4, 1956 Show #2128: Dilly and Capt. Scuttlebutt get ready to sail away in search of sunken treasure; Buffalo Bob and Mr. Cobb show how to have fun with music.

August 11, 1956 Show #2129: A statue comes to life just in time to save Doodyville from a shortage of water. Clarabell has a real trick up his sleeve which helps in solving the problem. Dilly Dally and Flub-A-Dub learn all about Peter, Peter, Pumpkin Eater from Buffalo Bob.

August 18, 1956 Show #2130: There is a big contest in Doodyville. Mr. Bluster and Clarabell conspire to win the prize by importing a dance instructor. The cartoon is "Ginger Nut."

August 25, 1956 Show #2131: Another Adventure Cartoon, an animated cartoon series featuring the Doodyville characters is shown. In the film, Capt. Scuttlebutt and Dilly Dally go off on a treasure hunt. Buffalo Bob is very impressed with their adventures.

September 1, 1956 Show #2132: Strange things happen in Doodyville today as a clown named Togo turns everything topsy-turvy. The clown appears in Howdy's dream and leads Howdy and all the other Doodyville characters on a trip to Clown Town.

September 8, 1956 Show #2133: Howdy and Buffalo Bob go down to the sea to look for sea shells, and Buffalo Bob puts on his skin-diving outfit to take a look at the ocean floor. But Mr. Bluster mistakes Buffalo Bob for a sea monster and soon all of Doodyville is hunting for the horrible sea monster; a Gumby cartoon is shown.

September 15, 1956 Show #2134: Everyone in Doodyville dresses up in Indian blankets and feathers to celebrate Indian summer. Mr. Bluster disguises himself as a totem pole and gives advice for money. The Gumby film is "Gumby in Mirror Land."

September 22, 1956 Show #2135: At a town meeting, everyone in Doodyville complains about the lack of luxuries; Buffalo Bob invites everyone up to his log cabin for the weekend.

September 29, 1956 Show #2136: Capt. Scuttlebutt and Dilly Dally are featured in the animated adventure cartoon, "Enchanted Treasure." The two adventurers board the Seven Seas and search for magic treasure.

October 6, 1956 Show #2137: Buffalo Bob and the gang have a welcome home cake for the Inspector, who is back from England with an assistant named Ginger Snapper with a Look-A-Crook machine. When clues are fed into the machine, out pops a picture of the crook. There is only one thing wrong with the machine: during the welcoming party it disappears.

October 13, 1956 Show #2138: Mr. Bluster scoffs at Columbus Day celebrations. Discovering America wasn't very much, says he, and takes off with Howdy and Dilly Dally to discover a new planet.

October 20, 1956 Show #2139: Howdy finds a bottle with a little man trapped inside. Buffalo Bob opens the bottle and becomes the victim of the genie's spell.

October 27, 1956 Show #2140: There is a convention in Doodyville and Howdy Doody is nominated. The second candidate is a mystery figure. Dilly's adventure with the Enchanted Treasure continues.

November 3, 1956 Show #2141: Today is election day in Doodyville. Bluster has a plan to make Howdy lose to the mystery candidate.

November 10, 1956 Show #2142: Howdy and Buffalo Bob decide to present their own version of Jack and the Beanstalk in honor of the forthcoming NBC Spectacular. Buffalo Bob sings *The Ballad of Jack and the Beanstalk* and Clarabell tries to get the part of the giant.

November 17, 1956 Show #2143: Mr. Bluster devises a plot to make Buffalo Bob leave Doodyville. The plan nearly works as Buffalo Bob leaves, thinking no one in the town likes him.

CANADA: Traffy, the cop, gives safety lessons.

November 24, 1956 Show #2144: Clarabell has opened a trick shop which has, as we see in flashback, affected Thanksgiving Day in Doodyville.

December 1, 1956 Show #2145: There is a contest in Doodyville to select the best dressed man; Mr. Bluster thinks up a trick so he can win.

December 8, 1956 Show #2146: Mr. Bluster obtains a crystal ball and starts telling everyone's fortunes. But when none of the fortunes sound right, the townspeople decide to put the crystal ball to a test.

December 15, 1956 Show #2147: Everyone in Doodyville is helping make toys for the needy, except Mr. Bluster, who has plans of his own.

December 22, 1956 Show #2148: After leaving Doodyville, Mr. Bluster travels to the North Pole.

December 29, 1956 Show #2149: To celebrate nine years on TV, Doodyville votes to award someone the best citizen award, but Mr. Bluster keeps finding something wrong with all the nominees; film clips from the past Howdy Doody shows are shown.

January 5, 1957 Show #2150: Everyone in Doodyville gets ready to welcome Flub-A-Dub's nephew, who is coming to town. Mr. Bluster thinks the preparations are for his nephew, who is also expected to arrive soon.

January 12, 1957 Show #2151: A painter is due to arrive in Doodyville to paint Howdy's picture. But a leprechaun disguises himself as an artist and causes all sorts of confusion.

January 19, 1957 Show #2152: Buffalo Bob returns from his trip to Gumbyland with a film to show everyone in Doodyville.

January 26, 1957 Show #2153: Today, the big snow carnival takes place in Doodyville, and everyone is busy competing in the snow statue contest. But Mr. Bluster and Clarabell are busy cooking up a sure way to win.

February 2, 1957 Show #2154: Today is Dilly's birthday and part of the celebration is the showing of a new Gumby film, "The Black Knight."

February 9, 1957 Show #2155: Liona, Heidi's jungle girlfriend, comes to Doodyville with a present from Heidi for everyone. Sly Mr. Bluster believes it is a diamond, so he schemes to get the present for himself.

February 16, 1957 Show #2156: Everyone in Doodyville, except Mr. Bluster, discovers that the present is truth water. After drinking it, if you aren't truthful you begin to hop on one foot until you tell the truth.

February 23, 1957 Show #2157: The old house on the hill in Doodyville will make a perfect clubhouse, but greedy Mr. Bluster wants it for his mayor's mansion. He plans a scheme using a tape recorder to discourage Buffalo Bob and Howdy, but his plan backfires.

March 2, 1957 Show #2158: Screaming Mr. Bluster plots with Mr. Cobb, the owner of the only general store in Doodyville, to raise his hamburger prices. Buffalo Bob hears about this and disguises himself as a traveling butcher to foil their plans.

March 9, 1957 Show #2159: After Howdy wins Doodyville's best all around athletics trophy, Mr. Bluster complains that any three year old could beat him. So Buffalo Bob sets up a contest between Howdy and the three year old that Mr. Bluster must provide.

March 16, 1957 Show #2160: Buffalo Bob is planning to read a story to the Doodyville gang, but they don't like what he has chosen, so they try their hands at story telling; a Gumby cartoon is featured.

March 16, 1957 *The Gumby Show* spins off from the Howdy Doody show. The program was first hosted by Robert Nicholson and later Pinkie Lee. It was canceled in November after eight months.

March 23, 1957 Show #2161: Buffalo Bob discovers that everyone in Doodyville is suffering from spring fever and tries to remedy the situation. But Leo the Leprechaun soon appears with his bewitching powers.

March 30, 1957 Show #2162: Suspicions arise after mysterious explosions are heard in Doodyville and Mr. Bluster is seen covered with dust.

April 6, 1957 Show #2163: After winning the spelling contest, Howdy is too proud of his new ability. When he goes to pick up the crate of dancing kangaroos from Australia, he corrects the label and the fun begins.

April 13, 1957 Show #2164: Buffalo Bob wants to color Easter eggs for the Easter bunny to hide for the big Easter egg hunt. Mr. Bluster sees a chance to make some money, so he buys up all the eggs in town.

April 20, 1957 Show #2165: Mr. Bluster's nephew, Petey tumbles down a hole and finds himself in Bunnyland. Before he can leave, he learns he must believe in the Easter bunny.

April 27, 1957 Show #2166: When Leona, the jungle girl arrives in Doodyville, she is greeted by Mr. Bluster and tells him about the balloon berries she brought with her. He learns that the berries make one blow up like a balloon.

May 4, 1957 Show #2167: Howdy and Buffalo Bob build a do-it-yourself soda fountain which they hope to sell to tycoon Andy Handy. Mr. Bluster hears about this, he makes a do-it-yourself clothes cleaner which he hopes to sell to Mr. Handy.

May 11, 1957 Show #2168: After the circus comes to town and Clarabell has a disagreement with Mr. Bluster, a new clown, Pesky, is hired. Pesky's pranks, though, soon bring about some changes.

May 18, 1957 Show #2169: When the kids of Doodyville decide to form a basketball team, Buffalo Bob and Mr. Bluster compete to see who will manage the team.

May 25, 1957 Show #2170: A circus ringmaster sees Mambo the Dancing Elephant and decides to buy him for his circus. When he approaches Mr. Bluster about it, Mr. Bluster sees an opportunity to make some easy money.

June 1, 1957 Show #2171: Buffalo Bob and the Doodyville gang are practicing in the firehouse for the competition of bands to lead the Memorial Day parade. When Mr. Bluster get the special favor he is demanding, he and Chief Thunderthud make some big switches.

June 8, 1957 Show #2172: After Clarabell plays some practical jokes on people, Buffalo Bob suggests that he learn magic tricks that won't hurt anyone. Clarabell then comes back to show him his magic-box trick, which makes people disappear.

June 15, 1957 Show #2173: After Mr. Bluster is frightened by a dog, he orders that any strange dog in Doodyville must be put in the dog pound. So Buffalo Bob organizes a hunt to find the dog before Mr. Bluster does.

June 22, 1957 Show #2174: When John J. Fedoozle, private eye, doesn't turn up a clue about Mr. Bluster's glasses, Mr. Bluster threatens to fire him. Buffalo Bob persuades him to give Fedoozle another chance by solving Doodyville's next crime.

June 29, 1957 Show #2175: The youngsters of Doodyville are told that they have to go back to school because they broke Mr. Bluster's window while playing ball. On their way to school, they meet the Pied Piper, who proposes to take them to Funland.

July 4, 1957 Judy Tyler was killed with her husband in an auto accident in Rock River, Wyoming.

July 6, 1957 Show #2176: Howdy has an "Alaskan Adventure" film where he and Dilly Dally rescue a professor lost in the frozen north and bring back a prehistoric Goola-Goola bear. In the last portion of today's show, Buffalo Bob and the gang find the best way to beat the heat.

July 13, 1957 Show #2177: There's a new fountain in Doodyville. Clarabell throws a penny into it, thinking it's a wishing well. Immediately Mr. Bluster takes it over and tries to make it a money making scheme.

July 20, 1957 Show #2178: When Clarabell wins Doodyville's Good Behavior medal, Petey runs into his uncle, Mr. Bluster. Mr. Bluster devises a scheme with Pesky the clown to fix things.

July 27, 1957 Show #2179: Since Clarabell left town, the Winder-Finder is being used to find him. While Buffalo Bob is working on the machine, Mr. Cobb is in his car trying to find him.

August 3, 1957 Show #2180: Now that Clarabell has been found, Pesky the clown leaves town. But he does send the Doodyville folks a gift they are not to open until 8:25 A.M.

August 10, 1957 Show #2181: Doodyville is putting on a play, Cinderella, but there are no parts in it for Clarabell or Mr. Bluster. To get revenge, Clarabell drinks some Vanishing Water and becomes invisible.

August 17, 1957 Show #2182: When Chief Thunderthud thinks no one in Doodyville likes him, he writes himself an anonymous letter, saying he is needed by his Indian tribe.

August 24, 1957 Show #2183: At the town carnival, Buffalo Bob and Howdy set up a shooting gallery with hopes of making money for a new Howdy Doody playground. But Mr. Bluster wants the playground for himself, so he cooks up a scheme with Clarabell to make the shooting gallery a failure.

August 31, 1957 Show #2184: When Mr. Bluster gets hold of a weather-making machine, he tries out a money-making scheme — selling hot chocolate at an outrageous price. Buffalo Bob tries to counter Mr. Bluster's scheme by having his own hot chocolate stand.

September 7, 1957 Show #2185: In preparing for Grandpa Doody's expected visit, everyone tries to clean things up, but Clarabell has trouble with confetti. A film feature of Capt. Scuttlebutt's treasure hunt is presented.

September 14, 1957 Show #2186: Buffalo Bob and Howdy have opened a lunchroom which uses electrical appliances throughout. As mayor of the city, Mr. Bluster thinks he should be allowed to cook the first meal. Actually he is hoping to win the best chef award from Duncan Hounds, who is soon to come to Doodyville.

September 21, 1957 Show #2187: There is a contest in Doodyville to find the town's oldest citizen. The prize is a TV set and naturally, Mr. Bluster wants to win it.

September 28, 1957 Show #2188: Mr. Cobb is having a sale in his general store. Mr. Bluster wants some ties and tries to get them at a lower price.

October 5, 1957 Show #2189: Pesky the clown drinks some Muscle-Berry Juice which has been given to him by Mr. Bluster. Then Mr. Bluster challenges Buffalo Bob to a weight-lifting contest, but sends Pesky in as his substitute. Kokomo, Jr., the comic chimp from the *Today* show pays a return visit.

October 12, 1957 Show #2190: Howdy and the gang celebrate Columbus Day with their version of the discovery of America. Mr. Bluster plays Columbus.

October 19, 1957 Show #2191: Mr. A.O. Todd has offered a prize to the Doodyville citizen who can go around the world the fastest. Howdy and Mr. Bluster enter the competition. Howdy is planning to use a flying balloon and Mr. Bluster hopes to use his flying harness. Kokomo Jr., the comical chimpanzee from the *Today* show, pays another visit.

October 26, 1957 Show #2192: Mr. Bluster and Howdy continue their race around the world. As gas is leaking from Howdy's balloon, he is forced to land in Arabia; a friendly maharaja offers some help.

November 2, 1957 Show #2193: Howdy arrives in China via the Flying Fish, but the fish is too tired to go any further. Howdy is sent onward on a Chinese box-kite. Mr. Bluster arrives on his magic rope. The Smile Contest is announced.

November 9, 1957 Show #2194: Clarabell is taking pictures for the big smile contest. Since his nephew Petey never smiles, Mr. Bluster decides to hold a frown contest.

November 16, 1957 Show #2195: Mr. Bluster decides he wants to become a partner with Howdy and Buffalo Bob in their restaurant business. When Buffalo Bob vetoes the idea, Pesky the clown gives him some Confusion Juice.

November 23, 1957 Show #2196: Capt. Scuttlebutt arrives on his boat with some mail from the smile contest. In a film feature, he and Dilly tell of their search for an enchanted treasure.

November 30, 1957 Show #2197: As everyone sits down to Thanksgiving dinner, strange things start happening. It is discovered that there is a witch who is causing the trouble. Buffalo Bob gives final warning that the Howdy Doody smile contest ends tomorrow night.

December 7, 1957 Show #2198: Howdy and Buffalo Bob go to Always Always Land to look for Mr. Bluster, who was taken away by the witches.

December 14, 1957 Show #2199: Doodyville is building a rocketship to send Howdy to the moon. Dilly is inside the ship when Mr. Bluster, not knowing Dilly is there, sends it off.

December 21, 1957 Show #2200: Mr. Bluster is lacking in Christmas spirit, but in a dream he sees things in a new light.

December 28, 1957 Show #2201: Today Howdy's 10th anniversary on TV is celebrated with an hour-long birthday party. The show's theme is based on the program *This Is Your Life,* but for Howdy. Billy Oltmann, Patchogue, NY, The Howdy Doody Boy of 1950, is another guest. Several of Howdy's friends visit, including Pierre the Chef.

December 31, 1957 Total Howdy Doody merchandise sales are estimated at $25 million.

January 4, 1958 Show #2202: Clarabell and Mr. Bluster open a barber shop. They cut Buffalo Bob's hair, hoping it will cause him to lose his strength.

January 11, 1958 Show #2203: Buffalo Bob and Mr. Cobb play the Swiss bells, after which Clarabell tries to play them. Another cartoon adventure of Dilly Dally, Capt. Scuttlebutt, and the hidden treasure is featured.

January 18, 1958 Show #2204: Pixie-Mixie Pie Pot a machine that makes pies, is invented by Buffalo Bob. Although Buffalo Bob doesn't want to sell the machine, Mr. Bluster invites pie maker Simple Simon from New York to see it.

January 25, 1958 Show #2205: Pesky the clown comes to town with the circus and brings along Mr. Ohms V. Watts, an electric man. Mr. Bluster plans to use the electric man to scare Buffalo Bob out of town so he can take over Doodyville.

February 1, 1958 Show #2206: When Buffalo Bob tries out Pesky's Guess The Weight game, he finds he weighs more than he realized and decides to take off some weight. Howdy tells him he invented a fat vat, a machine that will make Buffalo Bob weigh what he wants to weigh. While Buffalo Bob is in the machine,

Pesky sets the dial for 10 pounds. Kokomo Jr., the chimp, appears today.

February 8, 1958 Show #2207: Buffalo Bob invites Professor Whipporill to speak at a meeting of the Doodyville Bird Club. The Professor brings along a pet woodpecker named Pecky, which Mr. Bluster uses it to break up the meeting.

February 15, 1958 Show #2208: Mr. Bluster receives a valentine from a mysterious woman.

February 22, 1958 Show #2209: Buffalo Bob tries to find a clown to replace Clarabell while he is away. Bluster sends Pesky to be the clown, and Bob agrees to let him sign the contract if he makes one child laugh at him. None of the children laugh, but a very tall child that is planted by Mr. Bluster does, forcing Buffalo Bob to sign the contract.

March 1, 1958 Show #2210: Grouchy, deciding to take Pesky's place as clown, chases him out of town. Mr. Bluster joins Pesky in a scheme to get rid of Buffalo Bob so they can take over Doodyville.

March 8, 1958 Show #2211: Clarabell and the grand prize winner of the Smile Contest, Tammy Marihugh of Hollywood, CA, return from their tour. Buffalo Bob gets ready to present Tammy with her prizes, but he finds that they have already disappeared.

March 15, 1958 Show #2212: Buffalo Bob presents Clarabell with a gold key and a scrapbook from his recent tour. Buffalo Bob also tells Clarabell that he may push the flower cart in the Spring Festival Parade. But Pesky the clown comes back to town and gets Clarabell in trouble.

March 22, 1958 Show #2213: Leo the Leprechaun leaves a magic crock of gold dust in Doodyville, which causes people to disappear if it is sprinkled on them. Buffalo Bob and Clarabell wish themselves to Ireland to return the gold dust to the leprechaun.

March 29, 1958 Show #2214: Clarabell starts celebrating April's Fool day early. There is a flashback to last year's costume party, as Buffalo Bob describes why there will be none this year.

April 5, 1958 Show #2215: Grandpa Doody has hidden an Easter gift in an old house. While the kids are looking for it, Mr. Bluster hides in the attic with Prof. Jacquin DeBox, who is passing through Doodyville with his new invention, the electickle. The machine tickles everyone invisibly, and Mr. Bluster uses it to scare everyone out of the house so he can find the gift for himself.

April 12, 1958 Show #2216: Conrad Mann comes to Doodyville with phony diplomas. He tricks Mr. Bluster into stamping them with the official stamp and sells them to the kids.

April 19, 1958 Show #2217: Mr. Bluster decides to build a balloon to break an ascension record. Buffalo Bob tries to discourage the attempt by disguising him as the famous balloonist Prof. Von Sputnik.

April 26, 1958 Show #2218: Howdy makes a wooden man, Splinters, out of sticks. Sandra Witch brings Splinters to life on the condition that Howdy doesn't tell how it happened. But Splinters wooden brain causes trouble.

May 3, 1958 Show #2219: Today is Clean Up Day in Doodyville and Buffalo Bob is chairman of the committee. He wants to make sure everyone will be ready when the Mayor of Doodyville comes to visit.

May 10, 1958 Show #2220: Mr. Bluster answers an ad which seeks a man with nerves of steel for a special job. He uses trickery so Capt. Boone will hire him.

May 17, 1958 Show #2221: The Doodyville gang intends to celebrate Mr. Bluster's birthday with a surprise party. When Mr. Bluster's nephew, Petey, tells him of the plans, Mr. Bluster goes over to help them.

May 24, 1958 Show #2222: In part one of a two-part story, Buffalo Bob gets a cablegram from King Yodstik in Urli, Tibet, asking for help.

May 31, 1958 Show #2223: In the concluding part of a two part story, Buffalo Bob and Howdy arrive in Urli, Tibet, after being tricked into an airplane ride, and help King Yodstik search for his missing jewels.

June 7, 1958 Show #2224: Pesky decides to make a fortune by starting a zoo, so he lures all the Doodyville animals into cages.

June 14, 1958 Show #2225: To find a leader for a hike in the woods, Doodyville holds a contest in wood lore.

June 21, 1958 Show #2226: All of Doodyville is trying to find the best way to spend the summer. Howdy Doody finally comes up with a secret seven solution.

June 28, 1958 Show #2227: Con Mann and Louie think they have pulled a shrewd deal with a piece of real estate, but Doodyville benefits after all.

July 5, 1958 Show 2228: To celebrate Independence Day, Bob has a statue made of Doodyville's leading citizen. Mr. Bluster, thinking that it's a statue of Buffalo Bob, arranges to destroy it.

July 12, 1958 Show 2229: After Buffalo Bob's friends overhear him telling Clarabell all about his new club, they decide to ignore him because they feel left out.

July 19, 1958 Show 2230: Buffalo Bob tells the story of how Capt. Scuttlebutt came to Doodyville.

July 26, 1958 Show 2231: Clarabell decides to leave Doodyville after Buffalo Bob gets angry with him for making a mistake in the cafeteria. Buffalo Bob's friend, Mr. M. Ploy, tries to find Clarabell a job. The secret seven contest continues.

August 2, 1958 Show 2232: Clarabell signs up as a clown in the Val Carney carney-val so that he can go on all the rides without paying. He ends up on the high wire and Buffalo Bob has to come to his rescue.

August 9, 1958 Show 2233: Prof. Sy Ince gives Tizzy the Dinosaur a dinosaur egg to hatch, but Mr. Bluster steals it.

August 16, 1958 Show 2234: The Poofinwiff bird returns to Doodyville, the place of her birth, and lays some golden eggs.

August 23, 1958 Show 2235: Howdy Doody and Dilly Dally become prime suspects when a football is stolen. Called in to break the case is Detective Mike Hatchet.

August 30, 1958 Show 2236: Sandra Witch decides to make the Peanut Gallery disappear. When she refuses Buffalo Bob's pleas for the return of the gallery, he calls upon the Wizard of What.

September 6, 1958 Show 2237: Buffalo Bob holds an invention contest in Doodyville today. Included among the entries are Cobb's Hair Fair, Chief Thunderthud's Instant Toupee, and Flub-A-Dub's Do Nothing Machine.

September 13, 1958 Show 2238: Everyone in Doodyville takes out his camera today for the camera club contest. Mr. Bluster wants to be the judge but Buffalo Bob chooses Mr. Wong.

September 20, 1958 Show #2239: Howdy and Buffalo Bob act fast to help Oil Well Willie, Doodyville's friendly prospector, who dangles dangerously on a mountainside.

September 27, 1958 Show #2240: Howdy and Buffalo Bob save a bunyip from starvation and receive an unexpected favor as payment.

October 4, 1958 Show #2241: Doodyville wants to win the State Fair band contest, but the band members have very shabby uniforms and battered instruments; Simp Foney, a musician, offers a solution.

October 11, 1958 Show #2242: Trigger Happy, a western bad man, arrives in Doodyville. Buffalo Bob tries to protect Chief Thunderthud from the Indian-hating desperado.

October 18, 1958 Show #2243: Trigger Happy is locked up in jail when his pal Mad Meany comes to town to get him out of jail. But the Poofinwiff Bird who has magical powers foils Meany's attempt to spring Trigger.

October 25, 1958 Show #2244: Through an ingenious machine constructed by Doctor Ditto, exact duplications of Howdy and Clarabell are created. Buffalo Bob tries to learn the machine's secret.

November 1, 1958 Show #2245: Sandra Witch is furious at not being invited to the Halloween party, so she casts a spell on Howdy and Buffalo Bob, turning the pair into donkeys.

November 8, 1958 Show #2246: Clarabell proves to be a friend in need when Trigger breaks out of the Doodyville jail and tries to gain revenge on Buffalo Bob Smith.

November 15, 1958 Show #2247: Sandra Witch comes to Doodyville while a spelling bee is going on and counts Buffalo Bob as one of her victims.

November 22, 1958 Show #2248: Buffalo Bob and Howdy try to prevent a spaceman from taking Mambo the Elephant back to his planet.

November 29, 1958 Show #2249: A batch of eggs containing people's fortunes is laid by the Poofinwiff Bird. Mr. Horn finds only the first half of his fortune and is afraid to learn the second half.

December 6, 1958 Show #2250: Hollywood producer B.P. Borscht comes to Doodyville to shoot a picture. He plans to have an ape star in the movie.

December 13, 1958 Show #2251: Mr. Bluster and Petey snub Sandra Witch under the mistletoe at Doodyville's Christmas party, so she makes the decorations disappear.

December 20, 1958 Show #2252: Mr. Bluster is suspected of pilfering toys which are being repaired for poor people.

December 27, 1958 Show #2253: Today is the show's 11th anniversary and the annual Christmas party as well.

January 3, 1959 Show #2254: A strange Indian tries to get Buffalo Bob's Thunderbird blanket given to him by Osage Indian chief, Labadie.

January 10, 1959 Show #2255: Buffalo Bob decides to reopen the Doodyville theater, but everyone tells him that he shouldn't, because they feel the theater is haunted.

January 17, 1959 Show #2256: Hamlet Bone, the phantom of the theater, is found to be a secret agent who has been harming national defense.

January 24, 1959 Show #2257: Buffalo Bob is experimenting with Good Deed pills, but Pesky and Mr. Bluster dilute the preparation and begin to do bad things.

January 31, 1959 Show #2258: Prince Howl Vah of Turkey lands in Doodyville in a balloon. He is looking for a doctor to take back to Turkey. Mr. Bluster tells him that Buffalo Bob is a doctor, so the prince tries to get Buffalo Bob to go back with him.

February 7, 1959 Show #2259: Buffalo Bob follows Prince Howl Vah to Turkey to rescue Howdy. When he gets there he is surprised to find that Princess Summerfall Winterspring is held captive.

February 14, 1959 Show #2260: Mr. Bluster gets an unsigned Valentine's Day card from "Guess Who?" He assumes that Buffalo Bob sent it, so he persuades Sandra Witch to cast a spell over Buffalo Bob, making him a clown.

February 21, 1959 Show #2261: Heidi Doody returns and shows that she has picked up the habit of fibbing. Buffalo Bob, helping the Doodyville gang prepare for Washington's Birthday party, agrees to try to set her straight.

February 28, 1959 Show #2262: Clarabell stumbles upon a diamond smuggling racket while playing with a set of maracas. When the smugglers kidnap him, Buffalo Bob and Howdy try to find him.

March 7, 1959 Show #2263: Grandpa Doody visits Doodyville and offers a bag of silver dollars as the first

prize in a singing contest. Mr. Bluster, determined to win, sabotages Chief Thunderthud's voice.

March 14, 1959 Show #2264: Sandra Witch flies around the Arctic Circle on her broomstick and bends the North Pole when she crashes into it.

March 21, 1959 Show #2265: With everybody out of town, everyone dresses up as a clown to compete for the Hick Cup in the clown contest.

March 28, 1959 Show #2266: El Bandito, who has been elected revolutionary leader president of the South American republic of Amos, comes to Doodyville bent on killing Buffalo Bob.

April 4, 1959 Show #2267: Sandra Witch, angry because she was the victim of an April Fool's trick, casts a spell on everyone in Doodyville.

April 11, 1959 Show #2268: Everyone in Doodyville tries to be as quiet as possible to win the Noise Abatement Week award. Judge for the contest is the hard-of-hearing Mr. Bim Bam Boom.

April 18, 1959 Show #2269: Buffalo Bob falls asleep under a Japanese cherry tree. He dreams that he is in Japan and forced to challenge Japan's champion wrestler.

April 25, 1959 Show #2270: Sandra Witch brings her jack-in-the-box to Doodyville. Pesky and Mr. Bluster steal it but Sandra Witch accuses Clarabell.

May 2, 1959 Show #2271: A special election is held to determine whether the name of Doodyville should be changed to Blusterville. All the citizens of the town who have appeared in the past shows return to cast ballots.

May 9, 1959 Show #2272: Pesky the evil clown has mastered ventriloquism. Angry at Buffalo Bob for not letting him become the clown in the Doodyville circus, Pesky gets his revenge.

May 16, 1959 Show #2273: Mr. Bluster persuades Sandra Witch to help him become like King Midas, who was able to turn everything he touched to gold. However the results are disastrous.

May 23, 1959 Show #2274: Mr. Bluster and J. Cornelius Cobb conspire to fix a contest being held to choose an official flower. When Mr. Bluster develops an allergy to flowers, Mr. Cobb attempts to carry on alone.

May 30, 1959 Show #2275: Mr. Bluster and Clarabell pick up a newspaper and read about a gold strike in California. They quickly make preparations to join the gold rush.

June 6, 1959 Show #2276: Sandra Witch meets her match when Hazel Witch comes to Doodyville and places Sandra under a spell.

June 13, 1959 Show #2277: Hazel Witch uses her mysterious power to turn her pet bird, Screaming Mimi, into an invisible menace to Doodyville.

June 20, 1959 Show #2278: Clarabell gets a job in a summer camp. Buffalo Bob comes to visit him and finds out that a gang of thieves is trying to take over the camp.

June 27, 1959 Show #2279: Sandra Witch, on her way to Doodyville from Always Always Land, drops her broom in the forest. There she meets a dragon who tells her of a beautiful sleeping princess.

July 4, 1959 Show #2280: Buffalo Bob tries in vain to get some sleep while preparations are being made for Doodyville's Independence Day celebration. He is scheduled to lead the band in the celebration.

July 11, 1959 Show #2281: Trigger Happy and El Bandido join forces to get their revenge on Buffalo Bob and take over Doodyville.

July 18, 1959 Show #2282: Things begin to disappear mysteriously from Mr. Cobb's general store. He calls on Buffalo Bob and Howdy to help him catch the thief. Buffalo Bob and Howdy get a hidden camera to trap the thief by surprise.

July 25, 1959 Show #2283: Spin Platter, the disc jockey, holds a contest for the best recording; everyone wants to enter a song.

August 1, 1959 Show #2284: Clarabell visits the Catskill Mountain area, where legend has it that Rip Van Winkle slept for 20 years. The clown meets some dwarfs, who offer him a drink that puts him under a spell.

August 8, 1959 Show #2285: Under the mistaken impression that he is no longer wanted in Doodyville, Clarabell goes to Clown Town where he goes to work for Slapsy Sam. Buffalo Bob and Howdy go after Clarabell.

August 15, 1959 Show #2286: Jimmy Blaine and Jose the Toucan Bird of the *Rough and Ready* show pay a visit to Doodyville. Jose and Flub-A-Dub attempt to reach an agreement in their weeks old feud. Pesky the clown attempts to blame Jose when Buffalo Bob's ring is discovered to be missing.

August 22, 1959 Show #2287: Howdy, Buffalo Bob, and Clarabell go to the south sea island of Bali-Hoo for a vacation. Mr. Bluster, anxious never to see them in Doodyville again, contacts his friend Garfield Barge on the island and asks him to arrange for Howdy and his friends to never leave the island alive.

August 29, 1959 Show #2288: Cy Clone, an unscrupulous salesman, talks everyone in Doodyville into buying his feedbags at very high prices. Buffalo Bob, angered at the swindle, attempts to find a way to make Cy Clone buy back the useless articles.

September 5, 1959 Show #2289: Mr. I.M. Piggy comes to Doodyville to open the Piggy Bank. When the burglar doesn't arrive in time, Buffalo Bob devises his own protection system which uses laughing gas.

September 12, 1959 Show #2290: When the Doodyville water supply gets too low, Buffalo Bob decides to rub the magic lamp to get help from friendly Johnny Genie.

September 19, 1959 Show #2291: Flub-A-Dub is stricken with diesel measles, and learns that the only cure is to eat caboose cabbage. The precious vegetable can only be found in the cave of the dangerous Stick Men.

September 26, 1959 Show #2292: Mambo the Elephant dreams of a terrible looking man with a black beard and a star on his forehead that takes him away.

October 3, 1959 Show #2293: The Doodyville citizens don't know how to raise money to purchase football uniforms for the local children, until boxing promoter, Fred Fraud, comes to town.

October 10, 1959 Show #2294: Captain Bluster is captured by two Chinese thugs and carried off to the Orient aboard a Chinese ship. He gets word to Doodyville by hiding messages inside Chinese fortune cookies.

October 17, 1959 Show #2295: Theodore the Matador comes to Doodyville and shakes Clarabell's confidence in Buffalo Bob's bravery. Theodore dares Buffalo Bob to a bull fight.

October 24, 1959 Show #2296: When Mr. Bluster writes a history of Doodyville that glorifies him and his ancestors, Howdy dares him to use Clarabell's time machine to go back into history to see what really happened.

October 31, 1959 Show #2297: Pesky, the evil clown, uses Fred A. Stare's whammy eye to destroy the Halloween party decorations. Sandra Witch appeals to Buffalo Bob to outstare Mr. Stare and nullify the evil eye's power.

November 14, 1959 Show #2298: Clarabell accidentally eats some plant food which makes him grow into a clumsy giant. Soon he is so big that Howdy and Buffalo Bob begin to search for a way to shrink him back to normal size.

November 21, 1959 Show #2299: Hazel Witch tells Buffalo Bob that she has inherited a showboat and that it is now in the Doodyville harbor.

November 28, 1959 Show #2300: Citizens of Doodyville suspect that Clarabell has been turned into a turkey and they all stop their plans for a Thanksgiving dinner.

December 5, 1959 Show #2301: The Wizard of What visits Doodyville on his magic carpet. Soon Buffalo Bob and Clarabell find themselves on their way to a strange planet.

December 12, 1959 Show #2302: Hazel Witch changes herself into a beautiful girl with a chimpanzee. She frightens Buffalo Bob by making the monkey bigger and bigger.

December 19, 1959 Show #2303: Howdy, Buffalo Bob, and Clarabell come upon a Santa Claus who has been put to sleep by the elves of Rip Van Winkle mountain.

December 26, 1959 Show #2304: Sandra and Hazel Witch prepare to go to Howdy's party but leave their maid, Peppi Mint, behind. The Wizard of What finds the girl and transforms her into a beautiful princess; she takes her to the party, where she makes the witches jealous.

January 2, 1960 Show #2305: Captain Scuttlebutt plans to recover lost treasure.

January 9, 1960 Show #2306: Mr. Bluster visits a haunted house on a dare from Buffalo Bob and Clarabell.

January 16, 1960 Show #2307: The young girl whom Mr. Bluster and Howdy helped escape from Witch Hazel's house comes to Doodyville and offers to help in the work. The witch is determined to get her back.

January 23, 1960 Show #2308: Dance teacher Arthur Surry comes to Doodyville to find a new dance step. Soon the leading contenders appear to be Mr. Bluster's Hop and Buffalo Bob and Peppi Mint's Doodyville Glide.

January 30, 1960 Show #2309: King Boreas Rex of the St. Paul, Minnesota, Winter Carnival invites Buffalo Bob, Howdy, and Clarabell to visit the carnival next week.

February 6, 1960 Show #2310: Show from St. Paul, Minnesota, Carnival. In the St. Paul Auditorium, Clarabell is placed on trial before the festival's King Boreas and the Snow Queen for the disruption of some of last week's festivities.

February 13, 1960 Show #2311: Buffalo Bob makes plans for the annual Doodyville contest to find the Valentine Queen. Chief Thunderthud urges Cupid to fire his arrow into Peppi Mint so she will win.

February 20, 1960 Show #2312: Doodyville citizens plan their Washington's Birthday celebrations around a cherry blossom tree from Japan.

February 27, 1960 Show #2313: The Wizard of What visits Doodyville and brings a gold coin with him and says that it must be given to someone celebrating a 4th birthday; otherwise he will raise a great wind and blow the trees away.

March 5, 1960 Show #2314: Doodyville holds an art contest. Determined to win, the Wizard of What arrives in his magic paint set. But when he isn't looking, Pesky the Clown steals it.

March 12, 1960 Show #2315: Leo the Leprechaun visits Doodyville to march in the St. Patrick's Day parade. The witches, jealous because they can't participate in the festivities, steal his crock of gold.

March 19, 1960 Show #2316: Howdy and Buffalo Bob open their Reading is Fun campaign with their first list of recommended books.

March 26, 1960 Show #2317: El Bandidito and El Pupetero arrive in Doodyville with glints in their eyes. Fred Flipflop also arrives and flipflops at the smell of danger.

April 2, 1960 Show #2318: Larson E. Grand checks into Doodyville's new hotel with his St. Bernard dog. Later Buffalo Bob hears that a large gem, the Baseball Diamond, has been stolen by a thief with a large dog.

April 9, 1960 Show #2319: For breaking all of Gus Gasbag's balloons, Clarabell is kidnapped and taken to Baluna for trial.

April 16, 1960 Show #2320: Doodyville is preparing for the Easter Parade. Buffalo Bob tells Witch Hazel that she can't march in the parade with her football helmet. To get even, she and Sandra Witch put him under a spell.

April 23, 1960 Show #2321: Doodyville needs rain; Mr. Bluster hires two rainmakers.

April 30, 1960 Show #2322: The Doodyville band holds auditions in preparation for a performance at the state capital.

May 7, 1960 Show #2323: Doodyville is holding its annual scavenger hunt; Howdy and Clarabell come up with a nose cone and a missile.

May 14, 1960 Show #2324: Larson E. Grand talks Buffalo Bob into starting a circus using local talent to pay for their summer camp, including Fred Flipflop. Buffalo Bob and Peppi sing *Everyone Loves a Circus*.

May 21, 1960 Show #2325: Always Always land, the home of the witches, is attacked by Captain Hook and his pirates. Buffalo Bob and Peppi Mint sing *Read a Book*.

May 28, 1960 Show #2326: Clarabell and Buffalo Bob set out to catch a gang of counterfeiters.

June 4, 1960 Show #2327: A mysterious man comes to Doodyville and starts asking questions about Mr. Bluster; Buffalo Bob and Peppi Mint sing *Whistle a Happy Tune*.

June 11, 1960 Show #2328: The invisible man of Always Always Land decides to have some fun in Doodyville. Buffalo Bob and Peppi Mint sing *Look on the Bright Side*.

June 18, 1960 Show #2329: The Doodyville canteen runs out of straws and Mr. Bluster gets taken in by Con Mann who sells him real straw. Buffalo Bob and Peppi Mint sing *Sipping Soda Through A Straw*.

June 25, 1960 Show #2330: As a prelude to their visit to the Detroit International Freedom Festival, Mayor Bluster decides to have a Friendship Festival with the Clown Town.

July 2, 1960 Show #2331: The Doodyville gang is in Detroit for the International Freedom Festival; Clarabell has policemen from Detroit and Windsor Canada after him.

July 9, 1960 Show #2332: Diamond Jim Nasium hires Captain Windy Scuttlebutt to take his Golden Treasure to the Tennis Sea.

July 16, 1960 Show #2333: Clarabell is tired of having a shadow. He is surprised to learn that shaving cream is the answer. Buffalo Bob and Peppi Mint sing *Me and My Shadow*.

July 23, 1960 Show #2334: A band of gypsies is selling a cure-all medicine and come to Doodyville. Buffalo Bob and the Peanut Gallery sing *Peanut Band*.

July 30, 1960 Show #2335: Doodyville's Good Behavior Medal is awarded to the best youngster in town. Buffalo Bob and Peppi Mint sing *High Hopes*.

August 6, 1960 Show #2336: Gnik, a peddler, comes to Doodyville and gives Peppi Mint a full length mirror that has a strange power. Buffalo Bob and the Peanut Gallery sing *The Cheer Up Song*.

August 13, 1960 Show #2337: The Doodyville Doodlers, the local band, are going to sing a concert if they can decide who will have the solo parts. Peppi Mint sings *Wahoo*, then Peppi and Buffalo Bob sing *I Love a Band*.

August 20, 1960 Show #2338: Merlin the Magician makes Sir Laffalot invisible, but Buffalo Bob makes him visible again.

August 27, 1960 Show #2339: Doodyville is preparing for its annual square dance. Mr. Bluster wants to be the dance caller, but Buffalo Bob says no. So Bluster schemes to ruin the dance. Buffalo Bob and Peppi Mint sing *Friendship*.

September 3, 1960 Show #2340: Doodyville starts a book club and a Reading for Fun campaign for kids.

September 10, 1960 Show #2341: Sandra Witch now flies a jet propelled vacuum cleaner instead of a broom. Something goes wrong and she crashes into a monkey cage. Buffalo Bob sings *I Love a German Band*.

September 15, 1960 NBC announces that the *Howdy Doody Show* will terminate with the September, 24th program.

September 17, 1960 Show #2342: Buffalo Bob is going on vacation and tells Con Mann that this is the time to bring Benny Beat, a cool cat who looks just like Buffalo Bob to Doodyville.

September 24, 1960 Show #2343: Last network show. Special one-hour program as everyone in Doodyville is packed and ready to leave. Clarabell is telling everyone that he has a secret. That secret is that he can talk! Clarabell says, "Good-bye Kids!"

September 3, 1976 *Howdy Doody Time* begins again on TV, this syndicated revival consists of 130 programs.

December 31, 1991 John C. Walworth Jr. dies. He designed and created Howdy Doody premiums for Nabisco from 1951 to 1954.

July 15, 1993 Hal Schaffel dies.

September 23, 1993 Robert Bobby Nicholson dies. He was the third Clarabell, Corny Cobb, and the voice of Dilly Dally, Phineas T. Bluster, the Inspector, Flub-A-Dub, and Captain Scuttlebutt.

Badge, Flip-Up
Wonder Bread, ca. 1950 – 1954, 1¾" diameter Howdy, Clarabell, Bluster, etc. $25.00 – $35.00; 2½" diameter Howdy, Clarabell, Princess, Flub, etc. $24.00 – $45.00.

Ad, Page
Rice Krispies, 1953, page from *Life* magazine with Wild Buffalo Bill in 4 different poses. Copyright by Kagran Corporation. $18.00 – $20.00 each.

Art, Original
Milt Neil, 1993, Sketch of Howdy, Clarabell, or Bluster. $50.00 each.

Art, Original
Whitman, 1950s, Howdy face, 15" x 10", from a Golden Book. $95.00.

Article
Sunshine Book, 1958, *My Friend Buffalo Bob.* $20.00.

Badge, Tin
Rivers, 1954, Twin Pop or Fudge Bar. $50.00.

Bag, Cloth
17" x 20", terrycloth with Howdy, Dilly, Princess, and Clarabell. $50.00.

Bag, Plastic Fruit
Sanson, ca. 1950 – 1954, Little Chief Grapefruit. $3.00 – $13.00.

Bag, Plastic, Fruit
Sanson, ca. 1950 – 1954, Little Chief Orange. $3.00 – $25.00.

Bag, Plastic, Fruit
Sanson, ca. 1950 – 1954, Little Chief Apples plastic fruit bag. Copyright by Kagran Corporation. Manufactured for the J.F. Sanson & Sons Co. $9.00 – $25.00.

Bag, Plastic Fruit
Sanson, ca. 1950 – 1954, Little Chief Potatoes plastic fruit bag. Copyright by Kagran Corporation. Manufactured for the J.F. Sanson & Sons Co. $3.00 – $20.00.

Bag, Plastic Shopping
Plastic shopping bag, 22" x 13", Best Seal Corporation. $5.00.

Bag, Sleeping
Howdy Sleeping Bag. $89.00.

Bandana
Howdy on horse with lasso, 1988, 19" x 19". $2.00 – $50.00.

Bandana
Same as above, ca. 1948 – 1949, 18" x 20½". $75.00 .

Bank, Ceramic
Howdy on a pig, ca. 1948 – 1949. $145.00 – $250.00.

Bank, Ceramic
Vandor, Howdy's head. $75.00.

Bank, Ceramic
Howdy in space ship holding gun. $35.00.

Bank, Musical
Leadworks, 1988, Howdy coming out of piano. $65.00.

Barrette, Leather
Dubeliet, 1976, *It's Howdy Doody Time*. $13.00.

Barrette, Plastic
Set on card. $95.00.

Bandage Box, Display
Forest City, 1950s, empty counter display for 18 packages. $100.00.

Bandage Box, Empty
Foster City, 1950s, box only. $80.00 – $85.00.

Bandage Box, Full
Foster City, 1950s, with large and small bandages and picture. $40.00 – $150.00.

Bandage, Small Forest City
1950s, 2" in Howdy wrapper. $11.00 – $15.00.

Bandage, Large Forest City
1950s, 3¼" in Howdy wrapper. $11.00 – $13.00.

Banks, Plastic
1976, flock covered plastic banks. Mr. Bluster, Howdy, and Clarabell, 9" high. Copyright by National Broadcasting Co., Inc. Manufactured by F. J. Strauss Co., Inc. $10.00 – $75.00.

Barrette, Plastic
Clarabell. $20.00 – $85.00.

Barrette, Plastic
Howdy seated crosslegged, multicolored. $20.00 – $25.00.

Bib
White towelette, ca. 1950 – 1954, 10" x 18". Copyright Kagran. $8.00 – $20.00.

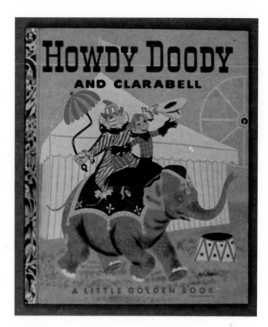

Book
Howdy Doody & Clarabell, a Little Golden Book, copyright 1952 by Kagran Corporation, published by Simon & Schuster. $7.00 – $21.00.

Book
Howdy Doody and the Magic Lamp, copyright 1954 by Kagran Corporation, published by the Whitman Publishing Company. $18.00.

Book
Tell-A-Tale, *Howdy Doody Famous TV Star.* $13.00.

Book
Howdy Doody Story & Show Book — has script. $25.00.

Book
Little Golden, 1955, *Howdy Doody & Santa Claus.* $5.00.

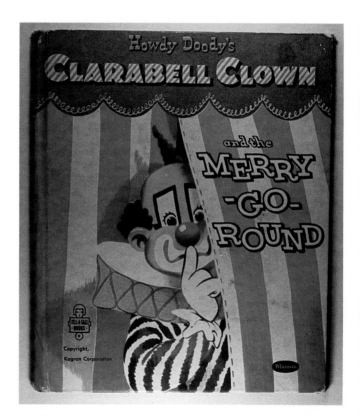

Book
Howdy Doody & Clarabell Merry Go Round, copyright 1955 by Kagran Corporation, a Tell-A-Tale Book published by the Whitman Publishing Company. $19.00 – $28.00.

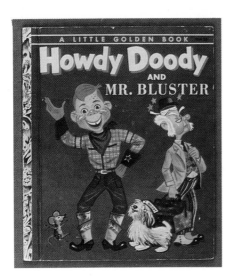

Book
Howdy Doody & Mr. Bluster, a Little Golden Book published by Simon & Schuster, copyright 1954 by Kagran Corporation. $15.00 – $20.00.

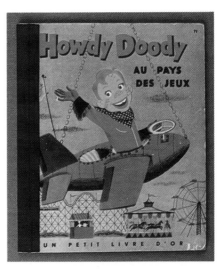

Book
Howdy Doody Au Pays Des Juex, library copy of the French version of *Howdy Doody in Funland*, Un Petit Livre D'Our published by Cocorico, copyright 1953 by Simon and Schuster. $15.00.

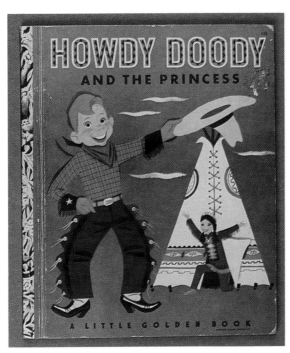

Book
Howdy Doody & The Princess, copyright 1952 by Kagran Corporation, A Little Golden Book published by Simon & Schuster, Inc. $15.00 – $20.00.

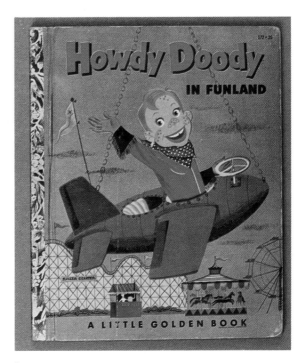

Book
Howdy Doody in Funland, copyright 1953 by Kagran Corporation, a Little Golden Book published by Simon and Schuster. $10.00 – $18.00.

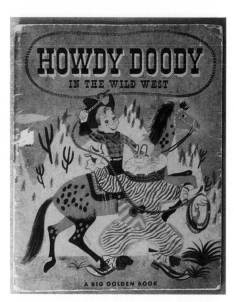

Book
Howdy Doody in the Wild West, copyright 1952 by Kagran Corporation, a Big Golden Book, published by Sandpiper Press. $25.00 – $75.00.

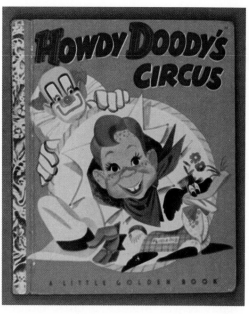

Book
Howdy Doody's Circus, copyright 1950 by Robert E. Smith, a Little Golden Book published by Simon & Schuster. $5.00 – $28.00.

Book
Howdy Doody's Animal Friends, a Little Golden Book published by Simon & Schuster, copyright 1956 by Kagran Corporation. $15.00.

Book
Howdy Doody's Island Adventure, copyright 1955 by Kagran Corporation, a Cozy Corner Book published by the Whitman Publishing Company. Robert Gribbroek illustration showed more mature Howdy. $20.00.

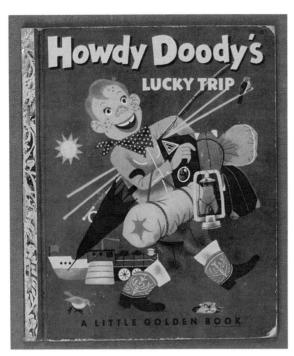

Book
Howdy Doody's Lucky Trip, copyright 1953 by Kagran Corporation, a Little Golden Book published by Simon & Schuster, Inc. $7.00 – $15.00.

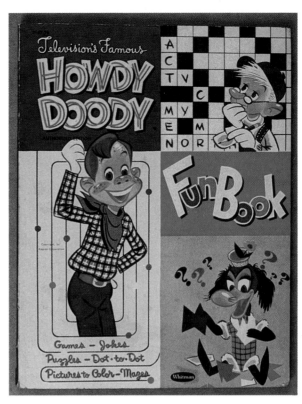

Book
Television's Famous Howdy Doody Fun Book, copyright, 1953 by Kagran Corporation, published by the Whitman Publishing Company. $42.00 – $45.00.

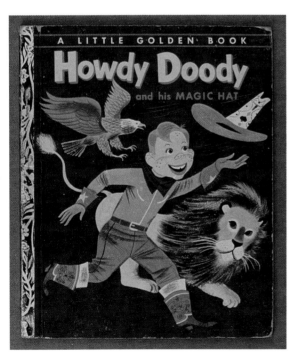

Book
Howdy Doody & His Magic Hat, copyright 1953 by Kagran Corporation, a Little Golden Book published by Simon & Schuster, Inc. $10.00 – $15.00.

Book
Howdy Doody & the Monkey Tale, copyright 1953 by Kagran Corporation, published by the Whitman Publishing Company. $9.00 – $22.00.

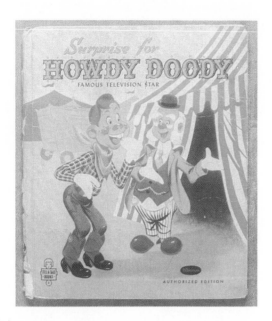

Book
Surprise for Howdy Doody, copyright 1951 by Kagran Corporation, published by the Whitman Publishing Company. Early editions are numbered 2573. $13.00 – $36.00.

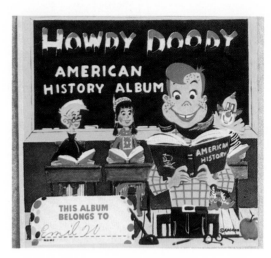

Book, Bread Label
Wonder Bread, ca. 1950 – 1954, *American History Album.* One of the several Wonder Bread end label albums. This album tells the story of the Revolutionary War. Copyright by Continental Baking Company, Inc./Kagran. $25.00 – $175.00.

Book
Little, Brown, 1987, *Say Kids, What Time is it?,* by Davis. $10.00 – $25.00.

Book, Activity
Make Your Howdy Doody Puppet Show. $265.00.

Book, Activity
Whitman, 1955, *Howdy Doody Follow the Dots.* $28.00.

Book, Coloring
Whitman, 1950s #2018. $24.00.

Book, Coloring
Whitman, #2093 *Howdy Doody Coloring Book,* copyright 1957 by California National Products, Inc. $20.00.

Book, Coloring
Whitman, 1951, little colored. $15.00 – $39.00.

Book, Activity
Funbook #2169, copyright 1951 by Kagran Corporation, published by the Whitman Publishing Company. $27.00 – $35.00.

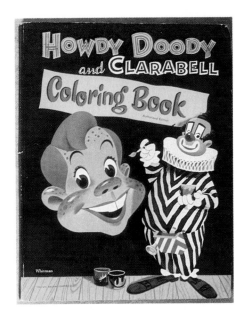

Book, Coloring
Whitman #1188, *Howdy Doody & Clarabell Coloring Book*, copyright 1955 by Kagran Corporation. $17.00.

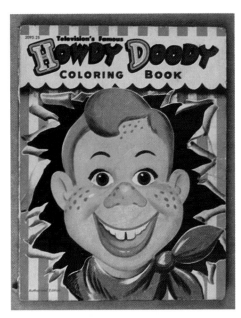

Book, Coloring
Whitman, #2093, *Television's Famous Howdy Doody Coloring Book*, copyright 1950 by California National Products, Inc. $20.00.

Book, Coloring
Whitman, 1954, #2918. $33.00 – $35.00.

Book, Coloring
Whitman, 1957, #2957. $13.00 – $27.00.

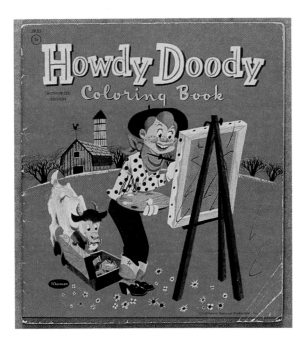

Book, Coloring
Whitman, 1957, #2953. $24.00 – $39.00.

Book, Coloring
Whitman, 1951, #2161. $15.00 – $33.00.

Book, Coloring
Whitman, 1952, #2176. $24.00 – $35.00.

Book, Coloring Comic
One of the several Blue Bonnet Coloring Comics. A 1953 Blue Bonnet Margarine premium. Copyright by Kagran Corporation. $30.00.

Book, Comic
Dell, 1949, #3 photo cover. $35.00 – $65.00.

Book, Comic
Dell, 1949, #4 photo cover. $25.00 – $65.00.

Book, Comic
Dell, 1951, # 8. $39.00.

Book, Comic
Dell, 1952, #20. $35.00.

Book, Comic
Dell, #30. $5.00.

Book, Comic
Dell, 1956, #36. $10.00 – $14.00.

Book, Comic
Howdy Doody Comic and the Spanish version *Jaudi Dudi*. Copyright 1953 by Kagran Corporation. Spanish version courtesy of Edward Kean who wrote the comic book stories. US Comic $14.00 – $35.00. Spanish version $50.00+.

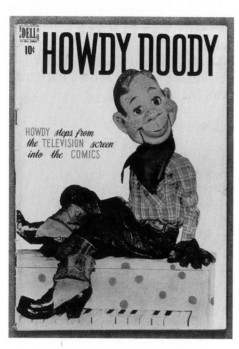

Book, Comic
Howdy Doody Comic, No. 1, copyright 1949 by Robert E. (Bob) Smith, published by Dell Publishing Co., Inc. $40.00 – $250.00.

Book, Fun
Whitman, 1951, some penciled in. $22.00 – $30.00.

Book, Punch Out
1950s, cardboard characters for puppet show. $95.00.

Bookends
Vandor, Howdy. $125.00.

Booklet
Welch's, 1951, for retailers *How To Conduct a Doll Promotion*. $300.00.

Book, Comic
Poll Parrot's Howdy Doody, Comic Book No. 4, copyright 1952 by Robert E. (Bob) Smith, 1951. $15.00.

Bottle
Welch's, ca. 1950 – 1954, Empty bottle with cap. (See photo page 122.) $40.00 – $60.00.

Bottles
Welch's, ca. 1950 – 1954, 4 pack, 2 still full and capped. $135.00 – $185.00.

Bowl, Ceramic
See Cup and Bowl.

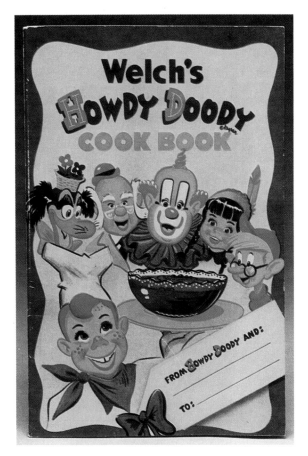

Book, Cookbook
Welch's, 1952, softbound, 36 pages, copyright by Kagran Corporation, produced by RCA Victor. $38.00 – $90.00.

Box, Pudding
Royal, ca. 1950 – 1954, unopened puddings/pie fillings with trading cards on back. There were several versions of this box. Copyright by Kagran Corporation, manufactured by Standard Brands, Inc. $25.00 – $90.00.

Box, Cereal
Kellogg, Rice Krispies Howdy doll (back only). $22.00.

Box, Gelatin
Royal, ca. 1950 – 1954, coloring card on back. $48.00 – $96.00.

Box, Grape Juice
Welch's, ca. 1950 – 1954, Doodyville Circus box with four empty bottles. $125.00.

Box, Margarine
Blue Bonnet, ca. 1950 – 1954, oleomargarine with playroom portrait. $15.00 – $35.00.

Box, Piano
Howdy Doody's Magic Piano and Xylo-Doodle Box. $35.00.

Box, Pudding
Royal, ca. 1950 – 1954, unopened, Howdy on front, no card. $35.00 – $45.00.

Box, Shipping
Burry, ca. 1950 – 1954, end flaps from Howdy Sandwich Cream Cookies. $75.00.

Box, Sports
Adco Liberty, ca. 1950 – 1954, metal outdoor sports box. $50.00 – $100.00.

Box, Tool
Adco Liberty, ca. 1950 – 1954, metal ranch house tool box with handle. $100.00 – $175.00.

Brooch, Pin
Howdy's face in molded plastic on or off card, ca. 1950 – 1954. $25.00 – $80.00.

Brooch, Pin
Princess, 1". $15.00.

Brooch, Pin
Chelsey, 3½", Howdy talking pin. $15.00.

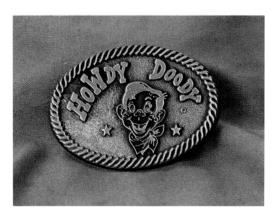

Buckle, Belt
Metal, 1976, 2½" long. $35.00.

Button, Metal
New York Sunday News, 1949, 1⅞", *Howdy Doody New Color Comic — Sunday News*. Produced in conjunction with the introduction of the Sunday Color Comics in November 1949. $50.00 – $75.00.

Button, Metal
It's Howdy Doody Time, 1988, 2¼". $5.00 – $7.00.

Button, Metal
Howdy Doody's 40th Birthday, Fries, 1988, 3½". $25.00.

Button, Metal
Red, Howdy in black and white, 1950s, 1" dia. $4.00 – $15.00.

Button, Metal
Howdy I, "I'm for Howdy Doody," 1948, 1¼". $25.00 – $75.00.

Button, Metal
Howdy says "Howdy," 1976, 1½". $10.00.

Button, Metal
It's Howdy Doody Time, black on orange, 1976, 1¾". Copyright by National Broadcasting, Inc. Manufactured by the Slater Corporation. $15.00.

Camera
Sun Ray, ca. 1950 – 1954, on illustrated card. $65.00 – $115.00.

Can, Juice
Welch's, 1955, Grape Juice Concentrate can, copyright by Kagran Corporation. $15.00 – $45.00.

Can, Snow Spray
Frosty Snow Spray, ca. 1955 – 1959, 7", copyright by California National Products, manufactured by U.S. Packaging Corporation. $75.00 – $95.00.

Can, Juice, Demo
Welch's, 1955, sealed marked "DUMMY," $150.00.

Card, Greeting
Hallmark, 1990, 2 different. $5.00 each.

Card, Picture
Forest City, ca. 1950 – 1954, 3½" x 4" from adhesive bandage strip box. (See photo page 113.) $35.00 – $40.00.

Card, Trading
Royal, ca. 1950 – 1954, cut from Royal Pudding boxes. $7.00.

Cards, Christmas
Mars, ca. 1950 – 1954, full set of 7 with original mailer & envelopes, copyright by Kagran Corporation. $3.00 – $35.00 individually; $81.00 set.

Card, Trading
Magic Trading Cards, perforated pairs, copyright 1951 by SAS NY. Two sets of cards were made, one distributed in pairs of cards by Burry's Howdy Doody Cookies, and the other as individuals with Howdy Doody Ice Cream. Although the magic tricks on the reverse use the same numbers on both sets, the obverse sides may be different. $45.00 – $50.00.

Chair, Rocking
Ringing bell on bottom rung, ca. 1948 – 1949. $150.00 – $250.00.

Chair, Stool
EZ Do, 1950s, Bluster Wooden Stool. $98.00.

Card, Playroom
Playroom Portraits, ca. 1950 – 1954, 10 different. These wax cards were cut from the backs of Blue Bonnet Margarine packages. The backs had collecting suggestions and replicas of other pictures. $16.00 – $46.00 each.

Clock, Alarm
Talking Alarm, Howdy and Clarabell, copyright 1974 by Janix Corporation. The alarm would say, "It's Howdy Doody Time." $15.00 – $100.00.

©BOB SMITH, FROM THE SCOTT BRINKER COLLECTION

Howdy and Mr. Bluster.

Clock, Alarm
Leadworks, 1976, brass, twin bells, Howdy as cowboy.
$35.00 – $55.00.

Clock, Alarm
Leadworks, 1988, Howdy on bronco, 4" x 7" x 10".
$25.00 – $65.00.

Clock, Wall
Hour classic, 1987, 26". $15.00 – $25.00.

Coin, Silver
1 Troy ounce. $30.00.

Coloring Set, Crayon
Ten crayons and pictures in TV-like box, ca. 1948 – 1949.
$42.00 – $125.00.

Costume
Clarabell costume with box. Bland Charnos, ca. 1950 –
1954, Howdy Doody in Wonderland. $100.00 – $175.00.

Costume
Princess or Clarabell with box, Wonderland, ca. 1950 –
1953. $125.00 – $190.00.

Crayon Set
1950s, crayons and book. $80.00.

Contest, Entry Blank
Blue Bonnet Sue and Howdy Doody Mystery Picture
Coloring Contest entry blank, copyright by Kagran,
printed by Blue Bonnet Margarine. $25.00.

Costume
Howdy Doody Official Collegeille Pl'a-Time Costume, copyright by Kagran. The box is rubber
stamped *2210, Princess Summerfall Winterspring,
Medium 8 – 10.* The box top tells the wearer that the
top is a cut-out mask. $75.00 – $175.00.

Clock, Cardboard
Howdy Doody Time Teacher, copyright by National
Broadcasting, Inc., 1976. $20.00 – $58.00.

Cup and Bowl
Howdy Doody children's cup and bowl, manufactured by Taylor-Smith Co. Cup is 2¾" high with 3⅜"
diameter; bowl is 2¼" high with 5½" diameter. Cup,
$70.00 – $75.00; bowl, $15.00.

Cup, Ice Cream
Dixie type ice cream cup, copyright by Kagran Corporation, manufactured by American Paper Goods Company. 2½" High x 4" diameter. $30.00 – $75.00.

Cup, Plastic
Ovaltine, 1950s, red or blue with decal. $30.00 – $50.00.

Cushion, Inflatable
Best Seal Corporation, 13" x 13". $10.00.

Cups
Howdy cups. Left: 3" high with Howdy face top and straw opening. $45.00 – $90.00. Right: Ovaltine drinking mug 3¼" high with Ovaltine decal on front. $24.00.

Curtain, Window
1950s, cloth pair, each 29" wide x 82" long. $250.00.

Curtain, Window
1950s, plastic. $95.00 – $500.00.

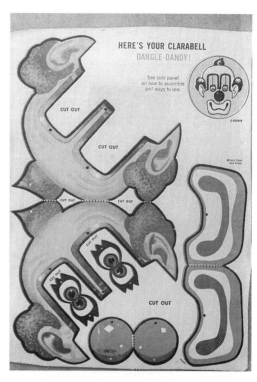

Cut-Out
Clarabell Dangle-Dandy, cereal box premium. Cut out and string the parts together. $75.00.

Cut-Out
Blue Bonnet margarine frequently had Howdy Doody collectibles on the back of the package. This example is part of the TV Studio series. $30.00 – $40.00 each.

Decals
Clarabelle and Mr. Bluster decals, copyright 1971 by NBC, Inc. $5.00.

Decoration, Cake
Six candle holders and a centerpiece, copyright by Kagran Corporation, ca. 1950 – 1954, pink, plastic. $25.00 – $200.00.

Desk Organizer
$42.00 – $50.00.

Display Board
Welch's, 1951, *Win a Howdy Doody Doll,* $350.00.

Display Card
Welch's, 1951, Howdy on arrow: *This way to the Welch's . . .* $175.00.

Display Card
Welch's, 1951, 6" x 11" *Howdy Doody Says It's my Favorite . . .* $150.00.

Display, Stand-up
Palmolive, 1950s, Colgate, 7", *Howdy says grime does not pay!* $15.00 – $70.00.

Decal
Howdy Doody decal, manufactured by the Myercord Co., 1950s. $5.00 – $35.00.

Decoration, Christmas
Vau-U-Form, 1950s, 10" x 1" Howdy on Santa's knee. $135.00.

Decoration, Christmas
Vau-U-Form, 1950s, 10" x 1" Howdy in chimney with Santa. $65.00 – $155.00.

Doll
Howdy, 8", celluloid head, ca. 1950 – 1954, with or without Bob Smith ventriloquist record. $125.00 – $225.00.

Doll
Eegee, 1987, 12". $35.00 – $40.00.

Doll
Ideal, 1950s, movable eyes and mouth with bandanna. $165.00.

Doll
Ideal, 1950s, 16", ventriloquist. $75.00.

Doll
Ideal, 1953, 20". $175.00 – $350.00.

Doll
Goldberger, 1976, 12", vinyl, ventriloquist, $30.00 – $65.00.

Doll
Goldberger, 1976, 19", vinyl, ventriloquist. $25.00.

Doll
Goldberger, 1976, 24", vinyl, ventriloquist. $135.00.

Doll
Goldberger, 1976, 30", vinyl, ventriloquist. $75.00.

Doll, Bean Bag
Howdy Doody. $20.00.

Doll, Inflatable
20". $75.00

Doll, Plush
Windy the dog with sailor cap, ca. 1950 – 1954. $250.00 – $300.00.

Doll, Nodder
Bobbin head doll, 6", 1976, manufactured by Leadworks. $18.00 – $85.00.

Dolls, Cloth
1988, 11" and 18", copyright NBC, Inc./KFS, Inc., manufactured by Applause, Inc. 11", $4.00 – $10.00; 18", $12.00 – $25.00.

Doll, Ventriloquist
Copyright by National Broadcasting Company, Inc., manufactured by the Milton Bradley Company. $21.00 – $55.00.

Doll, Wood
String joined Howdy, ca. 1948 – 1949. $395.00 – $495.00.

Ear Muffs
Furry with Vacu-form Howdy on each side, 1950s. $75.00 – $125.00.

Embroidery Kit
Milton Bradley, 1950s, Howdy and Princess kit complete, 7 pictures. $30.00 – $75.00.

Film, 8mm
A Trip to Funland, Castle, 1950s, copyright by Kagran Corporation. $25.00 – $65.00.

Film, Still
Howdy Doody at the Zoo, copyright by Kagran Corporation. Manufactured by the Silver-Rich Corp for their Sun-Ray cameras. Place these papers in the Howdy Doody camera with negatives provided, and expose to light.

Film, Still
Developing Papers for Sun-Ray Camera, ca. 1950 – 1954. Each envelope contained four pre-exposed photographic papers; when they were exposed to light, they produced a Doodyville picture. $15.00 – $30.00.

Figure
Flub, Hadley, ca. 1948 – 1949, 6½", unpainted. $75.00.

Game, B-B
Double sided B-B skill game, 2⅞" diameter x 1¼" high. Although this item was not an authorized toy, Howdy is unmistakably controlling the Mr. Bluster and Dilly Dally marionettes. Japan, 1950s. (Reverse is an unrelated hoop game.) $95.00.

Film, 35mm
Tru-Vue, 1950s, boxed black and white film strip. $25.00.

Flyer, Store
Welch's, 1951, 18" x 24", *Increase sales via a Doll Promotion.* $500.00.

Football
8" long with Howdy picture. $60.00.

Game, Howdy Doody's Beanbag Game
In original box. Parker Bros., 1951. $95.00.

Game, Boxed
Howdy Doody's 3 Ring Electric Circus, Harret-Gilman, 1950. $35.00 – $225.00.

Game, Boxed
Howdy Doody's Own Game, $75.00 – $175.00.

Game, Boxed
Milton Bradley, 1955, *Howdy Doody TV Game,* $40.00 – $136.00.

Book, Bread Label
Wonder Bread, ca. 1950 – 1954, *Howdy Doody Wonder Circus Album*. One of the several Wonder Bread end label albums, copyright by Continental Baking Company, Inc./Kagran Corporation. $25.00 – $75.00.

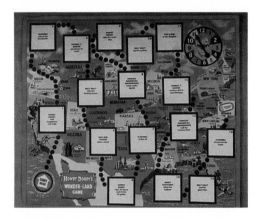

Game, Board
Howdy Doody Wonder-Land Game, copyright by Continental Baking Company, Inc./Kagran Corporation. End labels from loaves of Wonderbread had the 15 different pictures that could be trimmed and pasted to the map. $46.00 – $75.00.

Game, Boxed
Howdy Doody's Bowling Game, ca. 1948 – 1949, copyright by Bob Smith, published by Parker Brothers. $95.00 – $120.00.

Game, Dominos
Howdy Doody Dominos, Ed-U-Card, ca. 1950 – 1954. $80.00 – $350.00.

Game, Quiz
Howdy Doody Quiz Show, Multiple Products, ca. 1950 – 1954, round disk. $75.00.

Game, Sliding Tiles
Howdy Doody & His Famous TV Friends, Roalex, ca. 1950 – 1954. $75.00.

Game, Cards
Howdy Doody Card Game, 1955, copyright by Russell Manufacturing Co./Kagran Corporation. The deck had 42 cards with 14 different pictures. $28.00 – $60.00.

Game, Electric
Howdy Doody's Electric Carnival Game, copyright by Harett-Gilmar, Inc./Kagran Corporation. $35.00.

Game, Snap-A-Wink
Poll Parrot's Howdy Doody Snap-A-Wink game, copyright, 1953, Specialty Advertising Service, NY, C. Kagran. $65.00.

Glasses
Welch's, 1952 – 1953, jelly jar 1st or 2nd series, numerous varieties. One of the most common Howdy Doody items. $8.00 – $27.00.

Glasses
Welch's, 1952 – 1953, as above, but with Howdy lid. $44.00 – $45.00.

Handbag
Red child's handbag with Howdy face, 1950s. $95.00.

Game, Target
Target Game, Ja-Ru, #2312, copyright 1987 by National Broadcasting Co., Inc./King Features Syndicate. $7.00.

Handkerchief
Clarabell, copyright by Bob Smith. $25.00 – $35.00.

Handkerchief
Howdy on bronco, 8" x 8", multicolored, copyright by Bob Smith. $32.00.

Hat
Civil War style Howdy hats. Left: 1950s, cloth with plastic Howdy face. $29.00 – $125.00. Right: Felt, copyright by NBC. $18.00 – $35.00.

Handkerchief
Howdy and Elephant, ca. 1948 – 1949, 9" x 9", copyright by Bob Smith. $13.00 – $25.00.

Handkerchief
Howdy, ca. 1948 – 1949, 9" x 9". $13.00 – $25.00.

Handkerchief
Howdy, Flub, and Dilly, ca. 1948 – 1949, 9" x 9". $13.00 – $25.00.

Handkerchief
Howdy on yellow background, ca. 1948 – 1949, 9" x 9". $13.00 – $25.00.

Hat, Beanie
Gray felt with vinyl Howdy, 1950s, red & white stripes. $75.00.

Hat, Beanie
Red felt with white felt panel, 1950s. $50.00.

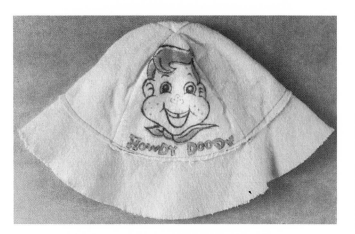

Hat, Beanie
Howdy Doody Make It Yourself Bee-Nee Kit, ca. 1950 – 1954. Conn. Leather. $35.00 – $85.00.

Hat, Paper
Welch's, 1951, 3½" x 11" *Howdy Doody Says Welch's . . .* $100.00.

House, Cut out
Welch's, 1953, Doodyville cut out houses. $19.00 – $65.00.

Iron-On Transfer
Howdy, 8" x 9". $9.00.

Key Chain, Flasher
1950s. $18.00.

Key Chain, Puzzle
Lido, 1970s, Howdy with microphone. $7.00 – $29.00.

Key Chain, Puzzle
Lido, 1970s, original 8½" x 12" full display with 12 chains. $75.00 each.

Key Chains
Copyright 1987 by NBC, Inc./KFC, Inc. $7.00 – $20.00.

Label, Bread End
Wonder Bread, 1950s, Howdy in blue circle. $30.00 – $35.00.

Lamp, Desk
Howdy sits on wood base. $40.00 – $165.00.

Lamp, Desk
Cosmic Scout above Howdy but with space helmet. $85.00.

Lamp, Desk
Leadworks, 1988, ceramic Howdy sits on a pig. $24.00 – $75.00.

Lamp, Wall
Vac-U-Form, 1950s, 14" x 8" Howdy sitting on chimney with Santa. $125.00 – $175.00.

Light, Night
Howdy Doody Night-Light, Leadworks, 1988, ceramic, copyright 1988 by NBC, Inc./KFS., Inc. $35.00 – $55.00.

Lamp Shade
Glass ceiling lamp shade, ca. 1950 – 1954, copyright by Kagran Corporation. $185.00 – $265.00.

Light, Night
Howdy Doody Night Lite with box, ca. 1950 – 1954, 2¼" x 3¼" x 1⅞", copyright by Kagran Corporation, manufactured by Leco Manufacturing Co. $50.00 – $150.00.

Light, Play
Play light, copyright 1987 by National Broadcasting Co., Inc./King Features Syndicate, Inc., manufactured by Ja-Ru. $7.00 – $10.00.

Magazine
The Billboard, 1948, Nov 27 issue. Cover pictures Bob Smith (as Santa), Clarabell (Bob Keeshan), Rhoda Mann (Howdy's puppeteer), and Howdy. Copyright 1948 by The Billboard Publishing Co. $40.00 – $60.00.

Lunch Box, Plastic
Howdy Doody & Pals lunchbox, 9" x 4½", copyright 1977 by National Broadcasting Company, Inc. Thermos, 1976, dome type without thermos. $25.00 – $55.00.

Lunch Box, Metal
Adco Liberty, 1955, steel box. $175.00 – $350.00.

Magazine
Castle Films, 1951, product catalog with Howdy cover. $22.00.

Magazine
Jack & Jill, 1960, January issue with cover photo. $12.00 – $25.00.

Magazine
New York City TV Guide. Top from left to right: September 2 – 8, 1950, $75.00; November 23 – 29, 1950, $50.00 – $300.00; August 31 – September 6, 1951, $50.00 – $300.00; bottom row: November 23 – 29, 1951, $75.00; November 21 – 27, 1952, $50.00 – $300.00. Photo courtesy of Bob Reed.

Magazine
TV Guide, 1948, July 26 issue, Howdy cover. $300.00.

Magazine
Philadelphia TV Digest. **Top from left to right: December 23 – 29, 1950; November 17 – 23, 1951; bottom row: June 21 – 27, 1952; December 27 – January 2, 1953. Photo courtesy of Bob Reed. $35.00 – $75.00 each.**

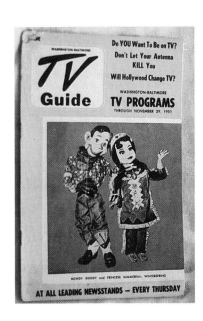

Magazine
Washington-Baltimore TV Guide, **November 23 – 29, 1951. Howdy and the puppet Princess Summerfall Winterspring. Photo courtesy of Bob Reed. $50.00.**

Magazine
TV Guide, 1952, December 19 – 25 issue, Howdy cover. $35.00.

Magazine
TV Guide, 1952, June 25 – July 1 issue, Howdy and Bob cover. $50.00 – $100.00.

Magazine
TV Jr., Howdy and Clarabell cover. $35.00.

Magazine
TV Preview, May 18 – 24, 1958, Clarabell cover. $25.00.

Marionette
Clarabell with or without box, ca. 1950 – 1954, copyright by Kagran Corporation, manufactured by Peter Puppet Play Things. $100.00 – $500.00.

Marionette
Dilly Dally with or without box, Peter Puppet, ca. 1950 – 1954. $600.00.

Marionette
Heidi by Peter Puppet, ca. 1950 – 1954, copyright by Kagran Corporation. $300.00.

Marionette
Howdy in box, ca. 1948 – 1949. $89.00.

Marionette
Howdy Doody by Peter Puppet, ca. 1950 – 1954, copyright by Kagran Corporation. $50.00 – $365.00.

Marionette
Princess by Peter Puppet, ca. 1950 – 1954, copyright by Kagran Corporation. $40.00 – $425.00.

Marionette
Flub-A-Dub with instructions, ca. 1950 – 1954, copyright by Kagran Corporation, manufactured by Peter Puppet Playthings. $300.00 – $403.00.

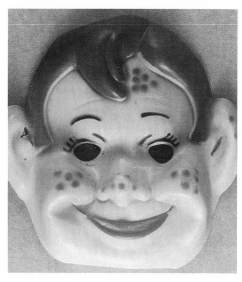

Mask, Rubber
Rubber mask with movable mouth. $50.00.

Mask, Cloth
Colorful with freckles and movable mouth, ca. 1950 – 1954. $35.00 – $65.00.

Mask, Paper
Kellogg, 1950s, Howdy from Wheaties box. $22.00 – $49.00.

Mask, Paper
Giles/Poll Parrot, 1950s, Howdy's face, 12" cut from card. $38.00 – $75.00.

Mittens, Kit
Howdy & Clarabell Puppet Mitten Kit, with yarn and instructions, Conn. Leather, ca. 1950 – 1954, copyright by Kagran Corporation. $50.00 – $65.00.

Modeling Kit, Clay
Howdy Doody Put-in-Head, 4 characters. $100.00.

Moccasin, Kit
Official Chief and Princess Moccasin Kit, with beaded and cloth accented leather pieces and instructions, ca. 1950 – 1954, copyright Kagran Corporation, manufactured by the Connecticut Leather Company. $150.00.

Money, Play
Burry premium, 1952, 18 pieces. Howdy Doody Play Money from the Doodyville bank. The money was produced via Advertising Specialty Service. Copyright by Kagran Corporation. Courtesy of Ralph MacPhail, Jr. $15.00 – $25.00 each.

Mug, Ceramic
1950s. $35.00 – $45.00.

Mug, Ceramic
1971, Shows six characters. $30.00.

Mug, Ceramic
Applause, 1988, coffee mugs, 3 different. $10.00 – $19.00 each.

Mug, Plastic
Ovaltine, ca. 1950 – 1954, Shaker mug with lid. $30.00 – $85.00.

Music Box
Vandor, Howdy playing piano. $125.00.

Napkin, Paper
Large Howdy. $16.00.

Needlepoint
Ca. 1950 – 1954, 3" x 4" cloth in kit. $100.00.

Note Pad
Two of a series of eight different notepad covers, copyright Bob Smith. These same photos were used with the Mars candy Christmas card premiums and the Forest City Bandages. 8" x 10", 1950s. $18.00 – $75.00 each.

Paint Set
Howdy Doody Paint Set, copyright by Kagran Corporation, manufactured by the Milton Bradley Company. $50.00 – $95.00.

Paint Set, Acrylic
Art Award, 1976, Howdy Doody Paint By The Number Set. $25.00.

Paint Set, Plaster
Marx, ca. 1950 – 1954, full set with figures. $65.00 – $115.00.

Paint Set, Plaster, Figures only
Marx, ca. 1950 – 1954, 60 mm figures only: Flub, Howdy, Clarabell, Bluster, and Dilly. $20.00 – $50.00 each.

Peg Board, Behavior
$75.00.

Patch
Joy, 1971, embroidered cloth, 2 different. Copyright by NBC, Inc. $10.00 – $15.00 each.

Pen
Copyright 1988 by NBC, Inc./KFC, Inc., manufactured by Leadworks, Inc. The rivets on Howdy's neck, two arms, and left leg allowed the character to be positioned. Pen is in Howdy's left leg. $10.00.

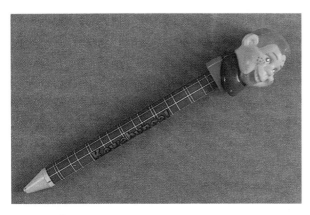

Pen, Kowabunga
Pen point retracts with a lever on the back of Howdy's head that also opens and closes his mouth. Copyright by NBC, Inc/KFS, Inc., manufactured by Leadworks, Inc., 5¼". **$3.00 – $10.00.**

Pencil
Howdy's head on top, ca. 1950 – 1954. $12.00 – $40.00.

Pencil
Assorted messages, 1988. $3.00 – $4.00 each.

Pipe, Bubble
Lido, 1950s, 4" Howdy or Clarabell. **$10.00 – $38.00 each.**

Placemat
Color Howdy and Friends, 9½" x 12". $25.00.

Placemat
Howdy Doody TV Merrimat Pictorial USA Map, 1952. $33.00 – $50.00.

Pencil Case/Bag
Transparent front and snap flap, 8¾" x 3½". Copyright by Kagran Corporation. **$28.00 – $120.00.**

Pencil Holder, Ceramic
Leadworks, 1988, 8" with box. $6.00 – $28.00.

Pencil Top
Leadworks, 1988, Howdy's head. $3.00 – $8.00.

Phonograph
Shura-Tone, ca. 1950 – 1954, Phono Doodle. $250.00 – $425.00.

Photo
1950, 8" x 10", Howdy and Bob. $10.00.

Photo Album
Poll Parrot, 1950, *Poll Parrot's Howdy Doody Photo Album*, 8 pages. $100.00.

Placemat
Howdy Doody Circus Placemat, copyright by Kagran. *This is a mat to place your dish upon, and Howdy Doody's watching till your food's all gone!* $10.00 – $35.00.

Planter, Ceramic
Lefton, Howdy seated on barrel, 5" x 5" x 6½". $100.00.

Plate, Ceramic
Smith-Taylor, 1950s, 8½" dia, Howdy as cowboy. $45.00 – $125.00.

Pocketbook
With shoulder strap and Howdy's raised face, 1950s. $145.00.

Pool, Wading
Ideal, ca. 1950 – 1954, 40" x 50" x 8" deep, vinyl. $100.00.

©BOB SMITH, FROM THE SCOTT BRINKER COLLECTION

Rhoda Mann and Howdy.

Polish, Shoe
Kunkel's Howdy Doody Shoe Polish, copyright by Kagran Corporation, ca. 1950 – 1954. $13.00 – $50.00.

Post Card
Howdy and Bob autographed, 5½" x 7". $35.00 – $40.00.

Poster, Ice Cream
Doughnut Corporation, 1954, vertical, 9" x 12", Howdy Doody Ice Cream Bars. $65.00.

Poster, Ice Cream
Doughnut Corporation, 1954, Howdy Doody Fudge Bar. $250.00.

Poster, Ice Cream
Doughnut Corporation, 1954, 9" x 12" Howdy Doody Ice Cream Sandwich. $65.00.

Prize Doodle List
Howdy Doody's Big Prize Doodle List, 1954 – 1955. Doughnut Corporation premium brochure. Copyright by Kagran Corporation. $9.00 – $60.00.

Prize Doodle List
Doughnut Corporation, 1957, *Jackpot of Fun* book. $75.00.

Proof Sheets
Doughnut Corporation, 1954, *Howdy Doody Ice Cream Circus* progressive proofs. $125.00.

Program, Souvenir
Lions Club, Nov. 20, 1954, event. $75.00 – $125.00.

Puppet, Finger
5" rubber Howdy, Clarabell, Dilly, and Bluster. $100.00.

Prize Doodle List
Howdy Doody's Big Prize Doodle List entry form, 1955, inside pages. Copyright by Kagran Corporation. $40.00.

Puppet, Finger
Latex Howdy finger puppet. Finger holes are behind the mouth, cheeks, and forehead. $10.00.

Puppet, Paper
Wonder Bread, 1950s, Princess, Howdy, Bluster, Flub, Inspector, Dilly, and Clarabell, 13" or 7½". Copyright by Kagran. Printed by Continental Baking Co. $15.00 – $75.00.

Puppet, Hand
Kaysam, 1950s, large Howdy in TV style box, latex. $95.00.

Puppet, Hand
Gund, 1950s, Howdy, Bluster, Clarabell, Dilly, Flub, or Princess with small vinyl head. $25.00 – $150.00.

Puppet, Hand
1950s, Bluster with googlie eyes. $60.00 – $85.00.

Puppet, Hand
1950s, Dilly with googlie eyes. $25.00 – $125.00.

Puppet, Hand
1950s, Flub with googlie eyes. $40.00.

Puppet, Hand
1950s, Princess with googlie eyes. $18.00 – $85.00.

Puppet, Plastic
Tee-Vee Toys, ca. 1950 – 1954, 3½" x 3¼" painted Flub with TV box. $75.00 – $156.00.

Puppet, Hand
Two different types of Howdy Doody hand puppets. The front row shows puppets with small rubber heads made by Gund in the 1950s. The back row shows puppets with large rubber heads and googlie eyes by Peter Puppet Playthings, 1950s. $25.00 – $125.00.

Puppet, Hand
1950s, Clarabell with googlie eyes. $30.00 – $95.00.

Puppet, Hand
1950s, Howdy with googlie eyes. $27.00 – $85.00.

Puppet, Plastic
These 4½" characters were available in many colors and also sold individually fully painted. One-color hard plastic, five pieces on card with movable mouth. $48.00 – $260.00.

Puppet, Plastic
Plastic puppets, painted hard plastic with moveable mouth. Howdy, Dilly, Bluster, or Princess, no box. Copyright by Kagran Corporation. Manufactured by Tee-Vee Toys. $18.00 – $65.00 each.

Puzzle
Howdy Doody and the Gang, copyright by Kagran Corporation, published by Milton Bradley from *3 Howdy Doody Puzzles* Box. $16.00 – $50.00.

Puzzle
Is that You Clarabell?, published by the Whitman Publishing Co., copyright 1952 by Kagran Corporation. $38.00 – $45.00.

Puzzle
Howdy Doody puzzle. Copyright by Kagran Corporation. $16.00 – $50.00.

Puzzle
Poll Parrot Howdy Doody Jig Saw Puzzle, copyright by Kagran, manufactured by Poll Parrot shoes, ca. 1950 – 1954. $90.00 – $100.00.

Puzzle
Princess Summerfall Winterspring, copyright by Kagran Corporation, published by Milton Bradley from *3 Howdy Doody Puzzles* Box.

Puzzle
Milton Bradley, ca. 1950 – 1954, #4121, boxed set of 3 puzzles. $48.00 – $150.00.

Puzzle
Milton Bradley, ca. 1950 – 1953, #4502, boxed set of 3. $58.00 – $75.00.

Puzzle, Frame Tray
Whitman, 1950s, #2628 Clarabell, copyright 1954 by Kagran Corporation. $33.00 – $38.00.

Puzzle, Frame Tray
Whitman, 1954, #301 *Howdy's One Man Band*, $19.00 – $60.00.

Puzzle, Frame Tray
Whitman, 1950s, *Skiing with Clarabell.* $12.00 – $45.00.

Puzzle, Frame Tray
Whitman, 1953, #4428 Howdy, Mr. Bluster, and Dilly in plane. $45.00 – $63.00.

Puzzle, Frame Tray
Whitman, *Howdy Doody at the Circus*, $25.00.

Puzzle Whitman
1950s, #4404 in box. $35.00.

Puzzle, Frame Tray
#2603 Ringmaster Howdy, published by the Whitman Publishing Co., copyright 1953 by Kagran Corporation. $20.00 – $46.00.

Puzzle, Frame Tray
Whitman, 1953, #2984 *Howdy Goes West*, $25.00 – $40.00.

Puzzle, Frame Tray
Whitman, 1950s, #2603 *Dilly Dally, the Human Bullet*, $33.00 – $38.00.

Puzzle, Frame Tray
Whitman, #4428 Howdy with skunk, copyright 1953 by Kagran Corporation. $25.00 – $65.00.

Ribbon
It's Howdy Doody Time, yellow and black, 3" x 3¾". $30.00.

Ring
1950s, silver, raised face *Howdy* and *Doody*, each shank. $95.00.

Ring, Horn
Clarabell, ca. 1950 – 1954. $395.00 – $525.00.

Ring, Flashlight
Raised Howdy face that lights, battery on ring, ca. 1950 – 1954. $95.00 – $250.00.

Ring, Flicker
Poll Parrot, 1950s, TV flicker ring in metal base. $50.00 – $400.00.

Ring, Flicker
Nabisco, 1950s, Clarabell, Bob, Howdy, Buffalo Bee, etc. $12.00 – $15.00.

Ring, Flicker
Nabisco, 1950s, same as above but set of 8. $100.00 – $200.00.

Ring, Flicker, TV
Poll Parrot, 1950s, set in TV set type frame. $100.00 – $400.00.

Ring, Photo
Howdy with red plastic base, 1950s. $165.00.

Ring, Photo Glow
Brass with convex dome over photo of Howdy. $100.00.

Record
Charles Dickens' A Christmas Carol, copyright by Kagran Corporation. A Little Golden Record published by Simon & Schuster, Inc. $25.00.

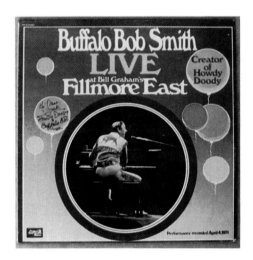

Record
Buffalo Bob Smith Live at Bill Graham's Filmore East, copyright 1971 by The Total Sound, Inc. An excellent sample of the Howdy Doody revival that brought Buffalo Bob to hundreds of colleges and universities in 1970 – 1971. This album has also been autographed on left ballon. $10.00 – $20.00.

Record, 6"
Golden Record, 1955, *Cowabunga/Big Chief.* $20.00.

Record, 6"
RCA, 1950s, *Howdy Doody & Mother Goose.* $50.00 – $70.00.

Record, 6"
RCA, ca. 1948 – 1949, *Howdy Doody & Santa Claus,* 45 rpm. $25.00.

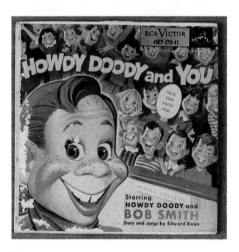

Record, 6"
RCA, ca. 1950 – 1954, *Howdy Doody and You,* copyright by Kagran Corporation, produced by RCA Victor. $21.00.

Record, 6"
Golden Record, 1955, *Laughing Song/John J. Fedoozle* in sleeve. $15.00.

Record, 6"
RCA, 1954, *It's Howdy Doody Time!* $15.00 – $50.00.

Record, 12"
Best of Howdy Doody. $10.00.

Record, 12"
History of the Howdy Doody Show, signed. $40.00.

Record, 12"
RCA, 1971, *It's Howdy Doody Time.* $15.00.

Record, 6"
RCA, 1950, *Howdy Doody's Laughing Circus*, 78 rpm. A Little Nipper Series, copyright 1950 by Bob Smith, produced by RCA Victor. $15.00 – $50.00.

Record, 6"
Golden Record, *Look! Look!/Will My Dog Be Proud of Me?*, copyright 1955 by Kagran Corporation, published by Simon and Schuster. $23.00.

Record, 12"
RCA, 1949, *Howdy & the Air-O-Doodle.* Jacket has wear, two records. Copyright by Bob Smith, 1949. A 78 rpm two-record set in fold-out jacket. $15.00 – $50.00.

Record, 12"
RCA, 1950, *Laughing Circus*, #Y414, two records. $75.00.

Record, 12"
1976, *Story of Howdy Doody*. $10.00.

Record, 12"
Be A Ventriloquist. Record from Goldberger Doll Manufacturing, Inc., designed to be sold with one of their ventriloquist dolls. Buffalo Bob, who was Howdy's voice, but not a ventriloquist, is pictured with one of the Goldberger Dolls. $28.00.

Sand Forms
Ideal, 1952, *Howdy Doody Sand Forms.* Four facial molds on card. $42.00 – $200.00.

Salt & Pepper Shakers
Peter Puppet, ca. 1950 – 1954, Howdy's head, 3" high, boxed. $75.00 – $250.00.

Seal, Wonder Bread
Howdy Doody's Favorite Wonder Enriched Bread.
One of the many Wonder Bread end wrapper seals
for Howdy Doody albums. Copyright by Kagran
Corporation. $30.00 – $35.00.

Sign, Advertising
Colgate, 1950s, 22" x 14" cardboard counter for Dental
Cream. $295.00.

Sign, Tin
Howdy Doody Twin Pop, ca. 1950 – 1954. $50.00.

Sign, Tin
AAA Sign Co., 1990, *Howdy Doody Twin Pop,* reproduction. $5.00 – $35.00.

Slide
Tru-Vue slides. Copyright 1954, 1955 by Kagran Corporation, a competitor to View-Master. The double
images travel down rather than around the viewer.
$15.00 – $25.00.

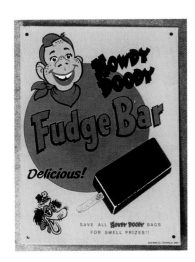

Sign, Tin
Howdy Doody Fudge Bar. Originally a 1954 ad from
the Doughnut Corporation of America, this example
is a 1980s reproduction manufactured by the AAA
Sign Company. $5.00 – $35.00.

Slide Viewer Kit
Howdy Doody and His Pals with Stori-Viewer with
slides and box, copyright by Kagran Corporation.
Kit K-60. The story was written on groups of six or
twelve individual slides. $100.00 – $200.00.

Slate
Doodle Slate with plastic cover, 1950s. $75.00.

Slide
Stori-View, 1955, *Howdy & His Toys* #1. $10.00 – $20.00.

Slippers
Howdy face figure on each, 1950s. $165.00.

Slipper box
Without slippers, cut-out pictures on side. $75.00.

Slipper Sock Kit
Howdy Doody and Clarabell Slipper Sock Kit, with yarn and instructions, Conn. Leather, ca. 1950 – 1954, copyright by Kagran Corporation. $35.00.

Spoon and Fork Set
Howdy Doody Educator Set, copyright by Kagran Corporation. Spoon and fork *Howdy Doody* on the handle and *Crown Silverplate* on the reverse. $195.00.

Slippers
Fun Feet cloth slippers with plastic Howdy head on each, copyright 1988 by Carousel by Guy™. $15.00.

Spoon, Metal
Sterling silver ice tea spoon with Howdy on handle, 9" long. Copyright by Kagran Corporation, manufactured by Crown, ca. 1950 – 1954. $10.00 – $90.00.

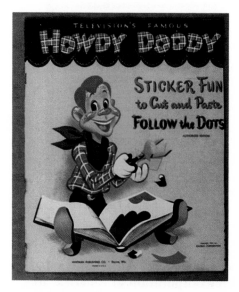

Stickers
Television's Famous Howdy Doody Sticker Fun, copyright 1952 by Kagran Corporation, published by the Whitman Publishing Company. $44.00.

Spoon, Wood
Rivers, 1950s, 3" for Howdy Doody Ice Cream cups, in wax paper. $15.00.

Spoonholder
Vandor, Ceramic Howdy. $35.00.

Sportsbox, Tin
Liberty Steel, 1950s, Howdy Doody Official Outdoor Sportsbox. $50.00 – $100.00.

Stationary
1971, stationary pack, sheets 6" x 8". $18.00 – $30.00.

Stencil
U.S. Packaging, ca. 1955 – 1959, Christmas from Frosty Spray Snow cans, full set. $12.00 – $75.00.

Stocking, Christmas
Red flannnel with felt graphics, ca. 1950 – 1952, 18" long. $75.00 – $100.00.

Suspenders
Howdy in green, white, and gold. $20.00.

Tag, Bottle
Welch's, 1951, from grape juice bottle, ½" x 6". $40.00 – $45.00.

Tag, Cupcake
Hostess, 1950s, Hostess cupcake label with Howdy picture. $50.00.

Tag, Talking
Wonder/Hostess, 1950s, *Howdy Doody Talking Tag* disk with rotating mouth. $75.00.

Towel, Bath
Howdy on horse, 38" x 21". $125.00.

Towel, Beach
1970s, 4 different. $10.00 each.

Toy, Acrobat
***Acrobat Howdy*, Arnold, 1950s. Tin frame, plastic head and hands, cloth body. Copyright by Kagran Corporation. $250.00 – $425.00.**

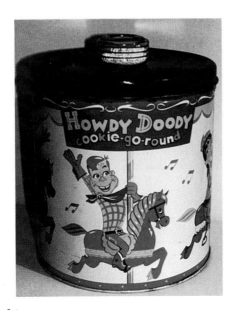

Tin, Cookie
Howdy Doody Cookie-Go-Round, copyright by Kagran Corporation, manufactured by Luce, 1950s. $90.00 – $200.00.

Toy, Dancer
***The Wonder Dancer*. Not sold as a Howdy Doody tie-in, but obviously it is Howdy. Copyright by Jaystik Sales, 1952. $39.00 – $75.00.**

Toy, Bendee
Howdy, rubber head, wire body with clothes. $30.00 – $95.00.

Toy, Gun
Ja-Ru, 1987, *Howdy Doody Western* gun with holster. $9.00.

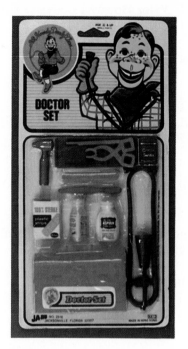

Toy, Gun
Sparkle Gun, Ja-Ru #2314, copyright 1987 by National Broadcasting Co., Inc./King Features Syndicate, Inc. $9.00.

Toy, Kit
Howdy Doody Make It Yourself Toy Kit, Flub and Clarabell. $65.00 – $75.00 each.

Toy, Pinwheel
Ja-Ru, 1987, blister pack. $10.00 – $25.00.

Toy, Pool
Ideal, 1950s, 21" diameter inflatable swim tube vinyl ring. $25.00 – $125.00.

Toy, Pop-up
Howdy with microphone, ca. 1950 – 1954. $95.00 – $165.00.

Toy, Power Tools
Ja-Ru, 1987, drill or saw, blister pack (MIP). $25.00.

Toy, Push-Up
Kohner, Flub-A-Dub. $160.00 – $250.00.

Toy, Doctor Set
Plastic medical kit, Ja-Ru #2307, copyright 1987 by National Broadcasting Co., Inc./King Features Syndicate, Inc. $7.00.

Toy, Kit
Howdy Doody Ready To Make Toy Kit, **copyright, Kagran. Clarabell Hug-Me Toy or Laundry Bag with Clarabell face pattern, red, white, and black yarn for embroidery; with felt nose, striped costume, and instructions. Box measures 9" x 11", ca. 1950 – 1954, Conn. Leather. $65.00 – $75.00.**

Toy, Paper
Howdy Doody's Comic Circus Animals, copyright 1954 by Roberts, Johnson & Rand/Kagran Corporation. Rotating the dials on the side created up to 810 different variations. $75.00.

Toy, Pinball
Pinball Game, blister pack, Ja-Ru #2312, copyright 1987 by National Broadcasting Co., Inc./King Features Syndicate. $15.00.

Toy, Paper
Rope-climbing Howdy, copyright 1951 by Kagran Corporation. $35.00.

Toy, Play Tools
Howdy Doody Play Tools, F. J. Strauss Co., Inc., copyright 1976 by National Broadcasting Company, Inc. $15.00.

Toy, Push-Up
Princess Summerfall Winterspring, copyright by
Bob Smith, manufactured by Kohner Products.
$68.00 – $325.00.

Toy, Sparkler
Sparkler, copyright 1987 by National Broadcasting
Co., Inc./King Features Syndicate, Inc. Manufac-
tured by Ja-Ru. $7.00.

Toy, Slot Machine
Mini Jackpot Game, Ja-Ru, copyright 1987 by
National Broadcasting Company, Inc./King Features
Syndicate, Inc. This was about the closest that
Howdy got to gambling. $7.00.

Toy, Squeeze
Peter Puppet, 8" Clarabell, soft vinyl with box. $375.00.

Toy, Squeeze
Spunky, rubber Howdy in an airplane. $95.00.

Toy, Squeeze
Spunky, 8½" Howdy standing, feet crossed. $98.00.

Toy, Squeeze
Spunky, 6" Rubber Howdy in raft. $125.00.

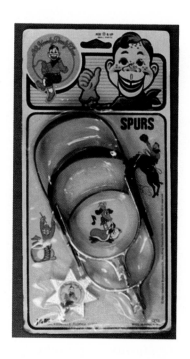

Toy, Spurs
Ja-Ru, #2318, 1987, copyright 1987 by National
Broadcasting Co., Inc./King Features Syndicate.
$15.00.

Toy, Tin
Remote Control Clarabell tin toy by Linemar Toys, 7", copyright by Kagran Corporation, ca. 1950 – 1954. Clarabell could walk across the floor by squeezing the control. $475.00 – $995.00.

Toy, Tin
Unique Art, 1948, *Howdy Doody & Buffalo Bob at the Piano.* $850.00 – $1,995.00.

Toy, Tin
Nylint, *Howdy Doody Pumpmobile.* $300.00 – $475.00.

Toy, Tin
Nylint copy, *Howdy Doody Pumpmobile.* $375.00.

Toy, Tin
From Japan, 1950s, *Jackie the Farm Boy on Trapeze* without box. Not an official Howdy Doody toy, but unmistakably it's Howdy, scarf, boots, and all. Photo courtesy of Gasoline Alley. $1,995.00.

Toy, Tin,
Camion de Juguetes, 1950s, 9¾" truck. Made in Argentina from Pepsi-Cola can with Celonese writing. Not sold as a Howdy Doody toy, but Flub-A-Dub is plainly visible. $335.00.

Toy, Top
Tin top, copyright by National Broadcasting Company, Inc. produced by LBZ in Western Germany. $32.00 – $150.00.

Toy, Toss
Flub-A-Dub Flip-A-Ring game, ca. 1950 – 1954, copyright by Kagran Corporation. $65.00 – $69.00.

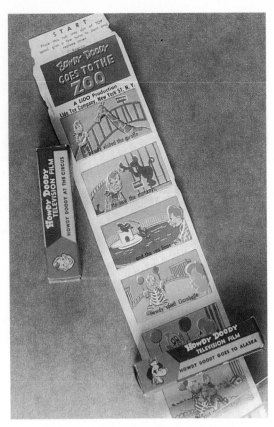

Ukulele
Emenee, ca. 1950 – 1954, *Howdy Doody Uke*, white or yellow, 17" with or without box. $95.00 – $100.00.

Toy, TV
Lido, ca. 1950 – 1954, *Howdy Doody Television Film* with box, copyright by Kagran Corporation. $15.00 – $49.00.

Toy, TV
Colgate, 1949, miniature TV with color viewing disk. $75.00.

Umbrella
Hollander, 1952, vinyl with Howdy head on handle and tag. The bag is a "face-go-round." The user can change the eyes, nose, and mouth of the Howdy by turning a dial. $185.00.

Utensils
Crown, ca. 1950 – 1954, spoon and fork *Educator Set*, boxed. $195.00.

Wall Plaque
Vandor, Howdy. $65.00.

Toy, Wall
Howdy Doody Wall Walker, with card, manufactured by Tigrett Enterprises. $35.00 – $89.00.

Wallet, Children's
Assorted pictures on front, ca. 1950 – 1954. Wallets used the pictures from the Magic Cards, but without the tricks on the back. There were a number of different cards on the back. $20.00 – $28.00.

Wallpaper
Strip from roll with the characters, ca. 1950 – 1954.
$20.00.

Washcloth
Ulmann, 1950s, Howdy, Clarabell terry cloth mitt.
$25.00 – $45.00.

Watch Set
Ja-Ru #2307, copyright 1987 Aby National Broadcasting Co., Inc./King Features Syndicate, Inc.

Watch
Oblong with Howdy's face, red band. $50.00.

Watch
Ingerhan, 1950s, eyes follow hand movements. $250.00.

Wrapper, Bread
Wonder, 1948, full wrapper with end seals. $100.00.

Wrapper, Candy
Cadbury, ca. 1950 – 1954, Howdy Doody Bar made for Canada. $125.00.

Wrist Band
Plastic Howdy. $75.00.

Watch
Official Howdy Doody Quartz Analog Unisex Watch with number dial, copyright 1987 by NBC/KFC, Inc., manufactured by Concepts Plus, Inc., 1988. $39.00 – $48.00.

Howdy Doody Ice Cream Wrappers, 1954. Top: Chocolate Covered Ice Milk, $20.00 – $25.00; Clarabell Banana Bar Ice Milk, $20.00 – $35.00; Chocolate Covered Ice Cream, $20.00 – $35.00. Middle: Cream Ice (Water Ice and Ice Milk), $20.00 – $35.00; Banana Fudge Bar Milk Sherbet, $20.00 – $25.00; Twin Pop, $10.00 – $25.00. Bottom: Fudge Bar Milk Sherbet, $20.00 – $25.00; Twin Ice Cream Sandwich, $20.00 – $25.00. Copyright by Kagran Corporation. Manufactured by Rivers Ice Cream Co. of Schlosser Brothers, Inc. Wrappers could be saved and traded for various toys.

Mid 1950s Christmas card.

"Firsts" From Doodyville

☑ First nationally syndicated TV show given the "George Foster Peabody Award for Children's Broadcasting."

☑ Pioneered the art of TV product merchandising.

☑ First to introduce the concept of face lift surgery on TV (March 1948).

☑ First split screen broadcast — Chicago and New York (June 23, 1949).

☑ First live broadcast of a total eclipse of the sun (March 4, 1951).

☑ First program to reach 1,000 performances (January 27, 1952).

☑ First regularly broadcast color TV program (June 26, 1953).

☑ First "Hot" Kines — filmed on 35mm rather than 16mm (1954).

☑ First TV program to be broadcast every day in color (September 12, 1955).

☑ First program to reach 2,000 performances (December 20, 1955).

☑ First show to have a giant mail response (12 million letters by December 31, 1955).

About the Author

The New England born author grew up during the times of Howdy Doody, Rottie Kazootie, the Mickey Mouse Club, and Froggie Gremlin. After serving in Viet Nam with the US Army, he rediscovered Howdy and Buffalo Bob first at the University of Massachusetts in 1972, while editing the campus humor magazine, and again at an antique "show signing" in 1993. An avid treasure hunter, his Howdy Doody collection includes hundreds of related premiums and uncountable related articles and magazines.

Author and Friend 1993.
This Doody is "Photo Doody." He is ball jointed and has no strings.

Books on Collectibles

This is only a partial listing of the books on antiques that are available from Collector Books. All books are well illustrated and contain current values. Most of the following books are available from your local bookseller, antique dealer, or public library. If you are unable to locate certain titles in your area, you may order by mail from COLLECTOR BOOKS, P.O. Box 3009, Paducah, KY 42002-3009. Customers with Visa or MasterCard may phone in orders from 7:00–4:00 CST, Monday–Friday, Toll Free 1-800-626-5420. Add $2.00 for postage for the first book ordered and $0.30 for each additional book. Include item number, title, and price when ordering. Allow 14 to 21 days for delivery.

DOLLS, FIGURES & TEDDY BEARS

2382	Advertising Dolls, Identification & Values, Robison & Sellers	$9.95
2079	Barbie Doll Fashions, Volume I, Eames	$24.95
3957	Barbie Exclusives, Rana	$18.95
3310	Black Dolls, 1820–1991, Perkins	$17.95
3873	Black Dolls, Book II, Perkins	$17.95
3810	Chatty Cathy Dolls, Lewis	$15.95
2021	Collector's Male Action Figures, Manos	$14.95
1529	Collector's Encyclopedia of Barbie Dolls, DeWein	$19.95
3727	Collector's Guide to Ideal Dolls, Izen	$18.95
3728	Collector's Guide to Miniature Teddy Bears, Powell	$17.95
4506	Dolls in Uniform, Bourgeois	$18.95
3967	Collector's Guide to Trolls, Peterson	$19.95
1067	Madame Alexander Dolls, Smith	$19.95
3971	Madame Alexander Dolls Price Guide #20, Smith	$9.95
2185	Modern Collector's Dolls I, Smith	$17.95
2186	Modern Collector's Dolls II, Smith	$17.95
2187	Modern Collector's Dolls III, Smith	$17.95
2188	Modern Collector's Dolls IV, Smith	$17.95
2189	Modern Collector's Dolls V, Smith	$17.95
3733	Modern Collector's Dolls, Sixth Series, Smith	$24.95
3991	Modern Collector's Dolls, Seventh Series, Smith	$24.95
3472	Modern Collector's Dolls Update, Smith	$9.95
3972	Patricia Smith's Doll Values, Antique to Modern, 11th Edition	$12.95
3826	Story of Barbie, Westenhouser	$19.95
1513	Teddy Bears & Steiff Animals, Mandel	$9.95
1817	Teddy Bears & Steiff Animals, 2nd Series, Mandel	$19.95
2084	Teddy Bears, Annalee's & Steiff Animals, 3rd Series, Mandel	$19.95
1808	Wonder of Barbie, Manos	$9.95
1430	World of Barbie Dolls, Manos	$9.95

TOYS, MARBLES & CHRISTMAS COLLECTIBLES

3427	Advertising Character Collectibles, Dotz	$17.95
2333	Antique & Collector's Marbles, 3rd Ed., Grist	$9.95
3827	Antique & Collector's Toys, 1870–1950, Longest	$24.95
3956	Baby Boomer Games, Identification & Value Guide, Polizzi	$24.95
1514	Character Toys & Collectibles, Longest	$19.95
1750	Character Toys & Collector's, 2nd Series, Longest	$19.95
3717	Christmas Collectibles, 2nd Edition, Whitmyer	$24.95
1752	Christmas Ornaments, Lights & Decorations, Johnson	$19.95
3874	Collectible Coca-Cola Toy Trucks, deCourtivron	$24.95
2338	Collector's Encyclopedia of Disneyana, Longest, Stern	$24.95
2151	Collector's Guide to Tootsietoys, Richter	$16.95
3436	Grist's Big Book of Marbles	$19.95
3970	Grist's Machine-Made & Contemporary Marbles, 2nd Ed.	$9.95
3732	Matchbox® Toys, 1948 to 1993, Johnson	$18.95
3823	Mego Toys, An Illustrated Value Guide, Chrouch	15.95
1540	Modern Toys 1930–1980, Baker	$19.95
3888	Motorcycle Toys, Antique & Contemporary, Gentry/Downs	$18.95
3891	Schroeder's Collectible Toys, Antique to Modern Price Guide	$17.95
1886	Stern's Guide to Disney Collectibles	$14.95
2139	Stern's Guide to Disney Collectibles, 2nd Series	$14.95
3975	Stern's Guide to Disney Collectibles, 3rd Series	$18.95
2028	Toys, Antique & Collectible, Longest	$14.95
3975	Zany Characters of the Ad World, Lamphier	$16.95

JEWELRY, HATPINS, WATCHES & PURSES

1712	Antique & Collector's Thimbles & Accessories, Mathis	$19.95
1748	Antique Purses, Revised Second Ed., Holiner	$19.95
1278	Art Nouveau & Art Deco Jewelry, Baker	$9.95
3875	Collecting Antique Stickpins, Kerins	$16.95
3722	Collector's Ency. of Compacts, Carryalls & Face Powder Boxes, Mueller	$24.95
3992	Complete Price Guide to Watches, #15, Shugart	$21.95
1716	Fifty Years of Collector's Fashion Jewelry, 1925-1975, Baker	$19.95
1424	Hatpins & Hatpin Holders, Baker	$9.95
1181	100 Years of Collectible Jewelry, Baker	$9.95
2348	20th Century Fashionable Plastic Jewelry, Baker	$19.95
3830	Vintage Vanity Bags & Purses, Gerson	$24.95

FURNITURE

1457	American Oak Furniture, McNerney	$9.95
3716	American Oak Furniture, Book II, McNerney	$12.95
1118	Antique Oak Furniture, Hill	$7.95
2132	Collector's Encyclopedia of American Furniture, Vol. I, Swedberg	$24.95
2271	Collector's Encyclopedia of American Furniture, Vol. II, Swedberg	$24.95
3720	Collector's Encyclopedia of American Furniture, Vol. III, Swedberg	$24.95
1437	Collector's Guide to Country Furniture, Raycraft	$9.95
3878	Collector's Guide to Oak Furniture, George	$12.95
1755	Furniture of the Depression Era, Swedberg	$19.95
3906	Heywood-Wakefield Modern Furniture, Rouland	$18.95
1965	Pine Furniture, Our American Heritage, McNerney	$14.95
1885	Victorian Furniture, Our American Heritage, McNerney	$9.95
3829	Victorian Furniture, Our American Heritage, Book II, McNerney	$9.95
3869	Victorian Furniture books, 2 volume set, McNerney	$19.90

INDIANS, GUNS, KNIVES, TOOLS, PRIMITIVES

1868	Antique Tools, Our American Heritage, McNerney	$9.95
2015	Archaic Indian Points & Knives, Edler	$14.95
1426	Arrowheads & Projectile Points, Hothem	$7.95
1668	Flint Blades & Projectile Points of the North American Indian, Tully	$24.95
2279	Indian Artifacts of the Midwest, Hothem	$14.95
3885	Indian Artifacts of the Midwest, Book II, Hothem	$16.95
1964	Indian Axes & Related Stone Artifacts, Hothem	$14.95
2023	Keen Kutter Collectibles, Heuring	$14.95
3887	Modern Guns, Identification & Values, 10th Ed., Quertermous	$12.95
2164	Primitives, Our American Heritage, McNerney	$9.95
1759	Primitives, Our American Heritage, Series II, McNerney	$14.95
3325	Standard Knife Collector's Guide, 2nd Ed., Ritchie & Stewart	$12.95

PAPER COLLECTIBLES & BOOKS

1441	Collector's Guide to Post Cards, Wood	$9.95
2081	Guide to Collecting Cookbooks, Allen	$14.95
3969	Huxford's Old Book Value Guide, 7th Ed.	$19.95
3821	Huxford's Paperback Value Guide	$19.95
2080	Price Guide to Cookbooks & Recipe Leaflets, Dickinson	$9.95
2346	Sheet Music Reference & Price Guide, Pafik & Guiheen	$18.95

OTHER COLLECTIBLES

2280	Advertising Playing Cards, Grist	$16.95
2269	Antique Brass & Copper Collectibles, Gaston	$16.95
1880	Antique Iron, McNerney	$9.95
3872	Antique Tins, Dodge	$24.95
1714	Black Collectibles, Gibbs	$19.95
1128	Bottle Pricing Guide, 3rd Ed., Cleveland	$7.95
3959	Cereal Box Bonanza, The 1950's, Bruce	$19.95
3718	Collector's Aluminum, Grist	$16.95
3445	Collectible Cats, An Identification & Value Guide, Fyke	$18.95
1634	Collector's Ency. of Figural & Novelty Salt & Pepper Shakers, Davern	$19.95
2020	Collector's Ency. of Figural & Novelty Salt & Pepper Shakers, Vol. II, Davern	$19.95
2018	Collector's Encyclopedia of Granite Ware, Greguire	$24.95
3430	Collector's Encyclopedia of Granite Ware, Book II, Greguire	$24.95
3879	Collector's Guide to Antique Radios, 3rd Ed., Bunis	$18.95
1916	Collector's Guide to Art Deco, Gaston	$14.95
3880	Collector's Guide to Cigarette Lighters, Flanagan	$17.95
1537	Collector's Guide to Country Baskets, Raycraft	$9.95
3966	Collector's Guide to Inkwells, Identification & Values, Badders	$18.95
3881	Collector's Guide to Novelty Radios, Bunis/Breed	$18.95
3729	Collector's Guide to Snow Domes, Guarnaccia	$18.95
3730	Collector's Guide to Transistor Radios, Bunis	$15.95
2276	Decoys, Kangas	$24.95
1629	Doorstops, Identification & Values, Bertoia	$9.95
3968	Fishing Lure Collectibles, Murphy/Edmisten	$24.95
3817	Flea Market Trader, 9th Ed., Huxford	$12.95
3819	General Store Collectibles, Wilson	$24.95
2215	Goldstein's Coca-Cola Collectibles	$16.95
3884	Huxford's Collector's Advertising, 2nd Ed.	$24.95
2216	Kitchen Antiques, 1790–1940, McNerney	$14.95
1782	1,000 Fruit Jars, 5th Edition, Schroeder	$5.95
3321	Ornamental & Figural Nutcrackers, Rittenhouse	$16.95
2026	Railroad Collectibles, 4th Ed., Baker	$14.95
1632	Salt & Pepper Shakers, Guarnaccia	$9.95
1888	Salt & Pepper Shakers II, Identification & Value Guide, Book II, Guarnaccia	$14.95
2220	Salt & Pepper Shakers III, Guarnaccia	$14.95
3443	Salt & Pepper Shakers IV, Guarnaccia	$18.95
2096	Silverplated Flatware, Revised 4th Edition, Hagan	$14.95
1922	Standard Old Bottle Price Guide, Sellari	$14.95
3892	Toy & Miniature Sewing Machines, Thomas	$18.95
3828	Value Guide to Advertising Memorabilia, Summers	$18.95
3977	Value Guide to Gas Station Memorabilia	$24.95
3444	Wanted to Buy, 5th Edition	$9.95

Schroeder's ANTIQUES Price Guide

. . . is the #1 best-selling antiques & collectibles value guide on the market today, and here's why . . .

Schroeder's ANTIQUES Price Guide

OUR #1 BEST SELLER!

Identification & Values Of Over 50,000 Antiques & Collectibles

8½ x 11, 608 Pages, $14.95

• More than 300 advisors, well-known dealers, and top-notch collectors work together with our editors to bring you accurate information regarding pricing and identification.

• More than 45,000 items in almost 500 categories are listed along with hundreds of sharp original photos that illustrate not only the rare and unusual, but the common, popular collectibles as well.

• Each large close-up shot shows important details clearly. Every subject is represented with histories and background information, a feature not found in any of our competitors' publications.

• Our editors keep abreast of newly developing trends, often adding several new categories a year as the need arises.

If it merits the interest of today's collector, you'll find it in *Schroeder's*. And you can feel confident that the information we publish is up to date and accurate. Our advisors thoroughly check each category to spot inconsistencies, listings that may not be entirely reflective of market dealings, and lines too vague to be of merit. Only the best of the lot remains for publication.

Without doubt, you'll find
SCHROEDER'S ANTIQUES PRICE GUIDE
the only one to buy for
reliable information and values.

COLLECTOR BOOKS
A Division of Schroeder Publishing Co., Inc.